Marginalized Voices

Marginalized Voices

A History of the Charismatic Movement in the
Orthodox Church in North America 1972–1993

Timothy B. Cremeens

FOREWORD BY
Vinson Synan

AFTERWORD BY
Bradley Nassif

PICKWICK *Publications* · Eugene, Oregon

MARGINALIZED VOICES
A History of the Charismatic Movement in the Orthodox Church in North America
1972–1993

Pickwick Publications
An Imprint of Wipf and Stock Publishers
199 W. 8th Ave., Suite 3
Eugene, OR 97401

www.wipfandstock.com

PAPERBACK ISBN: 978-1-5326-1708-9
HARDCOVER ISBN: 978-1-4982-4151-9
EBOOK ISBN: 978-1-4982-4150-2

Cataloguing-in-Publication data:

Names: Cremeens, Timothy B., author. | Synan, Vinson, foreword. | Nassif, Bradley, afterword.

Title: Marginalized voices : a history of the charismatic movement in the Orthodox Church in North America 1972–1993 / Timothy B. Cremeens; foreword by Vinson Synan; afterword by Bradley Nassif.

Description: Eugene, OR: Pickwick Publications, 2018 | Includes bibliographical references.

Identifiers: ISBN 978-1-5326-1708-9 (paperback) | ISBN 978-1-4982-4151-9 (hardcover) | ISBN 978-1-4982-4150-2 (ebook)

Subjects: LCSH: Eastern Orthodox Church—History | Orthodox Church in America | Pentecostalism | United States—Church history | Christianity—Canada

Classification: BX103.3 C725 2018 (print) | BX103.3 (ebook)

Manufactured in the U.S.A.   06/26/18

Dedication

The character of a man's life is formed by the lives of hundreds and thousands of others. I have been blessed by the many wonderful men and women that God has brought into my life over the past six decades. It is to these men and women that I dedicate this work. They include, but are certainly not limited to, the following:

- My parents—Louie H. and Velma I. Cremeens, who gave me life and introduced me to the Author of all Life. May their memory be eternal!

- To my wife—Tammy Kennedy Cremeens, for who I forsook all others and gave my heart only to her for all time and who supported me in times when I doubted myself.

- To my children—Timothy Gabriel, Zoe Christina and Magdalena Joy, in who's faces I have seen the unfathomable grace and love of Jesus Christ.

- To my sister—Pam Amlin, who's prayers and encouraging words have carried me through many dark days.

- To my numerous Brothers, Sisters and Friends in Christ—Orthodox, Catholic, Evangelical, Pentecostal, and Charismatic, who have walked beside me on my journey to the Kingdom

Contents

Foreword

FATHER TIMOTHY CREMEENS IS by all counts the most qualified person to write this book about Charismatics in the Orthodox tradition. His religious pilgrimage took him from his parent's Church of Christ in Christian Union, a small Holiness Church in Ohio, to the Assemblies of God, a Pentecostal church, to the Antiochian Orthodox Church, where he was ordained a priest in 1992, and finally to the Orthodox Church in America (OCA). He therefore knows firsthand the historical trajectory that led to the Charismatic Movement in the Orthodox Churches. He also knew personally many of the leading figures, especially Frs. Eusebius Stephanou and Athanasios Emmert, he has written about in this ground-breaking work, *Marginalized Voices: A History of the Charismatic Movement in the Orthodox Church in North America, 1972–1995*. At the time of the publication of this excellent history, he was serving as Dean of the Holy Resurrection Orthodox Cathedral (OCA) in Wilkes-Barre, Pennsylvania.

I first became acquainted with Timothy Cremeens as a sixteen-year-old student in my 1975-correspondence course on Pentecostal/Charismatic History in the Logos Institute of Biblical Studies, a "University without Walls," led by the late Dan Malachuk of Logos International Publishing. Fr. Timothy preserved all the course materials that now reside in the Vinson Synan Papers in the Regent University archives. Many years later, he enrolled in the first class of the new PhD program in Renewal Studies at the Regent School of Divinity. He earned the Doctor of Philosophy Degree in the History of Global Christianity at Regent University in 2011.

This book is a revision of his dissertation. It was my honor to direct the dissertation and host Father Cremeens in our home when he was in residence studying in the PhD program at Regent. In the years since, Father Timothy has taught classes in Church History and Biblical Studies at Regent University in Virginia Beach, Virginia, Assumption College in Worcester, Massachusetts, Anna Maria College in Paxton, Massachusetts, Olivet University and Seminary in San Francisco, California, and has served as Interim Dean of the Grace Graduate School of Ministry in Twin Falls, Idaho. He is married to Tammy Kennedy Cremeens and they have three adult children.

The reason for the title, *Marginalized Voices,* is because of the difficulties that Orthodox priests experienced while attempting to promote the Charismatic renewal in their churches. Unlike the Roman Catholic Charismatic movement that swept the globe after 1967 and counted some 120,000,000 followers worldwide after fifty years, the Orthodox Charismatics never gained the approval of the bishops, and some priests were indeed marginalized and in some cases punished for their charismatic activities. Perhaps it could be said that the book demonstrates that the Orthodox Churches were the most resistant to the Charismatic movement of any of the major Christian traditions. By the end of the 1990s the movement had practically disappeared from the world of Orthodoxy.

Cremeens has produced a thoroughly researched, well-written and very readable book that should be of concern to every Christian who sincerely wants to renew the face of Christianity in the twenty-first century. It is a ground-breaking work, in a never before explored area of the history of the Charismatic Renewal Movement.

Vinson Synan, PhD

Dean Emeritus, Regent University School of Divinity
Scholar in Residence at Oral Roberts University
July 17, 2017

Preface

IN THE LATE 1960s and early 1970s the Charismatic Movement broke upon the Christian Churches like mighty waves, successively crashing upon a sandy beach. And just like ocean waves breaking upon the sand, it made deep impressions and rearranged the landscape of the Churches. Church leaders, both clergy and laity alike, after brief periods of questioning, analysis and debate, acknowledged this movement as a gift of refreshing from the Holy Spirit. Still others rejected it, and put forth all their energies to combat it, seeing in it the seeds of Satan.

The Charismatic Movement, and its claim that a renewed outpouring of the Holy Spirit and His charisms were taking place, affected millions of Roman Catholics, and Protestants of all denominations. At the same time, the Movement's effect upon the Eastern Orthodox Churches was minimal, comparatively speaking. Instead of millions, only a few thousand people within the Orthodox Church embraced the Movement and its defining spiritual experience, the Baptism of the Holy Spirit. While the wider Charismatic Renewal's influence is seen around the globe, its manifestation among Orthodox Christians has been felt almost exclusively in North America.

Thousands, of dissertations, articles and monographs have been written about the Charismatic Renewal Movement from the perspectives of Protestantism and Roman Catholicism. Some have sought to analyze the Movement from a theological or historical perspective, others from a sociological and psychological viewpoint.[1] Likewise, many individuals have penned personal reflections and memoirs of their involvement in the Movement, most being written at the height of the Movement in

---

1. Goodman, *Speaking in Tongues,* Hunt et al., *Charismatic Christianity,* Kildahl, *Psychology of Speaking in Tongues*, Maloney and Lovekin, *Glossolalia.*

the 1970s and 1980s. While the Charismatic Movement, in the opinion of certain religious "experts," is over, or at the least has waned, it has not totally disappeared but has abated, among Protestants and Roman Catholics in North America, and in some cases morphed into a general emphasis upon spiritual renewal, shedding some of its emphasis upon "charismatic" manifestations, such as speaking in tongues. No studies of the Charismatic Movement in the Orthodox Church have been undertaken. This is a glaring hole in the field of understanding modern Church history in general, and of the Charismatic Movement in particular, which this work hopes to address.

CHAPTER I

The Beginnings

THE HISTORY OF CHRISTIANITY is marked by many defining moments. Beginning with the birth of the Christian Church on the day of Pentecost to the advent of Monasticism in the third century, the conversion of Constantine the Great, the schism between the churches of Rome and Constantinople, the nailing of Martin Luther's 95 theses to the door of the chapel at Wittenberg marking the beginning of the Protestant Reformation, all these events, and hundreds more, have contributed to the shape of contemporary Christianity. It could be asserted that each century contains at least one of these defining moments. The twentieth century is no exception. Possibly the greatest event in Christianity, at the beginning the twentieth century, was the birth of the Pentecostal Movement, its subsequent spread to every continent on the planet, and its further influence upon the wider Charismatic Movement, which dominated the religious news for the last forty years of the twentieth century and profoundly affected every Christian church and denomination. The Pentecostal and Charismatic Movements' emphasis upon the person and ministry of the Holy Spirit lends weight to Dr. Vinson Synan's apt description of the twentieth century as the "Century of the Holy Spirit."[1]

Considering the above facts, this work chronicles the advent, formation and early years of the Charismatic Movement among Orthodox Christians in North America.[2] Focusing on four primary leaders of the

---

1. Synan, *The Century*, ix.

2. Like the Charismatic Movement among Roman Catholics and Protestants, the Renewal counted adherents and participants among Orthodox Christians around the globe, however the scope of this study will only include Orthodox Christians within North America, i.e., the United States and Canada, between 1968 and 1993 (twenty-five years).

Charismatic Renewal among the Orthodox clergy: the Right Reverend Archimandrite Athanasios Emmert of the Antiochian Orthodox Christian Archdiocese of North America, the Right Reverend Archimandrite Eusebius Stephanou of the Greek Orthodox Archdiocese of North America, the Reverend Father Boris Zabrodsky of the Ukrainian Orthodox Church of America, and the Reverend Father Orest Olekshy, principle leader of Charismatic Renewal among the Orthodox in Canada and a priest in the Orthodox Church of America. This book presents a historical narrative of the Movement within the Orthodox Church in North America by looking at their lives, ministries, writings and personal reflections.[3] The main question it seeks to answer is: why was the Charismatic Movement not embraced by the hierarchy of the Orthodox Church in North America and as a result, repudiated by the vast majority of the Orthodox faithful, clergy and laity alike? The answers to this question, which the facts will bear out, is: First, the Charismatic Movement at its very core was perceived by the hierarchy of the Orthodox Church to be essentially rooted in evangelical Protestant spirituality and theology and therefore inconsistent and incompatible with an Orthodox approach to the Christian life. Second, the Movement, in the minds of a majority of the Orthodox Church's leadership, became synonymous with the person and ministry of Fr. Eusebius Stephanou, who was believed, in reality or perception, to be rebellious and arrogant and who consistently criticized the Orthodox Church leadership overall, especially the hierarchy of the Greek Orthodox Archdiocese of the Church, and persisted in using what was characterized as classical Pentecostal terminology and methodology in his ministry. Stephanou's weaknesses, initially in the mind of the Greek Orthodox hierarchy, and by extension, the remainder of the Orthodox hierarchs in North America, were the Movement's weaknesses. Third, and directly related to the first two, the Movement among the Orthodox, unlike its counterparts in the various Protestant traditions and Roman Catholic Church, failed to communicate itself successfully in an Orthodox Christian spiritual and theological idiom that was comfortable, familiar, and acceptable to Orthodox clergy and laity alike. This confirms what Pentecostal historian Vinson Synan has so accurately stated,

> Orthodoxy has always claimed to be charismatic in its worship
> and piety. At no time has it held to a theory of the cessation of the

---

3. Orthodox priests and laity, who were likewise involved in the Charismatic Renewal, will also be mentioned, especially regarding their interaction with the primary leaders of the Movement.

gifts of the Holy Spirit. Signs and wonders, including prophecy, healing, and miracles, have traditionally been accepted as a part of the heritage of the church. Despite this tradition, no major body of Christians in the world has been less affected by the charismatic movement of recent decades.[4]

Several types of sources have been employed in presenting the above-mentioned Orthodox Charismatic leaders. Articles and essays written by them, as well as several hours of personal taped interviews, present their thoughts and personal reflections. Stephanou is the author of several, all related to the subject of Charismatic or Spiritual Renewal in the Orthodox Church. In addition, in 1968, Father Eusebius began to publish and edit *The Logos*, originally a monthly, then quarterly, journal dedicated to Charismatic and Spiritual Renewal in the Orthodox Church. Over the three plus decades that *The Logos* appeared, Stephanou penned hundreds of articles. In addition, an authorized biography on Stephanou was published in 2008.[5] Taped sermons and lectures of Stephanou were also employed in writing this narrative. Zabrodsky, beginning May 1978, and the Service Committee on Orthodox Spiritual Renewal (SCOSR), which Zabrodsky chaired, published *Theosis* magazine. Initially edited by Zabrodsky, *Theosis* is the only written source for information regarding the activities and writings of Zabrodsky. In addition, several hours of interviews, regarding his involvement in the Charismatic Movement, were conducted with Zabrodsky and his wife, Jaroslava. The Movement in Canada will be chronicled mainly through the transcripts of personal interviews with Fr. Orest Olekshy and other lay eyewitnesses and participants of the Movement in Canada.

In addition to the leadership provided by Emmert, Stephanou, Zabrodsky, his wife Jaroslava, and Olekshy and his wife Oksana, several other Orthodox priests—Fr. Constantine Monios, Fr. David Buss, Fr. James Tavlarides, Hieromonk[6] Lazarus Moore, Fr. Anthony Morefesis, Fr. John Stinka (retired Metropolitan of the Ukrainian Orthodox Church of Canada), Fr. Constantine and Helen Kakalabaki, Fr. Svjatoslav and Eve Balevich and Fr. Maxym Lysack—as well as laymen—Charles Ashanin, Jordan Bajis, Demetrios Nicoloudakis (presently a priest of the Greek

---

4. Synan, *The Century*, 199. See also Synan, *The 20th Century*, 143–47.

5. M. Stethatos, *The Voice*. In reality, this is not a biography but an autobiography penned by Stephanou himself using "Maria Stethatos" as a pseudonymous pen name. Stephanou, Eusebius. 2008. Interview by author. Destin, FL. February 20.

6. The term" Hieromonk" refers to a male monastic who is also an ordained priest.

Orthodox Archdiocese, Metropolis of Pittsburgh), Gerald Munk (presently coordinator of the Work of Christ Community in East Lansing, Michigan), Gregory Gavralides, Dennis Pihatch (deceased Archpriest of the Archdiocese of Canada of the Orthodox Church in America), Philip (presently a priest in the Archdiocese of Canada of the Orthodox Church in America), and Barbara Ericson, Martin Zip, Vasil and Kathy Szalasznyj, John Syrnick, and James and Karen Davis—were deeply involved in the Movement. Some of their reflections will be presented to give a fuller picture of the Movement within Orthodoxy.

The Charismatic Movement among Orthodox Christians is tied organically and historically to the general Charismatic Movement, whose origins in turn are traced through the classical Pentecostal Movement. Likewise, the Pentecostal Movement has a three-fold connection; one, the eighteenth- and nineteenth-century Holiness Movement, second, the Revivalist Movement and third, the Higher Life or Keswick Movement, all of which flourished in the nineteenth century.[7] All three of these movements similarly find their roots in the Pietist Movement of the late seventeenth/eighteenth century; the Holiness Movement through John and Charles Wesley via the Methodists, the Revivalists through the Puritans via Jonathan Edwards and the ministry of Charles Finney, and the Keswick Movement through Quaker and Anglican Pietism. Therefore, it is necessary to present a brief historical, theological, and cultural backdrop of these spiritual movements and show how they in turn influenced one another and collectively shaped the spirituality of the Charismatic Movement.

7. Dayton, *Theological Roots*.

CHAPTER 2

Antecedents

The Charismatic Church

FROM ITS INCEPTION, THE Orthodox Christian Church has claimed to be charismatic (from the Greek term *charismata*, defined as "grace gifts"). The term is employed by the Apostle Paul in his first epistle to the Corinthians to refer to the manifestation of miraculous events and practices such as prophecy, healing, exorcism, and speaking in tongues, all inspired, and given, by the same Holy Spirit.[1] The second chapter of the Acts of the Apostles records that on the Day of Pentecost, traditionally celebrated as the birth of the Christian Church, was attended by the sound of rushing wind, flaming tongues of fire resting upon the heads of those present, and speaking in languages understood by the surrounding crowd but not learned by the speakers. The Acts of the Apostles further records that the disciples of Jesus continued to perform miracles of healing, casting out demons, and raising the dead to life. It seems clear from the New Testament writings that the early Christians expected charismatic manifestations to accompany their life in the Church. The charismatic element of the nascent Church was central to its very nature. This charismatic "tradition" continued in the Christian Church following the death of the first generation of believers.[2] However, by the beginning of the fourth and fifth centuries, following the "Peace of Constantine" and the First Ecumenical Council of Nicaea in 325, charismatic manifestations in the Church appear to begin to be limited to those in certain positions. Some scholars have proposed that the charismatic ministry, which initially was shared by all baptized Christians, clergy and laity, male and female alike, began to purposely be reserved only to

1. 1 Cor 12:4–11.
2. McGee, *Miracles, Missions*, 5–6.

5

the higher clergy, i.e., bishops, presbyters and monastics.[3] Other scholars of Church history would assert that those who exercised charismatic gifts were chosen to fill leadership positions, so that it only *appears* that they were limited to the hierarchy. We can glean from the writings of St. Symeon the New Theologian that by the eleventh century it was believed that the charismatic gifts were only for the early Apostolic days of the Church, a sort of "cessationism" held sway, at least among the hierarchy of the Church in Constantinople.[4] The approach to charismatic manifestations was somewhat different in the medieval Roman Catholic Church and the Protestant Churches of the Reformation. The medieval Roman Catholic Church, as can be attested in the writings of Thomas Aquinas, held to a similar position as the Orthodox Church of Constantinople of the eleventh century, in that the practice of charismatic gifts were relegated to the realm of the episcopacy and extraordinary monastics.[5] However, the Protestant churches, especially those of the magisterial Reformation, developed a full-blown theology of "cessationism," a doctrine that states that the spiritual gifts, especially those listed in St. Paul's first epistle to the Corinthians, were special gifts given to the Church in its infancy for the purpose of establishing it in the pagan world and until the canon of the written Scriptures was completed and received by the Church. Conversely the charismatic gifts were divinely removed from the Church and were no longer necessary or desirable. Thus, any charismatic manifestations, beyond those of the first through the fourth centuries, are automatically seen as human counterfeits at best, or demonic in origin at worst.[6]

The Importance of St. Symeon the New Theologian

St. Symeon the New Theologian (949–1022) became the "patron saint" of the Charismatic Movement within the Orthodox Church. Stephanou published the first article about St. Symeon in the November-December 1973 issue of *The Logos* (12–16), dubbing him "A Forerunner of Charismatic Revival."

---

3. Von Campenhausen, *Ecclesiastical Authority.*
4. Symeon the New Theologian, *Life, Times,* vol. 3, 38–53.
5. MacNut, *Nearly Perfect.*
6. Ruthven, *On the Cessation.* MacArthur, *Charismatic Chaos.*

St. Symeon's writings remained in obscurity in the English-speaking world until the advent of the Charismatic Renewal in the Roman Catholic Church. Fr. George Maloney, an Eastern-Rite Jesuit priest, involved in the Charismatic Movement, who taught at Fordham University in the Bronx, published the first biography of St. Symeon in English.[7] Maloney's biography, and his later translation of St. Symeon's *Hymns of Divine Love,* made a clear connection between the teachings of the "New Theologian" and the signature tenet of the Charismatic Movement, the baptism of the Holy Spirit.

St. Symeon the New Theologian born in 949, known as George before his monastic tonsure, lived in Constantinople in the middle tenth to early eleventh centuries. His family, who were lesser Byzantine nobles, turned George over to his uncle, who held a position at the Imperial Court, in hopes that he would be trained for Imperial service. However, after his initial education, George rejected his family's plans and decided to live a life of revelry in the Great City. While in Constantinople he met a monastic named Symeon, known as "the Pious," who resided at the famous Studion monastery in the capitol city. Symeon the Pious became George's spiritual father and trained him in classical Eastern Orthodox spirituality. At this time George claims to have had a profound "charismatic" experience in which he encountered the Lord in a vision of light.[8] He still felt the pull of the world and for a period of time wavered back and forth until finally he forsook the world, entered Studion monastery, was tonsured as a monk, taking the name of Symeon, in honor of his spiritual father, and was placed under the continued spiritual direction of Symeon the Pious.

Almost immediately the newly tonsured monk Symeon found himself in conflict with the abbot of the Studion monastery. Symeon the Pious gave spiritual directions that flew in the face of the stricter rules of Studion and the younger Symeon was asked to ignore the counsel of his spiritual father. To the contrary, Symeon the younger, who believed that his relationship with Symeon the Pious was a direct answer to prayer for a spiritual guide who would lead him to Christ, refused to forsake Symeon the Pious. As a result, Symeon the younger was expelled from the Studion Monastery.

7. Maloney, *Mystic of Fire and Light.* While Stephanou's introduction of St. Symeon the New Theologian to the readers of *The Logos,* preceded Maloney's biography by two years, it was Maloney's work, read by many Charismatic Catholics, that lifted St. Symeon out of the shadows in the Western world. St. Symeon the New Theologian's works were well known to both Greek and Russian-speaking monastics, however most Orthodox laypeople were unfamiliar with his life and teachings.

8. Krivocheine, *In the Light of Christ,* 17.

Relocating to the monastery of St. Mamas in western Constantinople, Symeon continued under the spiritual direction of Symeon the Pious, who remained at Studios. After the death of the abbot of St. Mamas, Symeon was elected to replace him and he was ordained to the priesthood. Symeon's biographer, St. Niketas Stethatos relates this story:

> When the most wise Symeon was being ordained priest by the patriarch and the latter was saying the prayer over him while he was bending his knee and bowing his head for the sacrament, Symeon beheld the Holy Spirit, pure and formless like boundless light, coming down and covering his most holy head. Indeed, during his forty-eight years as a priest, when he was celebrating the liturgy, he also used to see this light descending upon the eucharistic sacrifice he offered up to God. He would recount this story, but as though he were talking about someone else in order to conceal himself . . . .[9]

St. Symeon the New Theologian's teachings were based upon his many visions and direct encounters with the Lord. Instead of appealing to books of theology and or the opinions of religious philosophers, Symeon received revelations from the Holy Spirit regarding the theological inquiries put to him. One Stephen of Nicomedia, a bishop who served the Patriarch of Constantinople, jealous of Symeon's reputation as a spiritual father, undertook a campaign to besmirch the character and honor of the New Theologian. Stephen looked down on the simple monk and felt that he was theologically unlettered. Seeking to trip Symeon up, and feign spiritual humility, Stephen, at a public gathering, asked Symeon to answer an obscure question regarding the persons of the Holy Trinity. Symeon replied that he would give him an answer in due time. Symeon took the question to the Lord in prayer, and after being caught up in the Spirit in an experience of divine light, Symeon was given the answer. In addition, the Lord revealed to Symeon at least two other important teachings: one, that anyone who has not a personal experience of Christ or been initiated into the things of the Spirit cannot teach others. In other words, they cannot teach what they themselves have not learned experientially, and second, it is a heresy to state that the experiences of, and life in, the Holy Spirit, experienced by the first Apostles and the Apostolic Church, is no longer available today. It is these teachings that gained for Symeon the title of "New Theologian" in the Church. He did not appeal to scholastic texts or simple repeat the words of others. Rather, as is

9. N. Stethatos, *The Life of Saint Symeon*, 65–7.

true in Orthodox spirituality, a theologian is one who teaches theology not from the words of others but by his own experience of God.

Stephen of Nicomedia did not receive Symeon's words of instruction, but rather was inflamed with even greater jealousy. Symeon the Pious had since reposed in the Lord and his spiritual son sought to honor his memory, venerate his life, and seek for his further intercessions. Symeon the New Theologian commissioned an icon of his spiritual father to be painted and composed a service in his honor. On the anniversary of Symeon the Pious' death, the New Theologian would invite surrounding monastics to come and help him celebrate the Pious one's memory. Stephen of Nicomedia saw this as an opportunity to ingratiate himself with the Patriarch. He complained about this veneration of a man who had not been officially recognized as a saint by the Church. Symeon was summoned before an ecclesiastical tribunal. Initially the Patriarch commended Symeon for his veneration of his spiritual father. Stephen, however, did not cease to enlist others in his fight against Symeon. Once again, he was summoned before a Patriarchal synod at which time he was ordered to celebrate the services for Symeon the Pious privately. Symeon the younger refused and was banished from St. Mamas monastery and exiled from Constantinople.

Symeon crossed the Bosporus and found a small abandoned chapel outside the village of Paloukiton, which he rebuilt. Joined by several of his disciples, Symeon continued to pray, serve, and write. Within two years, after protests from his followers in Constantinople, the Patriarch reviewed the case and reversed the banishment. He recalled Symeon to the capital city, offering to elevate him as a bishop and compensate him for his troubles. Symeon refused and returned to his community outside Paloukiton. Following a prophetic utterance, in which Symeon foretold the exact date of his death weeks in advance, he laid upon his sick bed, levitating from it during his times of prayer. He fell asleep in the Lord, surrounded by many of his disciples, on March 12, 1022.

St. Niketas Stethatos, Symeon's disciple, biographer, and collector of his writings, records many charismatic manifestations during the New Theologians' life time. He not only exercised the gift of prophecy, but also the word of knowledge, healing, and casting out demons.[10] The bulk of Symeon's charismatic experiences lie in his numerous visions of God, usually manifested as what is called in the Orthodox Church, the "uncreated light."

10. Ibid., 265–99.

St. Symeon firmly believed that the all true Christians, whether they were monastics or laity, who properly prepared themselves, could experience the Holy Spirit in the same way as the first Apostles and early followers of Christ. He writes:

> Do not say that it is impossible to receive the Divine Spirit. Do not say that without Him you can be saved. Do not say, therefore, that one can possess Him without knowing it! Do not say that God is not able to be seen by men. Do not say that men do not see the divine light or that this is impossible in these present times! This is a thing never impossible, friends, but on the contrary it is very possible to those who wish, but only to those who lead a life purified of passions and have purified, spiritual eyes.[11]

St. Symeon's Teaching on the Baptism of the Holy Spirit

St. Symeon wrote considerably about having a conscious awareness of the Holy Spirit, even beyond the sacramental experiences of baptism in water and Chrismation (confirmation). This conscious awareness he attributes to what he called a "baptism in the Holy Spirit."[12] While stressing the conscious nature of the baptism in the Holy Spirit he does not deny the efficacy of sacramental baptism, which in his time would have mainly been performed for infants. He writes:

> We receive the remission of sins at our divine baptism and we are freed from the ancient curse and sanctified by the presence of the Holy Spirit.[13]

In his Discourse on Repentance, number 5, St. Symeon writes:

> The condemnation that was the consequence of our forefather's transgression he completely annihilated. By Holy Baptism He regenerates and refashions us, completely sets us free from the condemnation, and places us in this world wholly free instead of being oppressed by the tyranny of the enemy . . . . So we have been born again in Holy Baptism and have been released from slavery

---

11. St. Symeon, *Hymns*, 145.

12. St. Symeon, *Practical and Theological Chapters*, 84.

13. Ibid., 85.

and become free, so the enemy cannot take any action against us unless we of our own will obey him.[14]

However, St. Symeon is quick to point out that instead of remaining in the place of freedom, purification, and grace, we turn aside and, because of our continued sinful actions, the grace that we received in our baptism is transgressed so much that we put off that which we put on and was given to us, we turn away or ignore Christ and we are then in need of renewed purification. This purification comes only by deep and profound repentance accompanied by tears. In one of his hymns he pens:

> Assemble, children, come, women, hasten fathers before the end comes, and, with me, all weep, lament, since having received God in Baptism as infants, or rather, having become sons of God as little children, soon, sinners, we have been expelled from the House of David and that happened to us without our realizing it! Let us hasten by repentance since it is by it that all the expelled return and there is no other way . . . .[15]

This renewed purification St. Symeon call the "baptism in the Holy Spirit." While the mystery of holy baptism was efficacious, because it incorporated the faith of the Church and the sponsors, the infant was unconscious of it and depending upon the upbringing of their parents and the life lived afterwards may, or may not, have kept the deposit of grace and faith undefiled. Then there is a need for one to *consciously* receive the Holy Spirit that had unconsciously been given in holy baptism. In another hymn, St. Symeon states:

> For those who have received Your Baptism in infancy and have lived their life unworthily of that Baptism, their condemnation will be worse than that of the unbaptized, as You have said, since they have disgraced Your holy robe. And knowing, O Savior, this to be certain and true, You have given repentance unto a second purification and You have fixed it as a term for the grace of the Spirit that which we received before in the first Baptism, for it is not only "by water" as You have said that grace comes, but also rather "by the Spirit" in the invocation of the Trinity. Because therefore, we have been baptized as children with no awareness, having been imperfect, so we received imperfectly the grace when we received the pardon of the first transgression. . . . Such was Adam before his

14. St. Symeon, *Discourses,* 100–101.

15. St. Symeon, *Hymns,* 57.

sin, such also are all those who have been baptized and know the cause, but it does not apply to those who in their insensibility have not received the intellectual awareness which the Spirit brings about in coming by His works.[16]

St. Symeon teaches that the physical, outward evidence of this baptism in the Holy Spirit is the gift of tears. Concerning the two baptisms, he writes:

> But this is not yet the perfect grace of which the Scriptures speak: "I shall dwell in them and walk therein." This applies only to those who are strong in the faith and show it in their works, for if we fall back into evil and shameful deeds after our baptism, we completely throw away this very sanctification. It is in proportion to our repentance, confession, and tears that we receive the remission of our former sins, and as a consequence of this, sanctification and grace from on high.[17]

For St. Symeon, the water in baptism and the oil of chrismation are types that need to be fulfilled by being experienced consciously. He explains:

> Even though He is God who cannot be limited, he is limited by our weakness. But when a man suddenly lifts his eyes and contemplates the nature of reality in a way he has never done before, then he trembles and tears flood out spontaneously though he feels no sorrow. They purify him and wash him in a second baptism, that baptism our Lord speaks about in the Gospels: "If a man is not born of water and the Spirit, he will not enter the kingdom of heaven." And again he says: "If he is not born from on high." When he said "from on high," he signified being born of the Spirit. In the first baptism, water symbolizes tears and the oil of chrismation prefigures the inner anointing of the Spirit. But the second baptism is no longer a type of the truth, but the truth itself.[18]

The leaders of the Charismatic Renewal Movement in the Orthodox Church saw in St. Symeon the New Theologian a spiritual father who clearly taught that receiving the sacraments of baptism and chrismation in the Church were not sufficient, in and of themselves, but that those who had received those mysteries, efficacious though they be, were also in need of a "new" or "second" baptism. Because of their failure to ". . . preserve

16. St. Symeon, *Hymns*, 279–80.

17. St. Symeon, *Practical and Theological Chapters*, 3.45, 85.

18. Ibid. 1.35—1.36, 42.

[their] baptismal garment . . . undefiled . . . ," by giving themselves over to sin without repentance, not "having preserved the gift of Thy Holy Spirit," and because they have not "increased the measure of grace committed unto [them]"[19] they were in need of a renewal of the grace of the Holy Spirit, and that renewal needed to be a *conscious encounter* of the Holy Spirit. Orthodox participants in the Charismatic Movement witness that their "baptism in the Holy Spirit" was precisely this "renewal" or "second baptism."[20]

Likewise, the leaders of the Renewal in the Orthodox Church believed that the "baptism of the Holy Spirit," recently experienced by Pentecostal and Charismatic Christians, was a genuine manifestation of the grace of God, even outside the boundaries of the canonical Orthodox Church. They acknowledge this without fully endorsing Pentecostal or Charismatic theology and spirituality, which in some cases was contrary to the dogmatic teachings of the Orthodox Church. At the same time, they affirmed that there were Orthodox Christians who were experiencing the same "outpouring of the Spirit" and that this renewed experience of the Holy Spirit was not a denial of the initial reception of the Holy Spirit in baptism and chrismation, but rather their actualization.[21] They also affirmed that this "new" outpouring was the continuation of the promise of the Father given through the writings of the Prophet Joel and declared on the Day of Pentecost by the Apostle St. Peter, and that this continuation has ebbed and flowed throughout history and among all Christians who sincerely sought to walk in the gospel of Jesus Christ, even though at times their theology may not have been fully Orthodox, through no fault of their own.[22]

At no time, have the Orthodox Churches of the East ever officially articulated or adopted a theological stance akin to "cessationism." Rather, the Orthodox Church has consistently maintained a belief that genuine charismatic manifestations among its members, among the clergy and especially among monastics, is an abiding sign of the presence of the Holy Spirit in the Church.

> The charismatic phenomena of the first centuries of Christianity repeated themselves in . . . monasticism; the elders were bearers of these charisms—the special gifts of the Holy Spirit, given to man directly from God. . . . An ascetic is ideally a God-bearing

19. *Service Book*, 153, 156.
20. Nicoloudakis, "Release," 3–6.
21. Theosis, "Interview with Fr. Boris Zabrodsky," 1–6.
22. Emmert, "Orthodox Charismatic Renewal," 1–6.

and Spirit-bearing being. . . . As such, he receives spiritual gifts, an outpouring of which distinguished the first era of Christianity. The gifts of prophecy, casting out demons, healing sicknesses, and resurrecting the dead are not exceptional. They only disclose a normal step in the spiritual growth of a monk.[23]

The cessation of charismatic manifestations within the Orthodox Church is unthinkable. This would imply the departure of the Holy Spirit from the Church, the result being the demise of the Church. While the Orthodox Church does not have the bureaucratic apparatus employed by the Roman Catholic Church in its process of canonizing a saint, in which verifiable miracles are required, the Orthodox Church does nonetheless see the manifestation of miracles, coupled together with Orthodoxy of belief and moral, ascetical, and holy living, as signs of discerning the sanctity of a person. Numerous healers, wonderworkers, prophets, and Spirit-bearers are canonized saints venerated in the Orthodox Church. Some of the more recently saints, within the last century and a half, such as St. Herman of Alaska, St. Seraphim of Sarov, St. Nektarios of Aegina, St. Matrona of Moscow, St. Silouan of Mount Athos, St. John of San Francisco in America, and most recently St. Paisius of the Holy Mountain, St. Porphyrios the Wonderworker, and Mother Gabrielia, were practitioners of charismatic gifts in their lifetime, as well as having manifestations associated with them even after their repose.[24] Likewise, many of those departed who have not been canonized, as well as living men and women within the Orthodox Church, are venerated as holy elders/eldresses, and are believed to manifest charismatic gifts.[25]

23. Middleton, *Precious Vessels of the Holy Spirit,*" v. This quotation is attributed to S. I. Smirnov from the book, *The Spiritual Father in the Ancient Eastern Church.* No other information is provided.

24. Miracles of healings are reported to take place at the tombs of these saints, as well as associated with items directly associated with their person, such as their bones, clothing worn by them, oil that fuels the lamps that illumine their icons, etc. This is certainly considered charismatic phenomenon in the Orthodox Church.

25. Middleton, *Precious Vessels* and Papadopoulos, *The Garden,* and Agapios, *The Divine Flame.*

The Roots of a Movement: The Pietists and the Rise of Methodism

The Pietist Movement, a spiritual renewal movement that grew out of the Protestant Reformation of the sixteenth and seventeenth centuries, is in some ways the root of the contemporary Charismatic Movement. It was born out of a reaction to what many would characterize as an overly intellectual and confessional approach to the Christian Faith evidenced in "a new scholasticism of subtleties about 'ubiquity.'"[26] Phillip Jakob Spener, a seventeenth-century German Lutheran pastor and theologian, is considered the "father" of Pietism. Spener felt the German Lutheran church of his day to be in serious need of further reform due to:

> . . . that superficial security which is content with an external subscription to the orthodox Lutheran Church, and which is satisfied with, merely intellectual attachment to pure doctrine, outward participation in divine service and the sacraments, and abstinence from gross sins and vices.[27]

Spener believed that the most important thing necessary for salvation was personal conversion and change of heart, resulting in a life of holiness. By 1670, to provide an atmosphere for such conversions, Spener held weekly gatherings in his home during which he repeated his sermon from the previous Sunday's service. Discussion and questions were encouraged together with the study of Holy Scriptures. These meetings became known as "collegia pietatis" or the gathering of the pious. In 1675, Spener penned his most influential work, *Pia Desideria*, the full title being translated as *Earnest Desire for a Reform of the True Evangelical Church*. In this short work Spener

> . . . proposed the following helpful measures: the word of God must be more widely diffused among the people, this end being furthered by discussions on the Bible under the pastor's guidance; the establishment and maintenance of the spiritual priesthood, which is not possessed by the clergy alone, but is rather constituted by the right and duty of all Christians to instruct others, to punish, to exhort, to edify, and to care for their salvation; the fact must be emphasized that mere knowledge is insufficient in Christianity, which is expressed rather in action; more gentleness and love between denominations are needed in polemics; the university

26. McManners, *The Oxford Illustrated History of Christianity*, 292.
27. Schaff, *The New Schaff-Herzog Encyclopedia of Religious Knowledge*, Vol. IX, 54.

training of the clergy must be changed so as to include personal piety and the reading of edification, as well as intellectual knowledge and dogmatic controversies; and, finally, sermons should be prepared on a more edifying plan, with less emphasis on rhetorical art and homiletic erudition.[28]

In 1692, a Pietist theological and ministerial training seminary was established at the University of Halle. Through this institution, Pietism spread among the clergy of the German Lutheran Church. The school's greatest contribution to the Movement came through the ministry of Count Nicholas Von Zinzendorf, who embraced the principles and spirit of the Movement. Zinzendorf broke with the Lutheran Church and formed the Moravian Brethren, an intense Pietistic community which boiled down the entire Christian faith to the simple gospel of love evidenced in "heart religion."[29] Zinzendorf and the Moravian's established missions outside Bohemia and Poland in England and the American colonies, but the greatest and international impact of their influence was upon Anglican minister and founder of Methodism, John Wesley.[30]

It is no exaggerated claim that without the Moravians the name of John Wesley might be lost to history, and the several Methodist denominations who trace their spiritual legacy to Wesley may never have come into existence. Wesley's first encounter with the Moravians took place on his journey across the Atlantic from England to the North American colony of Georgia. The ship that Wesley and a band of Moravians shared ran into dangerous weather, so much so that the passengers feared for their lives. However, Wesley, an ordained priest in the Church of England, who should have had enough religious faith to comfort others, found himself in great dread and anxiety over his own eternal fate, while the Moravians engaged in prayer and hymn-singing, exhibiting a profound spirit of peace and tranquility in the midst of the raging storm. But it was not until Wesley's miserable failure at mission work in the colony of Georgia, his return to England, and the fateful evening of May 24, 1738, when he attended a Moravian meeting in the Aldersgate section of London, did the Moravian influence upon Wesley bear solid fruit. At Aldersgate, upon hearing the reading of Martin Luther's preface to his commentary on the Book of Romans, Wesley felt his heart "strangely warmed." Just a few days following this experience,

28. Ibid.
29. Ibid.
30. Ibid., 331.

Wesley embarked upon a pilgrimage to the center of the Moravian fellow-ship in Herrnhut, near Dresden, Germany. Upon Wesley's return he began to preach the message of salvation by faith to those who he felt needed it the most; the inmates at London's infamous Newgate prison. Wesley and Christianity would never be the same.[31]

Methodism coexisted alongside the Anglican Church for decades. John Wesley never intended on founding another denomination. Rather, Methodism was conceived as a spiritual renewal movement within the Church of England. However, as adherents of Methodism grew in number and influence, Wesley and his lay preachers came into open conflict with Anglican rectors and bishops who saw the Methodists as overly emo-tional, too attached to conversion experiences, and unconcerned with Anglican orthodoxy. George Whitfield—a Calvinist Anglican minister and Methodist enthusiast—embarked on preaching tours in the Ameri-can colonies that proved this point when he participated in holy commu-nion with Congregationalists in New England. The final break between the Methodists and the Church of England, however, did not take place until the end of the Revolutionary War in the American Colonies, with the disestablishment of the Anglican Church there and the organization of the Protestant Episcopal Church in the newly formed United States of America, and was assisted by the prolific preaching ministry of the first Methodist bishop, Francis Asbury.[32]

The Methodist Church and the Holiness Movement

John Wesley believed that Methodism was established by God in order that "scriptural holiness would be taught throughout the lands."[33] Beginning in 1760, Wesley sent "ordained" lay preachers to America to establish Method-ist societies, with the understanding they would work under the leadership of the Anglican Church in the colonies. At the outbreak of the Revolution-ary War many of the Methodist preachers returned to England. However, Francis Asbury, who came to America in 1771, remained. Wesley had pe-titioned the Anglican Bishop of London to ordain a bishop for America, to administer the sacraments to the Anglican Methodists, but his request

31. Ferguson, *Methodists and the Making of America*, 92–93.

32. Gaustad and Noll, *Documentary History of Religion in America to 1877*, 271.

33. Warner, "Spreading Scriptural Holiness," 115–38.

was rebuffed. Wesley "ordained" Thomas Coke, already an ordained presbyter in the Church of England, to go to the United States and to "ordain" Asbury. Together Asbury and Coke were to serve as co-superintendents. Asbury refused to accept the appointment until the American preachers confirmed Wesley's decision. The Methodist Episcopal Church came into existence at "The Christmas Conference," held in Baltimore, Maryland from December 25–27, 1784. Here, Coke and Asbury were chosen by the Methodist ministers as their leaders, and were "ordained" by the preachers as superintendents/bishops.

From the outset, the Methodist Episcopal Church committed itself to three tasks: one, preaching the gospel to everyone, everywhere; two, encouraging those who received the gospel to move on into an experience of sanctification or holiness; and three, to establish churches wherever their preaching travels took them. The growth of the Methodist Episcopal Church in the United States was meteoric.[34] Its phenomenal growth is attributed to its circuit riding preachers, who penetrated even the most backwoods regions of frontier America, and it organization of "class meetings." The class meetings were small groups led by laymen or laywomen, during which hymns were sung, the Scriptures were read, testimonies were heard, and sins were confessed.[35] This held the local Methodist flock together in between the visits of the circuit riding preachers.

Asbury was constantly encouraging his preachers to exhort the people to "holy living" and to proclaim the doctrine of sanctification. Simply put, the doctrine of sanctification taught that while a person might be redeemed, born again by faith in the work of Jesus Christ, and testify to being "saved," the "Adamic root of sin" was still active in the Christian believer. However, there is provided by the Lord another spiritual experience in which that Adamic root of sin is taken out of the believer and they are freed from the power of sin. This experience was referred to as "being sanctified," "made holy," or "baptized in the Holy Spirit."[36] The more radical wing of the Holiness Movement went so far as to claim that after one was sanctified, they could live a life of sinless perfection.[37]

This emphasis upon sanctification and personal holiness became the cornerstone of the Methodist Episcopal Church. However, it didn't end

---

34. Johnson, *Frontier Camp Meeting*, 67, 109.

35. Baker, *John Wesley and the Church of England*, 77–78, 87.

36. Wood, *The Meaning of Pentecost*.

37. Synan, *The Holiness-Pentecostal Movement*, 47.

there. The Christian experience of sanctification and holy living moved beyond the walls of the Methodist Church, touching Presbyterians, Baptists, and other Protestant denominations. Charles Finney, Congregationalist turned Presbyterian, and founder of Oberlin College in Ohio, latched onto the teaching of sanctification, adopting and adapting it in his ministry.[38] In his written testimony, Finney gave witness to a profound experience of sanctification, which he called the baptism of the Holy Spirit.[39] This language, equating the experience of sanctification with the baptism of the Holy Spirit, was not altogether new. John Fletcher, early Methodist theologian, and confidante and close friend of John Wesley, used this very terminology in his defense of the experience of sanctification.[40]

This trans-denominational reception of the Wesleyan emphasis on sanctification, as an experience following personal salvation, led to the growth of what became known as the Holiness Movement. Impetus was given to the Holiness Movement in a revival that broke out a few years prior to the American Civil War. Phoebe Palmer, a Methodist lay woman, living in New York City, held weekly meetings in her home for those seeking to be sanctified. Influential men and women attended Palmer's prayer meetings, some of them Methodist Bishops and leaders in other denominations.[41] This is only one of the catalysts leading to the national attention on Christian Holiness. With the Civil War, and the national divisions it spawned, the Methodist Church ended up splitting over the issue of slavery, and the Holiness Movement was likewise affected.[42] However, after the end of the war, the Holiness Movement continued unabated and even grew in strength. By the 1870s, the Movement had become nationwide. Holiness associations established Holiness camp meetings throughout the country, east and west, north and south. Holiness newspapers and magazines proliferated together with Holiness publishing concerns producing books on holiness. Evangelists and preachers were identified as Holiness evangelists and preachers.[43]

38. Gresham, Jr., *Charles G. Finney's Doctrine.*

39. Finney, *Memoirs of Rev. Charles G. Finney,* 20–21.

40. John William Fletcher, *Check to Antinomianism.*

41. Oden, *Phoebe Palmer: Selected Writings.*

42. Bucke, *History of American Methodism.* Vol. 2, 11–85. The Methodist Episcopal Church ended up splitting over the issue of slavery. In response, Southern Methodists organized the Methodist Church, South, which supported slavery.

43. Synan, *Holiness-Pentecostal,* 45.

The Holiness Movement began to collapse under its own weight of influence. By the 1880s, leaders in the Methodist Church, especially in the South, felt that the emphasis upon holiness had become overblown and in some cases devolved into legalism. The Methodist Church in the South had grown to the point where it was viewed as the church of the middle and upper class and the emphasis and culture of camp-meetings and emotional displays, so common in the Holiness Movement, were "old-fashioned" and "low class."[44] Also, many Methodist ministers began to question the Holiness Movement's interpretation of John Wesley's teaching on sanctification. One Methodist historian put it this way, "*Entire* and *instantaneous* became battles cries, answered by *progressive* and *gradual*."[45] By 1884, it was clear that the Methodist Episcopal (South), while affirming Wesley's teaching on perfect love, no longer supported the Holiness Movement's understanding of sanctification when at its General Conference, the bishops released a statement that in part read:

> But there has sprung up among us a party with holiness as a watch-word; they have holiness associations, holiness meetings, holiness preachers, holiness evangelists, and holiness property. Religious experience is represented as if it consists of only two steps, the first step out of condemnation into peace, and the next step into Christian perfection.[46]

The "nail in the coffin" however, came when the Methodist Episcopal Church (South) passed "Rule 301," which stated that no Methodist minister or evangelist could preach within the geographical territory of another Methodist minister's "circuit" without his express permission. This effectively curtailed the activities of Holiness Methodist evangelists, seeing that most anti-Holiness Methodist leaders were pastors of local congregations.[47]

The Pentecostal Revival of the Twentieth Century

Since entire and instantaneous sanctification, the landmark doctrine and experience of the Holiness Revival of the eighteenth and nineteenth centuries,

44. Stephens, *The Fire Spreads*, 141–45.

45. Norwood, *Story of American Methodism*, 298–99.

46. Journal of the General Conference, Methodist Episcopal Church, South (1894), 25.

47. Synan, *Old-Time Power*, 74.

was effectively jettisoned from the Methodist Episcopal Church (South), a host of breakaway Holiness denominations formed; the Pentecostal Church of the Nazarene,[48] the Church of God (Anderson), the Pilgrim Holiness Church, and the Fire-Baptized Holiness Church, only to name a few. These new Holiness denominations continued the traditions engendered by the earlier Wesleyan emphasis on the doctrine and experience of sanctification. Therefore, Holiness camp meetings and publications did not wane but rather proliferated. The preaching of sanctification continued in the parishes of the Methodist Episcopal Church above the Mason-Dixon line, but, like its Southern sister, it too finally repudiated the doctrine of entire sanctification as a definite experience subsequent to regeneration.[49]

In the middle decades, and waning days of the nineteenth century, a perceptible shift took place within the Holiness Movement, both among Wesleyans and adherents of Keswick doctrine.[50] Whereas earlier theological reflection on the doctrine and experience of entire sanctification was decidedly Christological in emphasis, a new shift, gradual but perceptive, took place in which more attention was given to the pneumatological aspects of the doctrine. Even the term "sanctification" began to be replaced by the phrase "baptism of the Holy Spirit." Holiness periodicals, and hymns made ample use of the word "Pentecostal" in their titles. Non-Wesleyan evangelists and teachers, such as Reuben A. Torey, Asa Mahan, and Dwight L. Moody, preached sermons and wrote books which emphasized the baptism of the Holy Spirit as the impartation of spiritual power to the Christian believer for victorious living, which was elevated over personal holiness and repudiated the "eradicationist" doctrine of many

48. As the word "Pentecostal" became progressively associated with those denominations that encouraged the practice of speaking in tongues, the Nazarenes dropped the word "Pentecostal" from their name in order not to be confused with those churches that practiced tongues-speaking.

49. Dieter, *The Holiness Revival*, 230–32.

50. Kostlevy, *Historical Dictionary of the Holiness Movement*, 20–21, 171–73, 274–76. The Keswick Movement, named for an annual "Higher Life" conference held in Keswick, England, beginning in 1873. Organized by American Quakers Robert and Hannah Whitehall Smith and Presbyterian minister W. E. Boardman, the conference repudiated the more radical teachings held by some proponents of the Holiness Movement that the experience of "second-blessing sanctification" resulted in a complete eradication of the sinful nature. Rather, those who held to a Keswick understanding of sanctification taught that the Christian believer received a "baptism of the Holy Spirit," subsequent to their salvation experience, in which the power of the Spirit "counteracted" the effects of the sinful nature. In the United States, the Keswick understanding of sanctification was promoted by D. L. Moody and A. B. Simpson, the founder of the Christian and Missionary Alliance.

radical Holiness proponents.[51] This new emphasis flowed from an increasing conviction of Evangelical and Holiness Christians that Christ's Second Coming was imminent and that a new outpouring of the Holy Spirit in apostolic power was necessary to equip the Church to engage in successful worldwide evangelization. Just as the Lord, in the first Christian century, poured out the Holy Spirit upon the 120 disciples gathered in the upper room, empowering them to carry the gospel to the ends of the earth, and confirmed their proclamation by signs, wonders, miracles, and mighty works, once again the Lord would do the same for the last days Church. The new twentieth century loomed before them and some eschatological enthusiasts predicted that the new century would be humanities' last, and that certainly by the year 2000 Christ would return and set up His millennial kingdom upon the earth. All of this created a heightened sense of expectation, especially among Holiness believers.[52]

One such Holiness believer, Charles Parham, formerly a Methodist preacher, like many others, departed the denomination after its hostile reactions to Holiness adherents within its ranks. Born in 1873 in Muscatine, Iowa, Parham was sickly as a child, contracting rheumatic fever at nine. At twelve years of age his mother died, which devastated him emotionally and contributed to his vow to "meet her again in heaven." This set him on a path of religious discovery. He attended a local Congregational Church where he committed himself to Christ. Later he joined the Methodist Church, where as a young teenager he taught Sunday school and began to preach.[53]

In 1890, Parham matriculated at Southwest Kansas College, initially hoping to study theology and enter the ministry; however, he changed his major to medicine. After a severe bout with his rheumatic fever, during which he feared for his life, Parham became convinced that it was God's punishment for not continuing his studies for the ministry. He repented for his disobedience and was miraculously healed. This experience led Parham to embrace the doctrine of divine healing. In 1893, he left college and for a short period of time pastored a Methodist church in Lawrence, Kansas. In 1895, Parham exited the Methodist Church and launched out upon an independent and itinerant ministry of preaching and praying for the sick. In 1898, he travelled to Illinois and spent time at Zion City observing the healing ministry of John Alexander Dowie. Zion, founded by Dowie as a

51. Gilbertson, *The Baptism*, 19–22.

52. Cox, *Fire*, 116–20.

53. Goff, Jr., *Fields White*, 17–31.

"Christian city," maintained several "Healing Homes" to which the sick were brought and intense, prolonged prayer was offered for their divine cure. This impressed Parham who returned west and opened Beth-el Faith Home in Topeka, Kansas. In 1900, he embarked on a tour of other divine healing centers in the United States; Frank W. Sandford's "Holy Ghost and Us" Community in Shiloh, Maine, A. J. Gordon's church in Boston, A. B. Simpson's work in Nyack, New York and D. L. Moody's mission in Chicago.[54] While at Shiloh, Maine, Parham encountered speaking in tongues among Sandford's followers. He began to contemplate that the gift of tongues might be restored to the Church in order that the gospel could to be preached around the world without the arduous and time-consuming process of learning a foreign language before going to the mission field.[55]

Parham returned to Topeka and opened Bethel Bible School, meeting in a large rented house. A castle-like structure, the house had a turret that served as a prayer tower and was known locally as "Stone's Folly," because the original builder, Erastus R. Stone, ran out of money before its completion. A faith school, Bethel provided classes in the Bible to train gospel workers in the doctrines of salvation by grace through faith, entire sanctification as a second definite work of grace, divine healing, and the imminent Second Coming of Jesus Christ. Approximately forty students gathered around Parham, the primary teacher at Bethel, who continued his itinerant preaching ministry in Holiness congregations. While Parham zealously embraced the doctrine of entire sanctification as a subsequent experience to salvation, he was beginning to entertain the possibility that there was a "third work of grace" subsequent to sanctification, which was the baptism of the Holy Spirit. There is evidence that Parham had visited some meetings of the Fire-Baptized Holiness Movement, which taught that the full Christian life consisted of personal conversion, followed by the experience of sanctification which then prepared the believer to the receive the baptism of the Holy Spirit and Fire.[56]

In the winter of 1900, before leaving on a preaching engagement, Parham assigned his students a research project. They were to ascertain, from studying the Scriptures, the physical sign or evidence that one had received the baptism of the Holy Spirit. Upon Parham's return to Bethel he gathered the students together to hear the results of their research.

54. Goff, *Fields White*, 53–60.

55. Faupel, *Everlasting Gospel*, 174–76.

56. Ibid., 166–67.

According to his report, almost every student came to the same conclusion; the sign of the baptism of the Holy Spirit was the act of speaking in other tongues, as recorded throughout the Book of the Acts of the Apostles. This engendered a great deal of expectation on the part of the student body because while many claimed to be saved and sanctified, according to this new understanding, neither Parham nor the students had received the baptism of the Holy Spirit.[57]

As was traditional at that time in many Evangelical and Holiness churches, New Year's Eve was celebrated with a worship, or "Watch Night" service, in which the New Year was ushered in with prayer. As students and friends gathered at Bethel in the tower for prayer on the evening of December 31, 1900, the eve a new millennium, one student, Agnes Ozman, approached Charles Parham and asked him to lay hands on her and pray that she might receive the baptism of the Holy Spirit as the Apostles and early disciples had. As Parham laid his hands on her head and prayed, Ozman almost immediately began to speak in what appeared to Parham to be a foreign language.[58] This was repeated throughout the night as other Bethel students received this experience of the baptism of the Holy Spirit and speaking in tongues. Thus, on January 1, 1901, the modern Pentecostal Movement was born.[59]

Most Pentecostals leaders in North America celebrate this event in Topeka as the beginning of their movement because of the connection between the experience of the baptism of the Holy Spirit and the accompanying manifestation of speaking in tongues as the "sign" or "evidence" of having received this experience. Many Christians had claimed to receive the baptism of the Holy Spirit previously, for most adherents of the Holiness Movement described their experience of sanctification as a "baptism of the Holy Spirit." However, Topeka was the first known time that the baptism of the Holy Spirit was linked directly to speaking in tongues.[60] From

57. Goff, *Fields White*, 66–86.

58. Marty, *Modern American Religion, Volume 1*, 240–41. There is a discrepancy between Ozman's early and later testimony about this event. In one place, she claims that she spoke in tongues as early as three weeks before the Topeka New Year's Eve event, while in another place she claims that this was the first time she had spoken in tongues.

59. Goff, *Fields White*, 66–67.

60. Flower, "The Birth," 3. Dories, "Edward Irving and the 'Standing Sign,'" 41–56. Edward Irving, a nineteenth-century Presbyterian minister in London and founder of the Catholic Apostolic Church, wrote an entire treatise on speaking in tongues as "the standing sign of the baptism of the Holy Spirit."

that moment Parham and his followers began to teach a three-stage process of Christian initiation; first, conversion, or personal salvation experienced through repentance and faith in Jesus Christ, second, entire sanctification, subsequent to salvation, in which the Christian believer's heart is cleansed from all sin and the "sin nature" or "adamic nature" is eradicated, and third, subsequent to salvation and entire sanctification, the baptism in the Holy Spirit, in which the Holy Spirit comes and takes up residence within the mind, body, and soul of the Christian, empowering them for Christian witness and mission, evidenced by the experience of speaking in tongues. Parham taught that the tongues phenomenon was that of xenoglossy, the miraculous ability to speak in a foreign language without any teaching or training on the part of the speaker.[61]

Parham took this new message of the "Apostolic Faith," as he called it, around the area of Kansas and Missouri and south to Texas. He organized "Apostolic Faith Bands" of men and women who played instruments, sang hymns, testified, and preached about the experience of the baptism of the Holy Spirit and the accompanying sign of speaking in tongues. However, he met with mediocre success. In 1906, he traveled south to Houston, Texas and opened a short-term Bible school. William J. Seymour, an African-America in the Holiness ministry, approached Parham and asked to attend the school. "Jim Crow" laws enforced in Texas, however, prohibited Seymour from sitting with whites in the same classroom.[62] Parham nonetheless accommodated Seymour and allowed him to sit outside the door in the hallway. Seymour became convinced of Parham's doctrine of the baptism of the Holy Spirit being subsequent to salvation and sanctification and also that speaking in tongues was the sign of having received the third experience. Yet Seymour did not receive the experience while attending classes in Houston. Before completing Parham's school, Seymour received an invitation to come to Los Angeles and take over the pastorate of a small Holiness congregation. Despite Parham's protests that Seymour needed more training and should remain at the Bible school until he completed the classes, Seymour accepted the invitation and headed west.[63]

William Seymour arrived in Los Angeles on Thursday, February 22, 1906.[64] He attended the small Holiness mission to which he had been

61. Cooper-Rompato, *Gift of Tongues: Women's Xenoglossia*, 10–17, 194.

62. Goff, *Fields White*, 106–7

63. Synan and Fox, Jr. *William J. Seymour,* 56–61.

64. Robeck, *Azusa Street,* 60.

invited and preached his first sermon on the baptism of the Holy Spirit and tongues as the evidence. The message met with a chilly reception among the leaders of the mission and the following service he found himself locked out of the building.[65] Seymour accepted the offer of Richard and Ruth Asberry, an African-American couple, to stay in their home at 214 North Bonnie Brae Street in Los Angeles, and hold prayer and preaching services in their house.[66] It was at one of these home meetings that Seymour himself received the baptism of the Holy Spirit and spoke in tongues.[67] Now that his preaching had become his own personal experience, Seymour's zeal increased. Many who attended the services at Bonnie Brae Street received the baptism of the Holy Spirit and spoke in tongues. The Asberry home became too small to accommodate the large number of people who attended the meetings. Several blocks from the Asberry's home stood an old, dilapidated African Methodist Episcopal Church building, which subsequently had been turned into a stable and was available for rent.[68] Seymour and the small band of "Apostolic Faith" people took possession of the building and the Apostolic Faith Mission, as it was called, began to hold services at 312 Azusa Street.[69] The Azusa Street building, a square, white clapboard building had a downstairs and upstairs floor. The upstairs floor was set aside as the chapel. Board planks were placed between old wooden nail kegs as pews and large wooden shoe boxes placed one on top of another became the pulpit.[70] From the outset the services at Azusa Street were unusual. While Seymour served as pastor of the Mission he very loosely regulated the services. Almost every recollection of Seymour testifies of his humility and gentleness. Many times, Seymour did not even seem to be "present" at the services, even though he was there in body. The wooden shoe boxes that served as the Mission's pulpit also served as Seymour's "prayer closet." More times than not eyewitnesses testified that they saw him on his knees with his head inside one of the shoe boxes praying during the service.[71]

Hundreds and thousands from all over Los Angeles, and eventually the United States and the world, heard of the outpouring of the Holy Spirit

---

65. Ibid., 62.

66. Ibid., 64.

67. Ibid., 69.

68. Ibid.

69. Ibid., 70.

70. Synan, *Century*, 52.

71. Bartleman, *How Pentecost Came*, 58.

taking place at Azusa. Many other hundreds and thousands traveled many miles to come and personally witness this revival. Services were held seven days a week from early morning till late in the night. Men, women, and children from all races and all socioeconomic and religious backgrounds came to investigate.[72] Each service was emotionally charged with intense expectation. The participants prayed, clapped, shouted, fainted to the floor, and stood in intense rapture with eyes closed while others around them danced with joyful frenzy. Many stood to testify that they had been "saved," or "sanctified" or "baptized and filled with the Holy Ghost," others witnessed to being healed of physical ailments. Many spoke in tongues and prophesied giving instructions to those around them. Those who heard the speaking in tongues claimed to recognize Chinese, Japanese, African dialects, Hebrew, Persian, and other languages. Many of those who spoke in tongues, and whose languages were understood, believed that this was a sign that they were being called as missionaries to the nations that spoke these languages. They believed that they had miraculously been given the ability to preach in these tongues without any academic study of the languages. In response, the people gathered at Azusa Mission collected funds in order to buy passage for these people to travel to foreign lands and sent them forth as missionaries of this new Apostolic Faith.[73] Unfortunately, most of these missionaries reported back to Los Angeles that when they preached "in tongues" to the indigenous people they were not understood. Several missionaries were left stranded and disillusioned when xenoglossia turned out to be glossolalia, or the speaking in an unknown language, both to the speaker and the hearer. Others were undaunted by these turns of events and continued to preach the Pentecostal message on the foreign fields to which they were sent.[74]

News of the events at the Azusa Street Mission were disseminated around the globe through the pages of *The Apostolic Faith*, a monthly newspaper mailed to thousands. In response, many places throughout the world which were also experiencing similar revivals wrote to Seymour and the reports were published in *The Apostolic Faith*. Personal testimonies of divine healing, miracles, the baptism of the Holy Spirit, announcements of camp-meetings and special evangelistic services, small homilies and sermonettes, filled the pages of the newspaper. Because of the paper, men and

72. Ramírez, *Migrating Faith*, 206–7.

73. Espinosa, *William Seymour*, 74–76.

74. McGee, *Miracles, Missions*, 61–76.

women from across the United States, Canada, and the world converged on Los Angeles, resulting in the message of the baptism of the Holy Spirit, speaking in tongues, and similar charismatic phenomenon becoming international. Charles Harrison Mason, founder and overseer of the black Holiness denomination, The Church of God in Christ, travelled from Memphis, Tennessee to Azusa and there received the baptism of the Holy Spirit and spoke in tongues. Returning to Memphis he shared his experience with his people.[75] As a result, the Church of God in Christ split between those who remained in the Holiness movement and the larger segment which identified themselves with the Pentecostal message.[76] Gaston Barnabas Cashwell of North Carolina, a preacher in the Fire-Baptized Holiness Church, traveled to Los Angeles to investigate and as a traditional Southerner was initially put off by the inter-racial character of the Azusa services. After days of struggling with his cultural prejudices, he finally submitted to prayer and received the baptism of the Holy Spirit and spoke in tongues. On his return to North Carolina, he stopped off in Cleveland, Tennessee and preached to a gathering of the Church of God at the invitation of A. J. Tomlinson, the General Overseer of the denomination. During Cashwell's sermon, in which he related his experiences at Azusa, Tomlinson and many of his people received the baptism of the Holy Spirit and spoke in tongues, effectively making the Church of God, like their black counterparts in Memphis, a Holiness Pentecostal denomination.[77] Cashwell proceeded home to North Carolina where he held large preaching crusades in Dunn and Durham bringing thousands of Holiness ministers and lay people into the experience of the baptism of the Holy Spirit and speaking in tongues.

Within a short period of time, several Holiness denominations, both black and white, accepted the Apostolic Faith message and joined the ranks of the Pentecostal Movement. The Fire-Baptized Holiness Church, with communities primarily located in the Midwest, merged with the Holiness Church, with congregation located principally in the South, to become the Pentecostal Holiness Church. Likewise, the United Holy Church, predominantly a black Holiness Church headquartered in North Carolina, embraced the teachings from Azusa and became Pentecostal. Several Free-Will Baptist associations in North Carolina accepted the Pentecostal message and formed the Pentecostal Free-Will Baptist Church. It cannot be overstated

75. Smith, *With Signs Following,* 64–68.

76. Robins, *Pentecostalism*, 43.

77. Conn, *Like A Mighty Army,* 84–85.

that the Holiness Movement in the southern states of United States almost *en masse* embraced the message of the Apostolic Faith.[78]

Pentecost Comes to Canada

While the revival at Azusa Street was in progress, a similar phenomenon took place in Toronto, Ontario. In 1906, Arthur and Ellen Hebden, English immigrants to Canada, opened a faith healing mission on 651 Queen Street. Called the Hebden, or East End Mission, the couple began to pray for revival and like the events in Los Angeles the Hebden's experienced a "Pentecostal" revival. Ellen Hebden testified that on November 17, 1906 she experienced the baptism of the Holy Spirit and spoke in tongues. The curious thing is that the Hebden's were totally unaware of the events taking place at Azusa Street. Quickly the East End Mission became the center of the Pentecostal Movement in Canada. Like Azusa, people from all backgrounds came to the storefront mission to witness the spiritual events. By 1910 there were fourteen Pentecostal Churches in Ontario alone. George Chambers, who became the first general superintendent of the Pentecostal Assemblies of Canada in 1919, attended the Hebden Mission. Two other men on furlough from the foreign mission field, Herbert Randall from Egypt and H. L. Lawler from North China, received the baptism in the Holy Spirit at East End Mission and upon returning to their foreign mission assignments took the message of Pentecostalism with them. The Hebden's organized several Pentecostal rallies in Toronto that sponsored speakers such as William Durham, Robert and Aimee Semple (McPherson), and Frank Bartleman, chronicler of the revival at Azusa Street. Just as the Azusa Street Mission became the "Jerusalem" of the Pentecostal Movement, the Hebden Mission became the "Upper Room" of Pentecostalism in Canada.[79]

Back at Azusa

The revival at Azusa Street continued unabated for three years. Simultaneously, other Pentecostal missions opened throughout Los Angeles and the surrounding area. While some of these new missions were obvious overflows of the revival at Azusa Street, others were set up as rival ministries,

78. Synan, *The Holiness-Pentecostal Movement*, 117–39.
79. Stroud, "The Hebden Mission," *Testimony*, 27.

hoping to steal "sheep" away from the Apostolic Faith Mission. Charles Parham, Seymour's former teacher, heard of his pupil's success and travelled to Los Angeles to investigate. When he arrived at Azusa Street he was appalled. Parham was put off by the inter-racial character of the services. As a man deeply influenced by the segregationist opinions of the times, he could not tolerate the sight of black women praying for white men, black men praying for white women, and the open, integrated seating and space for prayer at the altar area. Neither could he abide the emotional fervor and outburst of the services, which he attributed to African slave paganism infiltrating the meetings because of Seymour's laxness.

Parham tried to close down the Azusa Mission by verbally condemning what he believed were abuses, claiming to be the spiritual father of the Movement and by opening a rival Pentecostal mission just a few blocks from Azusa. Parham's attempts were short lived and he returned to Missouri. Reports were later disseminated that Parham was arrested on charges of sodomy during a preaching tour in Texas. As a result, Parham lost credibility among Pentecostals and was marginalized by the Movement for the remainder of his life.[80]

Trouble in Paradise

While rivalry among Pentecostal leaders developed early, the nascent Pentecostal Movement, as a whole, was strongly unified in its teachings and emphasis. This changed with the ascendancy of William Durham among Pentecostals. Born in Kentucky in 1873, Durham pastored the North Street Mission, a Holiness church in Chicago. As a young man, he became a Christian in the Baptist Church and early on came under the influence of the Holiness Movement, and professed the experience of entire sanctification. Not long after this, Durham entered the preaching ministry. While pastor of the North Avenue Mission in Chicago, Durham heard reports of the revival at Azusa Street and decided to go and investigate it for himself. He arrived in Los Angeles in late April 1907, and after days of prayer and "tarrying," received the baptism of the Holy Spirit and spoke in tongues. At Azusa, Seymour prophesied that Durham would be the cause of many people receiving the baptism of the Holy Spirit.

Durham returned to Chicago and almost immediately Seymour's prophecy began to be fulfilled. Through Durham's ministry at North Avenue

80. Anderson, *Vision,* 140, 160, 167, 252, 272–73.

Mission some of Pentecostalism's earliest leaders received the baptism of the Holy Spirit. Robert and Aimee Semple (McPherson), healing evangelist and later founder of the Four-Square Gospel denomination, as well as leaders among immigrant Persian, Norwegian, and Italian Pentecostals received the baptism of the Holy Spirit at North Avenue Mission. [81]

In May 1910, the Stone Church, a prominent Pentecostal congregation in Chicago, sponsored a Pentecostal conference attended by hundreds of people from the United States and Canada. Since Durham's preaching acumen was legendary throughout the infant Movement, he was tapped as one of the featured speakers.[82] Durham's sermon at the conference proved to be so controversial that it led to the split of the Pentecostal Movement into two separate theological camps. Even though Durham claimed to have received the experience of entire sanctification earlier in his life, his sermon at the Stone Church repudiated the experience of sanctification as subsequent to salvation. The sermon, entitled, "The Finished Work of Calvary" stated that sanctification takes place at the moment of conversion and continues to develop in the life of the Christian, as long as they apply the "finished work of Christ." Therefore, it is not necessary for a Christian believer to first seek the experience of sanctification before they pray to be baptized in the Holy Spirit with the evidence of speaking in tongues. Durham challenged the Holiness doctrine of entire sanctification by stating that it was not supported by holy Scripture, but rather on the teachings of John Wesley, godly though he may have been. Durham's new approach struck at the very heart of the Pentecostal Movement. To this point all Pentecostals affirmed a three-stage *ordo salutis*, salvation/conversion and then sanctification, after conversion, and then the baptism of the Holy Spirit, subsequent to sanctification. Durham did not question the need of sanctification in the Christian life, rather he challenged the insistence upon the subsequence of the experience to salvation, and the interpretation by more radical Holiness teachers that without the second experience of sanctification a Christian would be prevented from entering heaven. He stated that this was a repudiation of the finished work of Christ accomplished on the Cross.

Durham's "Finished Work" doctrine, as it came to be known, rocked the unified world of Pentecostalism. Immediately the "Finished Work" doctrine came under attack from many leaders within the Movement. Charles

81. Riss, "Durham, 594–95.
82. Blumhofer, "William H. Durham," 123.

Parham, self-proclaimed "father" of the Apostolic Faith Movement challenged Durham, calling on the Lord to justify Parham's teaching of "second blessing sanctification" over against Durham's "Finished work" doctrine by taking the life of the one who was teaching false doctrine. A. J. Tomlinson, overseer of the Church of God in Cleveland, Tennessee, Joseph Hilary King of the Pentecostal-Holiness Church and Florence Crawford, founder of the Apostolic Faith Mission in Portland, Oregon, condemned the new doctrine in strong terms. All Pentecostal organizations which had originally been a part of the Holiness Movement, prior to 1901, repudiated the "Finished Work" and continued to teach the Wesleyan doctrine of post-conversion sanctification as a requirement for receiving the baptism of the Holy Spirit. Nonetheless, Durham's preaching met with great success and hundreds of thousands of individual Pentecostals and congregations embraced the message of the "Finished Work."[83]

Durham cast his eyes towards Los Angeles and the Azusa Street Mission. He hoped to convince Seymour and the "Mother Church of Pentecostalism" of the validity of the "Finished Work" message. Durham arrived in the "city of angels" while Seymour was away from Azusa on a preaching tour. Welcomed by the people at Azusa, Durham began to teach them his new doctrine. Some accounts record that during Durham's time at Azusa the Mission returned to its former glory and that the Holy Spirit once again fell upon the people as in the early days. However, upon Seymour's return to Los Angeles he locked the doors of the Apostolic Faith Mission to Durham and publicly denounced his preaching. Undaunted by Seymour's rejection, Durham continued to travel and proclaim the "Finished Work."

Durham's grueling preaching itinerary finally took its toll on his health. On July 7, 1912, a mere two years after he began to proclaim the "Finished Work" doctrine, Durham died in Los Angeles. Parham lost no time in claiming victory and stating that the Lord had spoken and taken Durham's life as a confirmation that the "Finished Work" was a false doctrine, and a vindication of those who taught "second-blessing" sanctification. While Durham's untimely demise came as a great blow to the nascent Pentecostal Movement, it was only the beginning for those who embraced his doctrine of the "Finished Work." The largest white Pentecostal denomination, the Assemblies of God, embraced the "Finished Work" as did Aimee Semple McPherson's Church of the Four-square Gospel, the

83. Riss, "Finished Work," 638–39.

Pentecostal Church of God and other newer Pentecostal denominations and ministerial fellowships.

Another Dividing Issue

While the Pentecostal Movement was still reeling from the divisions caused by the proclamation of the "Finished Work," the infant movement shuddered under the burden of another theological controversy. In April 1913, Pentecostals on the West Coast organized a "Worldwide Pentecostal Campmeeting." Held in a grove of trees in the Arroyo Seco section just outside Los Angeles, the Worldwide Camp-meeting drew large crowds to hear such renowned speakers as healing evangelist Maria Woodsworth-Etter. After several days, the Campmeeting closed with a water baptism service at which Canadian Pentecostal R. E. McAlister preached. McAlister pointed out in his sermon that the Book of Acts records that the Apostles baptized converts in the "Name of Jesus" and that the traditional Trinitarian formula is not mentioned outside of Matthew 24. The seemingly harmless commentary led to great controversy. John Scheppe, a German immigrant attending the Campmeeting, was moved by McAlister's words and decided to pray through the night and search the Scripture concerning the subject of baptism in Jesus' name. Early the following morning, Scheppe went running through the campgrounds, shouting that he had received a "revelation" in the night that the scriptural formula that should be used in water baptism was "in the name of Jesus." Many Pentecostals, who were open to new "revelation" and who believed that all Christian practices should be as obedient as possible to the literal word of the Scriptures, expressed a desire to be re-baptized. However, the controversy did not just involve the debate on what baptismal formula was most scriptural, it evolved in a full-blown theological issue over the very nature of the Godhead, the traditional teaching of the Trinity.[84]

Frank Ewart, assistant pastor of Seventh Street Pentecostal Mission in Chicago, originally established by William Durham, also attended the Campmeeting and was duly impressed by Scheppe's "revelation" and sought to harmonize the baptismal formula instituted by Christ in Matthew 28:19 and that introduced by the Apostle Peter on Pentecost recorded in Acts 2:38. After a year of study, Ewart concluded that the only way they could be harmonized was a radically different understanding of the nature of the

---

84. Foster, *Their Story*, 88–90.

person of Jesus Christ. Ewart reasoned that the Apostle Peter would never disobey the command of Christ given in the Gospel of Matthew. Therefore, how was the Apostle Peter's command to be baptized "in the name of Jesus" a fulfillment of Jesus' instructions to baptize "in the name of the Father, and of the Son and of the Holy Spirit?" Ewart came to the conclusion that the *name* of the Father, and the Son, and the Holy Spirit *was* Jesus. Hence, Jesus was the Father *and* the Son *and* the Holy Spirit. In the Old Testament Jesus was the Father. In the Gospels Jesus was incarnate and came to earth as the Son. After his death, burial, resurrection, and ascension, he returned to earth again, on the Day of Pentecost, as the Holy Spirit. Therefore, there were not three persons in the Godhead, but rather one person, Jesus, who changed his form according to his ministry at the time. There was no Trinity of persons, only a trinity of offices, or manifestations. Historically known as Modalism or Sabellianism, unbeknownst to Ewart, he resurrected a heresy regarding the Godhead that was soundly condemned by the early Church.[85] Ewart developed an entirely new doctrine of salvation based upon this new "revelation" centered on the text of Acts 2:38. The process of salvation consisted of three inseparable parts: first, repentance, second, baptism by immersion using the formula "in Jesus' name" or "in the name of Jesus" and third, receiving the gift of the Holy Spirit with the initial, physical evidence of speaking in tongues. Ewart erected a tent in Los Angeles provided with a portable baptismal tank and preached his first public sermon on baptism in Jesus' name and the nature of the Godhead on April 14, 1914. Joined by Glenn Cook, a well-known Pentecostal evangelist, they re-baptized each other in Jesus' name and thus began the "Oneness" or "Jesus-Only" schism in the Pentecostal Movement.[86]

The Formation of the Assemblies of God

While the Oneness teaching rapidly spread through the ranks of the Pentecostal Movement, others attempted to organize a national Pentecostal fellowship. Pentecostal leaders, Eudoras N. Bell, originally a Baptist minister who pastored a Pentecostal congregation in Malvern, Arkansas, and Howard Goss, converted under Charles Parham and pastor of a Pentecostal mission in Hot Springs, Arkansas, issued a call through the pages of the Pentecostal newspaper *Word and Witness*, edited by Bell. The call invited

85. Hanson, *Search for the Christian Doctrine,* 287–88.
86. Riss, "Cook, Glenn A.," 559–60.

"laymen and preachers . . . elders, pastors, ministers, evangelists and missionaries . . . [from] all the churches of God in Christ . . . all Pentecostal or Apostolic faith Assemblies" to convene in Hot Springs, Arkansas at the Grand Opera House, April 2–12, 1914. The purpose of the gathering was sixfold: first, for attendees to better understand the message of the movement and to heal any divisions; second, to study the Scriptures and pray together for unity; third, to ascertain the needs of churches and missionaries at home and abroad and how to improve those ministries; fourth, to ascertain how they might better financially support Pentecostal foreign missions; fifth, to charter a fellowship with local government authorities in order to put the movement on a legal footing; and, sixth, to explore the possibility of establishing a Bible training school.[87] Over 300 people came to Hot Springs, 128 registered as missionaries or ministers. They hailed from several foreign countries, twenty different states, primarily from the Midwest and predominantly white males.[88] The absence of blacks may be attributed to two issues, first the newspaper *Word and Witness* was not distributed among black Pentecostals, and second, Hot Springs being in Arkansas was under the pall of Jim Crow laws and would have presented black Pentecostal travelers with many legal difficulties. While Bishop Charles Mason, overseer of the Church of God in Christ in Memphis, did not attend the meeting, he did give his complete support to the gathering. In spite of the difficulties, Garfield Thomas Haywood, black pastor of Christ Temple in Indianapolis, Indiana, attended and played a very important role in the deliberations at Hot Springs.[89]

The Hot Springs convocation opened on Thursday, April 2, 1914. The first four days were set aside for worship, prayer, and fellowship. On Monday April 6 the business session was called to order by Eudoras N. Bell, who acted as chairman. A resolution was brought to the floor and, in spite of the presence of many who strongly opposed any "organization" of the Movement, was adopted unanimously. The resolution affirmed that God established the Church through Jesus Christ, who was the only head of the Church. Secondly, that the Old and New Testament Scriptures were the only sources of all faith and practice. Third, that Jesus Christ had forbidden the Church to be divided by schism. And fourth, no denomination or organization should be formed that is sectarian in nature or institutes

87. Goss, *Winds of God,* 280.

88. Menzies, *Anointed,* 97.

89. Golder, *History of the Pentecostal Assemblies,* 31–39, 48.

rules or laws or establishes unscriptural tests of fellowship.[90] The convention steered clear of establishing an authoritarian organization and rather adopted a mixture of presbyterian and congregational polity, in which each individual congregation was autonomous, while at the same time participating in a voluntary cooperation of likeminded fellowships. The new body voted to incorporate under the name "The General Council of the Assemblies of God." Congregations in different regional and geographical locations were encouraged to organize local or district councils that undergirded the work of the General Council.[91]

The strong and positive beginning of the Assemblies of God was soon challenged. During the remainder of 1914 and 1915 the message of Oneness Pentecostalism continued to spread and in its wake many congregations split over the "new issue," and left others in confusion and disarray. Old friends who shared the Pentecostal experience now became enemies over the issue of Jesus' name baptism and the doctrine of the Trinity. Oneness preachers especially found a willing audience in the congregations that had affiliated with the recently organized Assemblies of God. By the summer of 1915, four influential Assemblies of God leaders; Eudorus N. Bell, Garfield Haywood, Howard Goss, and Daniel Opperman, were re-baptized in the name of Jesus. This sent shock waves throughout the member congregations of the Assemblies of God. Bell later repudiated Oneness doctrine, but Haywood, Goss, and Opperman remained in the ranks of the "Jesus-Only" Pentecostals.[92]

In October 1916, the second meeting of the General Council of the Assemblies of God met in St. Louis, Missouri. The Oneness doctrine was foremost on every delegates' mind. It must be decided whether the newly formed fellowship would be Oneness or Trinitarian. Contrary to early sentiments against writing a creed, a committee was formed to draft a doctrinal statement agreeable to those gathered. Oneness delegates fought tenaciously to have Trinitarian language dropped, but to no avail. As the delegates gathered for the general business meeting many of their voices broke out in song, singing the familiar hymn, "Holy, Holy, Holy, Lord God Almighty . . . God in three persons, blessed Trinity."[93] The doctrinal agreement, known as the "Statement of Fundamental Truths" became the closest thing to a creed,

90. Menzies, *Anointed*, 99–100.
91. Kendrick, *Promise Fulfilled*, 87–88.
92. Foster, *Their Story*, 94.
93. Ibid., 117.

which articulated the theological foundations of the Assemblies of God. The largest section of the statement was dedicated to affirming the Assemblies of God's acknowledgement and confession of the traditional, orthodox Christian doctrine of the Holy Trinity and clearly delineates between its beliefs and that of the Oneness Pentecostals.

With the adoption of the "Statement of Fundamental Truths" at the 1916 meeting of the General Council of the Assemblies of God, the third breach within the Pentecostal Movement was finalized. Over one hundred ministers defected from the Assemblies of God because of the Oneness issue. Oneness ministers, evangelists, and missionaries began a long, arduous, and divisive process of forming their own organizations. For the first two decades, following the St. Louis Council, the Oneness movement proliferated into numerous organizations and fellowships, which in turn, divided among themselves over several issues. Presently the two most prominent worldwide Oneness Pentecostal denominations are the Pentecostal Assemblies of the World,[94] predominantly a black organization, and the United Pentecostal Church International, while inter-racial in nature, has a preponderance of white ministers and congregations.[95] Over the years the Trinitarian Pentecostal bodies continued to grow and advance, in spite of predictions of their demise by Oneness Pentecostals. The Oneness Pentecostal Movement has also continued to grow, but at a somewhat slower rate than their Trinitarian counterparts. The Oneness Movement has shown the most numerical gains among its foreign missions works, especially in South America and Southeast Asia. Over the past several years an informal theological dialog, bringing together Oneness and Trinitarian Pentecostals, has opened some new doors of conversation between the two groups.[96]

The 1920s, 30s, and 40s saw Pentecostalism continuing to develop and impact North America and the world. Pentecostal denominations, fellowships and missionary organizations proliferated and earlier formed organizations split along racial lines and became new denominations. Other Pentecostal organizations divided over power struggles between personalities and parties. Overall Pentecostalism was rejected by the remainder of

94. Clanton, *United We Stand*, 25–28. The Pentecostal Assemblies of the World (PAW), founded in 1906 by Garfield Haywood prior to the Oneness controversy, was swept into the Oneness camp due to Haywood's influence.

95. Hall, "United Pentecostal Church," 1160–65.

96. The Society for Pentecostal Studies sponsored an informal dialog between Oneness and Trinitarian Pentecostal theologians from 2002 and 2007. The results of each study topic have been published in *Pneuma* 30 (2008) 203–24.

Christendom: Roman Catholic, Orthodox, and Protestant. Conservative and fundamentalist Evangelicals and Holiness denominations, which share much in common with Pentecostalism, were some of its harshest critics. The secular world dismissed Pentecostals as religious charlatans, fanatics, cranks, or psychologically aberrant.

The Pentecostal Movement spread across North America and the entire globe. Beginning at Topeka in 1901 and then "super-charged" at the Azusa Street Apostolic Faith Mission in Los Angeles in 1906, and despite leadership and theological divisions, Pentecostalism became a global movement, present on every continent and in every nation. Its message of the baptism of the Holy Spirit as a spiritually empowering experience for all Christians, as well as its insistence that the charismatic gifts are a normative manifestation of that empowerment for Christian service, is the impetus behind its massive missionary success. Whether in the rainforests of South America, the frozen territories of northern Canada, the savannahs of Africa, the jungles of southeast Asia, the countless towns and villages of China and India, and the inner-city streets of the United States, Pentecostals have preached the gospel of Jesus Christ, convinced that they are endued with the same Holy Spirit and power as the Apostles received on the Day of Pentecost. This is what marks the growth of Pentecostalism.[97]

97. Anderson, *Spreading Fires*, 65–67.

CHAPTER 3

The Charismatic Movement

UNLIKE THE PENTECOSTAL REVIVAL of the early twentieth century, born out of the Holiness Movement of the nineteenth century, and divided into a multitude of Pentecostal denominations and independent churches, the Charismatic Movement of the 1960s, 70s, and 80s thrived among members of the established churches: Roman Catholic, Protestant, and Orthodox. Whereas the leaders and participants of Pentecostalism, who for the most part were Evangelical Protestants, were forced or volunteered to abandon the denominations of which they were members (be it Methodist, Baptist, or Holiness), Charismatic Roman Catholics, mainline Protestants, and Orthodox Christians remained faithful and zealous members of their respective traditions and denominations.

"Charismatics" before the Charismatic Movement

While most Church historians of the Charismatic Movement agree that 1960 is the year in which the Movement claims to have begun, there were Charismatics (i.e., non-Pentecostals who witnessed to having an experience of a baptism of the Holy Spirit accompanied by speaking in tongues or another of the charismatic gifts, and remained within their non-Pentecostal church or denomination) before 1960. One spiritual renewal movement, and another a spiritual renewal organization, both born within Pentecostalism in the 1940s and 50s, were catalysts in bringing the Pentecostal experience of the Holy Spirit outside of classical Pentecostal ranks to the wider church: the Healing Movement and the Full Gospel Business Men's Fellowship.[1]

1. Synan, *Under His Banner.*

The Healing Movement

From the beginning, Pentecostals were strong believers in the doctrine and experience of "divine healing." Pentecostalism's spiritual mother, the Holiness Movement, bequeathed to her daughter the practice of praying for the sick and believing that God desired to manifest His power by healing them in a divine manner. Some proponents of "divine healing" believed that this was the only way that God intended for His people to live in this fallen world and that the use of medicine and other human medical arts was forbidden for they were a sign of little faith, or even among some extremists, demonic in origin.[2] However, other practitioners of "divine healing" did not take such a strident position, but believed that God made use of both prayer and medicine, that divine intervention should be sought before medical options were pursued. The Holiness Movement produced healing evangelists such as John Alexander Dowie, originally from Australia, and the proliferation of "healing homes" throughout the United States. Healing homes were places where the sick could come, be attended to by ministers and laypeople, who would through a regime of Bible reading, encouraging and faith-building exhortations and teaching, and daily prayers, seek healing through the supernatural power of God in Jesus Christ by the Holy Spirit. Many of those who practiced the ministry of healing among the Holiness people were easily drawn to the message of Pentecostalism. Charles Parham's views on "divine healing" were extreme in nature, repudiating all use of medicine. Maria Woodsworth-Etter, a nationally known healing evangelist in the Holiness Movement, embraced the Pentecostal teaching on the baptism of the Holy Spirit. The birth of the Pentecostal Movement saw an increase in the ministry of "divine healing." Individuals such as Dr. Finis Yoakum, Dr. Lilian Yeomans, Carrie Judd Montgomery, Dr. Charles Price, John G. Lake, F. F. Bosworth, and Aimee Semple McPherson, carried the message and ministry of "divine healing" across the nation, almost exclusively among Pentecostals. Early in its formative years the Assemblies of God adopted a doctrinal statement confessing their belief that "divine healing" was provided by Christ in the Atonement.[3] This doctrine was based on Isaiah 53:5, "But He *was* wounded for our transgressions, *he was* bruised

2. Alexander, *Pentecostal Healing,* 58–63. This was the position of the very colorful nineteenth-century healing evangelist, John Alexander Dowie, founder of the Catholic Apostolic Church and the planned city of Zion, Illinois. Many early Pentecostal leaders were influenced by Dowie in one respect or another.

3. Horton, *Systematic Theology,* 489–523.

for our iniquities; the chastisement for our peace *was* upon Him, and by His stripes we are healed." And upon the New Testament quotation of this passage in 1 Peter 2:24, "who Himself bore our sins in His own body on the tree, that we, having died to sins, might live for righteousness—by whose stripes you were healed."

By the late 1940s, a new generation of Pentecostal healing evangelists came upon the scene. These healing evangelists fanned out throughout the United States holding crusades in churches, auditoriums and huge tents, seating thousands, set up in open fields and on vacant city lots. Jack Coe, A. A. Allen, T. L. Osborn, Gordon Lindsay, William Braham, and Marjoe Gortner, dominated the Healing Revival Movement, as it has come to be called. Gordon Lindsay published a magazine entitled *Leaves of Healing* which publicized the itineraries of the healing evangelists, as well as printed testimonies of those who claimed to be healed during these crusades. This new band of healing evangelists made use of the "secular" media (i.e., the radio and television) to spread the message of "divine healing."[4] While Aimee Semple McPherson was the first to successfully venture into radio, establishing the first Pentecostal radio station, KFSG, in Los Angeles, it was young Pentecostal-Holiness healing evangelist Oral Robert who skillfully made use of the new medium of television.[5] The Healing Revival Movement began to wane by the late 1950s. Those healing evangelists who would survive turned to new avenue and methods. Oral Roberts founded his own university in Tulsa, Oklahoma. The mission of Oral Roberts University (ORU) was committed to train young men and women to carry the message of Christian healing to the world.[6]

Charismatic Forerunners

In 1936, South African Apostolic Faith Mission minister David Du Plessis received a unique call from God in the form of a personal prophetic message given to him. British Pentecostal evangelist and healer, Smith Wigglesworth, delivered a prophetic word to Du Plessis, which at the time seemed beyond belief: soon God would bring to the historic Roman Catholic and Protestant denominations a pentecostal outpouring and Du Plessis would

4. Synan, *The Century*, 326–27.

5. Harrell Jr. *All Things*, 135–37.

6. http://www.oru.edu/about-oru/mission.php (accessed June 27, 2017).

be an important part of the revival.[7] The prospect of such an event was nothing short of impossible. The Pentecostal Movement had been roundly rejected by the Christian mainstream, judged as fanatical at best and heretical and demonic at the worst.

Du Plessis immigrated to the United States and affiliated with the Assemblies of God. In 1951, as an initial fulfillment of Wigglesworth's prophecy, Du Plessis sensed a strong urge to visit the headquarters of the World Council of Churches in New York City. He met with the leadership and shared with them his testimony of Jesus Christ and the baptism of the Holy Spirit, reaching out to mainline Protestants, as well as Roman Catholics, with the message of the pentecostal experience.[8] His "unofficial" forays into the Ecumenical Movement secured an invitation as the only Pentecostal observer at the Second Vatican Council. Because of Du Plessis' ecumenical ministry many Protestant and Roman Catholic leaders received the baptism of the Holy Spirit.[9]

In 1946, Lutheran pastor Harald Bredesen received the baptism of the Holy Spirit, spoke in tongues, and remained within the Lutheran Church.[10] Later Bredesen moved to the ministry of the Dutch Reformed Church and in 1957 began pastoring a parish of that denomination in Mount Vernon, New York, which held weekly charismatic-style prayer meetings. Pat Robertson, founder of the Christian Broadcasting Network (CBN) and Regent University, was at the time attending seminary in New York City and came under Bredesen's influence, receiving the baptism of the Holy Spirit.[11] In 1951, Tommy Tyson, a North Carolina Methodist pastor, received the baptism of the Holy Spirit, without any connections to any Pentecostals or Charismatics, and remained in the ministry of the Methodist Church. One of the most influential forerunners among mainstream Protestants was Agnes Sanford. The wife of an Episcopal priest, Sanford, around 1953, began experiencing a very strong working of the Holy Spirit in her life which eventually led her to a prayer ministry of healing. In 1955, Sanford and her husband, established the weeklong Schools of Pastoral Care in which those involved in all aspects of healing ministry came for training in ministering healing in a Christian context. Sanford

7. Howard, "David Du Plessis," 274.

8. Du Plessis, *The Spirit*, 15–16.

9. Hocken, "The Charismatic Movement," 477–78.

10. Bredesen, *Yes, Lord*, 55–60.

11. Robertson, *Shout it*.

was likewise involved in the interdenominational Order of St. Luke; whose membership was primarily Episcopalian. While the purpose of the Order was to encourage the restoration and practice in the Church of prayers for the healing of the sick, in 1963 the Order came out strongly against the practice of glossolalia. However, the very nature of the Order caused its members to be open to the gifts of the Holy Spirit.

In the spring of 1956, Fr. Richard Winkler, an Episcopal priest and member of the Order of St. Luke, received the baptism of the Holy Spirit while attending a service held by an Assemblies of God evangelist. In the fall of 1956, Winkler, began holding prayer meetings in his home and then moved them to his parish, Trinity Episcopal Church in Wheaton, Illinois. Also in 1956, Presbyterian minister James Brown, pastor of Upper Octorara Presbyterian Church in Parkesburg, Pennsylvania, received the baptism of the Holy Spirit and began having prayer meetings in which the gifts of the Holy Spirit were practiced.

Another spiritual venue which led many into an early charismatic awareness was the Camp Farthest Out, founded in 1930 by Glenn Clark. A Presbyterian influenced by Christian Science and New Thought religious philosophy, Clark's camp introduced many to the mystical stream of Christianity.[12] In the 1950s and 1960s Camp Farthest Out sponsored conferences where Agnes Sanford, Tommy Tyson, Harald Bredesen, James Brown, and Derek Prince, a British Pentecostal teacher, taught.[13] It was at one of these conferences, in the early 1950s, that Don Basham, later of Christian Growth Ministries, received the baptism of the Holy Spirit.[14] In 1967, prominent Charismatic Catholic priest and healer, Fr. Francis MacNutt, received the baptism of the Holy Spirit at Camp Farthest Out.[15]

Fr. Dennis Bennett and the Episcopal Church

However, even with all of these Charismatic "forerunners" mentioned above, the beginning of the modern Charismatic Movement is celebrated on Sunday, April 3, 1960, when Father Dennis Bennett, Episcopal priest and rector of St. Mark's Episcopal Church in Van Nuys, California, stood before his congregation to announce that he had received the baptism of the Holy

12. De Arteaga, *Agnes Sanford*, 137–68.

13. De Arteaga, "Glenn Clark's Camps," 265–88.

14. Hocken, "The Chrismatic Movement," 478.

15. Christian Healing Ministries http://www.christianhealingmin.org/about/.

Spirit and spoke in tongues. This sent shockwaves through his parish community and subsequently throughout the Episcopal Diocese of Los Angeles and then throughout the United States and abroad.[16]

Bennett's confession at St. Mark's, however, had been preceded by several months of charismatic activities around him. Father Frank McGuire, rector of Holy Spirit Episcopal Church in nearby Monterey Park, had contacted Bennett to seek his advice in dealing with members of his parish, John and Joan Baker, who claimed that in the spring of 1959 they had received the baptism of the Holy Spirit and spoken in tongues, while visiting a Pentecostal church. Unlike many who had received this experience previously, and had left their home denominations for Pentecostal congregations, the Bakers returned to their Episcopal parish. The Baker's shared their experience with other members of Holy Spirit parish and at least ten other parishioners also received the baptism of the Holy Spirit and spoke in tongues. McGuire was concerned. However, by the fall of 1959, Fathers McGuire and Bennett also received the baptism of the Holy Spirit and spoke in tongues. Members of St. Mark's, Van Nuys, began to visit Holy Spirit in Monterey Park and by the spring of 1960 at least seventy members of St. Mark's, many of them lay leaders of important parish organizations, likewise received the baptism of the Holy Spirit, and many of them spoke in tongues.[17]

Bennett and McGuire's bishop, however, was not happy about the developments in their parishes. Several non-Charismatic members of St. Mark's parish called for Bennett's resignation, which he offered. The Episcopal Bishop of Los Angeles sent a directive forbidding any group to meet at St. Mark's that encouraged or allowed speaking in tongues. Two new groups were formed, as a result of the charismatic events at St. Mark's; one, a local prayer group and the second, "Blessed Trinity Society" founded by Jean Stone, which became a national organization.[18] Articles in both *Newsweek*[19] and *Time*[20] magazines gave national coverage to the events in California.

Father Dennis Bennett's testimony of the baptism of the Holy Spirit, covered by *Time* and *Newsweek*, launched him into national fame. While Bennett and his testimony and teaching of the baptism of the Holy Spirit,

16. Hocken, "Charismatic Movement," 479.
17. Bennett, *Nine O'Clock*.
18. Balmer, "Blessed," 84–85.
19. "Rector and a Rumpus" 77.
20. "Speaking in Tongues," 1960.

speaking in tongues, and the exercise of other spiritual gifts, was force-fully rejected by the Episcopal Bishop of Los Angeles, he was invited by the Episcopal Bishop of Olympia, Washington to come north and take the reins of St. Luke's Episcopal Church, a small and struggling parish in Seat-tle. Within a year of Bennett's arrival, attendance at St. Luke's skyrocketed from seventy-five to 300. The spread of the charismatic experience among Episcopalians gained further impetus when Bennett shared his testimony at meetings of priests from the dioceses of Olympia and Oregon. As a result, St. Luke's in Seattle became a Charismatic center of pilgrimage for Christians from all denominations, laity and clergy, who came and sought the baptism of the Holy Spirit.[21]

"Blessed Trinity Society" founded by Jean Stone also became a strong voice for the Charismatic Movement. Through the Society's quarterly jour-nal *Trinity*, which first appeared in fall 1961, thousands of Episcopalians and other mainline denominational Christians heard about the message of the baptism of the Holy Spirit and charismatic gifts.[22] Members of the board of directors of the magazine were all communicants of the Epis-copal Church, except for David Du Plesis and Harald Bredesen. "Blessed Trinity Society" also published another periodical, *Voice*, which printed articles from both classical Pentecostals and Charismatics, and had a larger circulation. *Trinity* was more geared to members of historic mainstream Protestant churches.

The Charismatic Movement among Mainline Protestants

The influence of the ministry of Fr. Dennis Bennett upon the Charismatic Renewal among other mainline Protestant denominations cannot be un-derestimated. Bennett's parish in Seattle not only became central in provid-ing a venue for leading many Episcopalians in receiving the baptism of the Holy Spirit, many other mainline Protestants, clergy and laity, visited St. Luke's and returned home to their congregations to spread the Charismatic message and experience. Bennett also travelled widely sharing his testimo-ny and teaching on the baptism of the Holy Spirit and the charismatic gifts. The Movement among Episcopalians was further enhanced by the writings and ministry of Agnes Sanford and Jean Stone.[23]

21. Bennett, *Nine O'clock,* 201–5.
22. Irish, "Blessed," 435.
23. Sanford, *Healing Light.* Sanford, the wife of an Episcopal priest, began her writing

Outside of the Episcopal Church one of the first Protestant denominations to be exposed to the Charismatic message was the American Baptists. As early as 1963, beginning at their national convention in Detroit, American Baptist pastors who had received the baptism of the Holy Spirit came together to hear further teaching regarding the Movement and to worship together.[24]

The Movement among Lutherans can be credited to the early leadership of American Lutheran pastor Larry Christenson. In August 1961, while pastoring in San Pedro, California, Christenson received the baptism of the Holy Spirit after being prayed for by a Pentecostal. He made his experience public on Pentecost Sunday, 1962, which almost cost him his ministry in the Lutheran Church. Christenson, however, was adept at making strong connections between the Pentecostal experience and Lutheran tradition and theology. The American Lutheran Church (ALC) became the first mainline Protestant denomination to officially respond to the Charismatic Movement. In 1962, in response to complaints that ALC evangelist Herbert Mjorud, as a result of receiving the baptism of the Holy Spirit at St. Luke's in Seattle, was teaching positively on the experience of speaking in tongues, the leadership of ALC formed a Committee on Spiritual Gifts to study the issue. The Committee studied the phenomenon of glossolalia, as well as the other charismatic gifts, and made recommendations to the denomination. In 1963, the ALC issued an official statement to its churches and clergy, forbidding the promotion of the gift of tongues and restricting its exercise to personal and private devotion. By the 1970s the ALC was much more positively disposed to the Charismatic Movement. In 1974, the Lutheran Charismatic Renewal Services was organized and an annual Lutheran renewal conference convened in Minneapolis, attracting thousands of participants. By 1987 the Charismatic Renewal was so well accepted among Lutherans that Larry Christenson's book, *Welcome, Holy Spirit: A Study of Charismatic Renewal in the Church*, was published in Minneapolis by Augsburg Press, the official publishing house of the American Lutheran Church. Charismatics within the Missouri Synod Lutheran Church did not fare as well as their American Lutheran brethren. In 1964, Missouri Synod pastor, Donald Pfotenhauer of Minneapolis, received the baptism of the Holy Spirit. In spring 1965, he was suspended from his pastoral position, beginning a five-year battle in ecclesiastical courts that finally ended in him

---

ministry on healing in the decades before the Charismatic Movement.

24. Hocken, "American Baptist," 312–13.

being defrocked by the Missouri Synod Lutherans. The ecclesiastical officials rejected Pfotenhauer's teaching on the gift of prophecy, stating that it called into question the authority and sufficiency of written Scripture for the Church. Despite the open hostility of the official leadership of the Missouri Synod, other pastors and theologians, such as Theodore Jungkuntz, Rodney Lensch, Don Matzat, and Delbert Rossin, continued to testify to their experience of receiving the baptism of the Holy Spirit.

Like the Missouri Synod Lutherans, Presbyterian Charismatics in the early days of the Renewal suffered persecution from their denominational leaders. United Presbyterian pastor Robert Whitaker received the baptism of the Holy Spirit in 1962 and after years of disputes with Church officials was removed from his pastoral ministry in 1967. In 1966, together with other Charismatic Presbyterians, Whitaker and J. Brown of Parkesburg, Pennsylvania formed the Charismatic Communion of Presbyterian Ministers (CCPM), the first Charismatic fellowship to be formed within a Protestant denomination. "Brick" Bradford served as CCPM's secretary and as a former lawyer represented Whitaker in his victorious legal battle with denominational officials overturning his expulsion from Presbyterian ministry. A watershed meeting for Charismatic Presbyterians was held in Austin, Texas in 1967. Organized by Bradford, the meeting featured two prominent Presbyterian theologians positively disposed to the Renewal, John Mackay, one-time president of Princeton, and J. Rodman Williams, later professor of theology at the Charismatic Melodyland School of Theology and Dean of the School of Divinity at Regent University in Virginia Beach. The reputation of these two men brought enough pressure on the United Presbyterian Church for it to seriously investigate the Movement and eventually led to one of the most thorough denominational studies of the Charismatic Renewal.[25]

25. McDonnell, *Presence, Power, Praise*, 221–82.

CHAPTER 4

The Charismatic
Catholic Movement

WHILE THE CHARISMATIC RENEWAL among mainline Protestant denominations was monumental and led to a new form of ecumenism, it was the reception of the Renewal in the Roman Catholic Church that opened the floodgates and became the catalyst for the spread of the charismatic experience in every Christian denomination and tradition.

The watershed event in the life of the Roman Catholic Church in the 1960s unarguably was the Vatican II Council called by Pope John XXIII. In 1958, upon the death of Pope Pius XII, the College of Cardinals elected Angelo Giuseppe Roncalli, then Cardinal-Patriarch of Venice. Thinking him to be a short-term Pope, because of his advanced age, the Cardinals did not expect him to live long enough to institute any major policy changes in the Vatican. However, far from being a "stop-gap" Pontiff, John XXIII convoked the great council known as Vatican II, which radically altered the Church in many ways and paved the way for the Charismatic Movement in the Roman Catholic Church.

On January 25, 1959, Pope John XXIII announced his call for a General Council to convene in Rome to "update" the Church.[1] In preparation for the council, John XXII prayed, "Renew Your wonders in our day, as by a new Pentecost."[2] Those involved in the Charismatic Renewal in the Roman Catholic Church believe that the Renewal is a direct answer to his prayer. Because of the council several documents stated clearly that the Roman Catholic Church was not only comprised of the Pope, bishops, and other clergy, but also included lay men and women who were possessors of the

1. Hatch. *Man Called John*, 219–20.
2. Abbott, *Documents of Vatican II*, 793.

48

gift of the Holy Spirit and were the recipients of those spiritual gifts for the purpose of glorifying God and edifying the Church.[3] This new emphasis upon the "apostolate of the laity" was joined by a new approach to Protestant Christians. No longer labeled as "heretics" but rather as "separated brethren," Protestants, while holding to certain theological errors, still retained a residue of the "Catholic" faith that enabled them likewise to be the bearers of certain spiritual gifts that could even benefit members of the Roman Catholic Church. These changes in attitude provided a new openness, not only within the Roman Catholic Church but also among Protestants.[4]

The birth of the Roman Catholic Charismatic Movement is traced to the campus of Duquesne University in Pittsburgh, Pennsylvania. In August 1966, Ralph Keifer, Patrick Bourgeois, and other lay faculty members at Duquesne met Steve Clark and Ralph Martin, recent graduates of Notre Dame University, at a National Cursillo Congress.[5] Clark was reading a book that both excited and bewildered him. *The Cross and Switchblade,*[6] an autobiographical sketch written by Pentecostal minister David Wilkerson, who in answer to a call from God, relocated from Western Pennsylvania to inner-city Brooklyn to minister to gang members caught up in drug abuse and violence.[7] Wilkerson related in his book that a spiritual experience, the baptism of the Holy Spirit, enabled him to minister to the troubled youth of New York City and in turn empowered those gang members who turned to Christ to live a victorious Christian life, overcoming drugs and violence.[8] Keifer, in turn came across a similar book, *They Speak with Other Tongues,* which described the baptism of the Holy Spirit and the spiritual gifts that accompanied its reception. The contents of the books caused these two Roman Catholic laymen to question whether this baptism of the Holy Spirit was what they lacked in their own Christian life. This was their introduction

---

3. Flannery, *Vatican Council II,* 766–98.

4. Ibid., 452–70.

5. Marcoux, *Cursillo,* 192–212. Cursillo, a spiritual renewal movement predominantly led by Catholic lay people, started in Spain following the Spanish civil war, in an attempt to reconnect men and boys, who participated in the fighting and left their faith, to the Catholic Church. The full title of the movement translated from Spanish is "A Short Course in the Way of Christianity." Many early leaders of the Charismatic Renewal in the Catholic Church were previously participants in the Cursillo Movement.

6. Wilkerson and Sherrill, *Cross and the Switchblade.*

7. Ranaghan, *Catholic Pentecostals,* 9.

8. Wilkerson, *David Wilkerson.*

to Pentecostalism.[9] They felt it was time for them to personally investigate these matters. Rev. William Lewis, rector of Christ Episcopal Church, who once gave a lecture to the students at Duquesne, put them in touch with Betty Schomaker, a member of Christ Church and a participant in a local Charismatic prayer group.

January 6, 1967, Keifer and other Duquesne lay teachers met with Schomaker in Fr. Lewis' office, where she shared her testimony of being baptism in the Holy Spirit and about her experience with the Charismatic prayer group she attended. The following Friday, January 13, the day on which the Roman Catholic Church commemorates the baptism of Jesus in Jordan and the resting of the Holy Spirit on Him, Keifer and friends attended this prayer group, which met in the home of Florence Dodge, a Presbyterian laywoman. Keifer returned the following week and brought Bourgeois with him.[10] At the conclusion of the meeting they both asked for the prayer group members to pray for them to receive the baptism of the Holy Spirit. Keifer states,

> They simply asked me to make an act of faith for the power of the Spirit to work in me. I prayed in tongues rather quickly. It was not a particularly soaring or spectacular thing at all. I felt a certain peace—and at least a little prayerful—and truthfully, rather curious as to where all this would lead.[11]

Within the next week Keifer prayed for two other Duquesne professors, who also received the baptism in Holy Spirit in a similar manner. This set the stage for a monumental spiritual earthquake that eventually rocked the worldwide Roman Catholic Church.

The weekend of February 18–19, 1967, thirty Duquesne students, together with several of their professors, went on a retreat to The Ark and the Dove retreat center just outside Pittsburgh. In preparation for the retreat the students were encouraged to read the book of the Acts of the Apostles, *The Cross and the Switchblade*, *They Speak with Other Tongues* and to regularly recite the "Veni, Creator Spiritus" prayer. Friday evening of the retreat a meditation on the Virgin Mary, as well as a service of Penance was offered. On Saturday, a member of a local Protestant prayer group

---

9. Laurentin, *Catholic Pentecostalism*, 11–12.

10. Ranaghan, *Catholic Pentecostals*, 12–13.

11. Ibid., 15.

addressed the students on the subject of Acts 2. Patti Gallagher-Mansfield, who attended the retreat writes,

> Saturday when I heard that the talk on Acts 2 was being given by an Episcopalian woman, I must admit that I was skeptical. My skepticism increased when she began by saying, "I don't know what to say, but I've prayed for the Holy Spirit to lead me." Indignantly, I thought, "Why didn't she have the courtesy to prepare a talk?" I sat there thinking, "Impress me with your Holy Spirit." Yet, as this beautiful woman spoke, God was moving. Really moving. At first I thought she couldn't be for real as she spoke about knowing Jesus personally. She said that the power of the Holy Spirit could be experienced in our daily lives. "It can't be that easy," I reasoned. "She looks old enough to know that life isn't that simple." But before she finished speaking I was longing to have what she had and I wrote in my notes, "JESUS, BE REAL FOR ME."[12]

Saturday evening a birthday party was held for three people attending the retreat.[13] One of the engaged couples, Paul Grey and Maryanne Springle, sought out Keifer to ask him to pray for them to receive the baptism of the Holy Spirit. They went upstairs to the chapel to pray, as did Patti Gallagher. Before the evening had ended, all those attending the retreat spontaneously wandered one by one into the chapel. All of them, as they entered, testify to the fact that they sensed a powerful presence of God, and all of them, as a result, received a baptism of the Holy Spirit and many of them also spoke in tongues. Now referred to as the "Duquesne Weekend," this event is celebrated as the official beginning of the Charismatic Renewal in the Roman Catholic Church.[14]

From the "Duquesne Weekend" the Charismatic Renewal rapidly spread throughout the Catholic Church. In less than ten years after Duquesne the Charismatic Renewal Movement grew so strongly among Catholics that they met in St. Peter's Basilica in Rome and were welcomed by Pope Paul VI.[15] The Charismatic Catholic Renewal was endorsed by Popes John Paul II, Benedict XII, and Francis. Paul VI appointed Cardinal Archbishop Leon Joseph Suenens of the Netherlands to serve as liaison between the Papacy and

---

12. Patti Gallagher Mansfield, *As By a New Pentecost*, 73.

13. Ranaghan, *Catholic Pentecostals*, 26.

14 Ibid., 6–23.

15. O'Connor, *Pope Paul and the Spirit*, 45–55.

the Movement.[16] The International Catholic Charismatic Renewal Services became a department of the Pontifical Commission of the Laity.[17] Throughout the globe, thousands of Catholic parishes hosted weekly Charismatic Prayer Groups. Catholic Charismatic Conferences were held annually throughout several different regions of the world and many bishops created diocesan Charismatic committees and commissions. Charismatic Catholic magazines, *New Covenant* and *Pentecost Today*, as well as Charismatic Catholic publishing concerns, such as Servant, published literature that served the Movement. The Movement gave birth to new religious orders and new radio and television ministries, like Mother Angelica's Eternal Word Television Network (EWTN)[18] in the United States and Canção Nova in South America.[19] It inspired the development of the "Life in the Spirit Seminar," a program to introduce Catholics to the baptism of the Holy Spirit.[20] The Movement also inspired the establishment of thousands of intentional lay communities throughout the world and organized into several different associations, such as the Catholic Fraternity and Sword of the Spirit.[21]

2017 marked the 50th anniversary of the beginning of the Catholic Charismatic Renewal. Celebrations took place in Pittsburgh at the Ark and Dove Retreat Center as well as other sites throughout the world. Pope Francis hosted an international commemoration of the Movement at the Vatican the weekend of Pentecost. Millions of Charismatic Catholics participated in person or by televised broadcasts.[22] The growth of the Charismatic Movement among Roman Catholics throughout the world shows no signs of abating. Rather, in the continents of South America, Africa, and Asia most Roman Catholics claim to be participants in the Charismatic Movement. Likewise, Catholic immigrants from these continents to North America continue to be strongly involved in the Movement in their local parishes.[23]

16. Suenens, *Memories and Hopes.*

17. Pontifical Council for the Laity. *Movements in the Church.*

18. http://www.ewtn.com/

19. http://www.cancaonova.com/

20. n.a., *Life in the Spirit Team Manual.*

21. http://www.catholicfraternity.org/ and http://www.swordofthespirit.net/about-sword-of-the-spirit/.

22. https://cruxnow.com/vatican/2017/06/03/jubilee-rome-highlights-charismatic-fruits-franciss-pentecost-papacy/.

23. Charlotte Saikowski, "Impact of the Charismatics" *Christian Science Monitor.* December 23, 1987

CHAPTER 5

Charismatic Renewal among Orthodox Christians

THE ORTHODOX CHURCH IN North America is a relatively recent religious newcomer to America's shores, especially compared with Protestant denominations and the Roman Catholic Church. The first Orthodox Christians arrived, in what would become the United States and Canada, in the late seventeenth century to Spanish Florida from Greece and to Russian Alaska in the late eighteenth century.[1] Whereas the Orthodox Greeks, who came to St. Augustine, Florida, came as ship-hands and never settled permanently in Spanish Florida, the Orthodox Russians who came to Alaska not only settled there but undertook the work of converting the Alaskan natives to the Orthodox Christian Faith.[2] The missionary work of Orthodox Russians spread south from Alaska to San Francisco and then across the United States and Canada. The earliest recorded Orthodox parish of Greeks was Holy Trinity in New Orleans in 1864, while throughout the late nineteenth and early twentieth century Russian, Ukrainian, Serbian, Carpatho-Russyn, Bulgarian, Romanian, Albanian, and Syrian Orthodox Christians immigrated to North America by the thousands and established parish communities wherever they settled. Initially arriving on the eastern seaboard, they made their way across North America, arriving in California and British Colombia and settling everywhere in between, and where they settled they established Orthodox communities and built Orthodox churches.

In almost every case, the first Orthodox Church churches were built around the ethnic community that established them. Orthodox worship

1. Stokoe and Kishkovsky, *Orthodox Christians*, 22.
2. Oleksa, *Alaskan Missionary Spirituality*.

was conducted in the language of the immigrant community, whether Greek, Church Slavonic, Arabic, or Albanian.[3] The people banded together and organized mutual aid societies, burial associations, Church and language schools for their children. In most cases, each ethnic group lived in its own separate neighborhoods. Initially social interaction was minimal. The Greek community was almost exclusively Orthodox, while Russian and Eastern European immigrants were typically Eastern Rite Catholic, Orthodox, Lutheran, or of some other Protestant denomination. The public-school system became the place of enculturation. Orthodox young people interacted with Irish, Polish, and German Catholics and a host of other ethnic and religious groups. While the first generation was more apt to marry within their own ethnic group, the second and third generation embraced a multi-cultural society and married outside the ethnic clan, in many cases defying the wishes of their parents.[4]

In these early days, before the reforms of Vatican II, Roman Catholics were forbidden to visit an Orthodox or Protestant Church. Likewise, marriage between a Roman Catholic and non-Catholic was religiously taboo. By the 1960s the social and religious landscape of North America had changed. While the Russian Orthodox were in some quarters still looked at with suspicion, with rumors of loyalty to Soviet Russia, after thousands of Orthodox young men served and died in World War II and the Korean War fighting for the Allies, the Orthodox, including those who had family ties to counties that were now behind the Iron Curtain, were accepted as a part of the American and Canadian social and religious mainstream. By the 1970s many Orthodox communities were using English in their services and the former Russian Orthodox Church in America was given independence from the Russian Mother Church in Moscow and adopted the name "Orthodox Church in America."[5] Likewise, in the early 1970s, the Syrian Orthodox Church in the North America changed its name from its ethnic identification to "The Antiochian Orthodox Church," English being the predominant language used in worship.[6] However, the Greek Orthodox Church in North America still holds tenaciously to its native culture and language.

3. Stokoe and Kishkovsky, 45–53.
4. Gabriel, *Ancient Church,* 10–11.
5. Ibid., 94–106.
6. Ibid., 63–5.

The Antiochian Connection:
Archimandrite Athanasios Emmert

Born November 16, 1934 in Hagerstown, Maryland, Franklin Stuart Em-mert, the only son of Edwin Ashman Emmert and Mary Virginia, was baptized as an infant at St. John's United Lutheran Church in Hagerstown. Educated in the public schools of Berks County, Pennsylvania, Emmert showed an interest in spiritual things at an early age. A pre-theological student his freshman and sophomore years at Muhlenberg College in Allentown, Pennsylvania, his junior and senior years he attended Concordia Theological Seminary in St. Louis, Missouri graduating with a Bachelor of Arts degree in 1956. He attended one more year at Concordia after which he joined the Orthodox Church.

On May 27, 1957 Emmert was Chrismated by Fr. George Mastran-tonis[7] into the Orthodox Church at St. Nicholas Greek Orthodox parish in St. Louis. Fr. George gave Emmert a new name, Athanasios, after the great champion at the First Ecumenical Council of Nicaea, St. Athanasios of Alexandria.[8] Emmert entered Holy Cross Greek Orthodox Seminary in Brookline, Massachusetts and studied there as a special senior student from September 1958 to December 1959. He continued theological studies at the Theological School of the University of Athens and Rizarion Seminary (at which St. Nektarios of Aegina served as headmaster) in Greece.[9] From 1967–68 he did further graduate studies at St. Vladimir's Orthodox Theological Seminary in Crestwood, New York.

On January 17, 1960, Metropolitan Anthony Bashir, primate of the Syrian Antiochian Archdiocese of North America, ordained Athanasios to the Diaconate.[10] This was followed on February 28 of the same year

---

7. Fr. George Mastrantonis, a prolific writer and Greek Orthodox priest, was the founder of one of the first English language Orthodox publishing ventures, in the United States, O LOGOS Publishing. He wrote hundreds of English language pamphlets and books on the Orthodox Faith. He was a proponent of spiritual renewal in the Greek Orthodox Archdiocese of North America.

8. It is customary in the Orthodox Church to give the name of an Orthodox saint to a person who is baptized and/or chrismated in a Church, especially if their name is not that of one of the saints of the Orthodox Church.

9. Chondropoulos, *Saint Nektarios,* 91–92. St. Nektarios is greatly revered throughout the Orthodox Church as a "wonder-working" saint. Numerous healing miracles are attributed to his prayers and intercessions. His grave, on the Greek island of Aegina is a site visited by thousands of pilgrims from all over the world.

10. The name of the Syrian-Antiochian Orthodox Archdiocese was changed to the

by ordination to the priesthood at St. Mary's Orthodox Church in Bay Ridge, Brooklyn. The newly ordained Fr. Athanasios became the personal secretary to Metropolitan Bashir and from January to May of 1961 served as assistant pastor to Fr. Wakeem Dallack at St. Nicholas Orthodox Cathedral in Brooklyn.

Fr. Athanasios served several parish communities within the Syrian Antiochian Archdiocese. Emmert served as priest at St. Mary in Johnstown, Pennsylvania (1961–63), during which time he also served as prefect and taught at Christ the Savior Seminary of the Carpatho-Russyn Orthodox jurisdiction; St. Nicholas, Beckley West Virginia (1963–64), St. George in Toronto, Ontario (1964–67), and St. George, Danbury, Connecticut (1967–68). He was the founding pastor of Holy Spirit, Huntington, West Virginia and served St. Elias, Syracuse, New York, St. Mary, Cambridge, Massachusetts, and St. George in Oak Park, Cicero a suburb of Chicago.

While each one of these pastorates testifies to Emmert's dedication to ministry in the Orthodox Church, it was his short tenure as priest at St. George parish in Danbury, Connecticut that forever changed his life and ministry. In Emmert's own words he states:

> I was having real serious problems dealing with personal issues, psychological and otherwise, and I was drinking heavily . . . actually it was so serious that I would get in my car and drive for hours at night and I'd be drunk or out of my head and the fact that I didn't end up wrecking somewhere is just a miracle of God. But the situation was so bad that I was going to commit suicide, I had it all done, I had a whole bottle of phenol barbital pills and I was all set to just down all of them when I was super, super drunk and end it all. And I told some people that I was in such a bad way that I am just going to pull the blinds shut, take the pills and end it all. That's when one of the nights when I was really, really bad I happened to stop at the Connecticut Turnpike rest area restaurant, near Bridgeport. And who should be in the restaurant when I got in but Stephen Barham. Now I had met Stephen Barham at Metropolitan Anthony's funeral in '65. I didn't like him; I didn't like him at all. I didn't like his ways, his manner, but he was just extremely friendly. He came over to me and sat down and we began to talk and I told him I was in bad shape. He asked me to come home to his apartment in Bridgeport, which I did. He handed me the scriptures and he handed me Psalm 38, and he said, "This is

---

Antiochian Orthodox Christian Archdiocese of North America in 1970, owing to the ethnic diversity of the clergy and laity in the Archdiocese.

you, isn't it?" And I read and I was still drunk and I stayed with him. Now he and Fr. Michael Stott, for almost over a week I did not go, I came back from Danbury to Bridgeport. They would not let me stay by myself in Danbury. Fr. Michael Stott was at St. Nicholas Syrian Church and Stephen was at St. George Albanian in Bridgeport. . . . I stayed either with Fr. Michael and his wife or at Stephen's . . . because of my condition . . . with the help of Stephen, showing compassion, concern and Fr. Stott to some degree more, but Stephen principally, and then it's when Stephen started to talk to me about the baptism in the Holy Spirit. . . . I had heard about it . . . and Schneirla[11] had told me about it and he was violently opposed to anything like that at the time. Schneirla knew Stephen as a student at St. Vladimir's and did not like Stephen's Pentecostal ways. Eventually they explained it to me I remember reading Kelsey's *Tongues Speaking* book and also *They Speak with Other Tongues* by Sherrill. And so one evening we were praying together, it was Fr. Michael and Fr. Stephen, and I asked them, "Would you please lay hands on me that I might receive the baptism in the Holy Spirit," which they did and that happened to me; . . . it was a tremendous experience, I did speak in tongues. . . . I didn't have any physical sensations, but I will say this, and I told many, many people at the time, and later on when I would tell this story, I gave my story how many times at Full Gospel's meetings in Virginia, quite a few different places. It was like I'd been living in a world of black and white and suddenly it was like everything became, as we called it back then, Technicolor. I felt a tremendous sense of relief, a tremendous sense of God's presence that I had not experience since I was a youth, a child, when I got "saved," so to speak. It was a tremendously moving experience.[12]

Following Emmert's experience of the baptism of the Holy Spirit he sought additional help in dealing with his psychological problems by visiting a psychiatrist in New York City who specialized in working with clergymen. He further comments that:

11. Gabriel, "Lest We Forget," 10–12. The Very Rev. Paul Schneirla, one of the early converts to Orthodoxy from the Lutheran Church, pastored St. Mary's Antiochian Orthodox Church in Bay Ridge, Brooklyn and Old Testament professor at St. Vladimir's Orthodox Theological Seminary. Schneirla was the first Secretary of SCOBA (Standing Conference of Orthodox Bishops in America), Vicar General of the Western Rite of the Antiochian Archdiocese, Secretary of the Antiochian Archdiocese Board of Trustees for many years and Chair of the Office of Ecumenical Affairs for the Antiochian Archdiocese.

12. Emmert, Fr. Athanasios. 2008. Interview by author. Price, UT. August 16.

I would come from Danbury and I would have a session . . . then I would leave . . . and went to Fr. James Griffith for Confession and counsel at the ROCOR Cathedral.[13] Fr. Griffiths was from England, and also close to the author of Peter the Great and Nicholas and Alexandria.[14] They were interested in each other because Fr. Griffiths had a hemophiliac boy, so did the author. . . . I told Fr. Griffiths all about what had happened to me and he was very supportive. He did not say, "Oh, this isn't Orthodox," or anything like that. He prayed with me and he was a tremendous help. So, the two of them [the psychiatrist and Fr. Griffiths] and at the same time of course Fr. Barham, they got me through that period from February through July.[15]

Fr. Athanasios related that his life and ministry were never the same after his experience of the baptism of the Holy Spirit.

In July of this same year, Emmert related that as he was standing before the altar at St. George, Danbury, Connecticut, presiding at a Divine Liturgy, the voice of the Lord came to him and told him to go to Huntington, West Virginia and begin an Antiochian Orthodox parish. He approached Metropolitan Philip, primate of the Antiochian Orthodox Christian Archdiocese of North America, and asked for a blessing for an extended vacation in Huntington. The Metropolitan granted his request.

13. ROCOR is the acronym for the Russian Orthodox Church Outside Russia.

14. Massie, Nicholas and Alexandria.

15. Fr. Athanasios Emmert, 2008. Interview by author. Price, UT. August 16.

CHAPTER 6

Greek Orthodox Involvement

Archimandrite Eusebius Stephanou

THE SPIRITUAL LIVES OF Fr. Athanasios Emmert and Fr. Eusebius Stephanou and their involvement in the Charismatic Renewal in the Orthodox Church are intricately interconnected. Through the testimony and ministry of Emmert, Stephanou became involved in the Charismatic Movement. As a result, Stephanou's participation in the Movement in many ways eclipsed Emmert, in that Stephanou becomes the most prolific and vocal defender of the Charismatic Movement in the Orthodox Church.

Agamemnon Papastephanou was born on Sunday, June 15, 1924 in Fond du Lac, Wisconsin, the third son of seven children, to Father Alexander and Presbytera Marika Papastephanou.[1] In 1906, Alexander Papastephanou immigrated to the United States from the Greek town of Philiatra. Alexander's father Stylianos had been an Orthodox priest as had his father before him. Agamemnon's early life centered on the activities of his father's priestly ministry which meant serving as an acolyte for all the liturgical services and moving around to the several different parishes he served. From Fond du Lac they moved to Detroit, to Lorain, Ohio, Pontiac, Michigan and then back to Detroit.[2] While Agamemnon attended local public schools, at home Greek was the spoken language, while in Church liturgical Greek was used in the Byzantine chants and in the texts of the services. This was also the time of the Great Depression in the United States and Agamemnon's family suffered the same economic hardships as other families and even more so since the salary of an Orthodox priest was meager. On many occasions, the only food available was the prosphora bread left over from Holy Com-

1. The Greek word "Presbytera," the feminine rendering of presbyter, is the title given to a priest's wife in the Greek Orthodox Church.

2. Stethatos, *Voice of a Priest*, 15–17.

59

munion.[3] Agamemnon's father had not had the chance for any advanced education and he encouraged his son to enter the medical or law profession in order that his son not suffer the same hardships he had suffered as a result of being a poor priest. However, this was not to be. In 1941, Agamemnon's senior year, a pamphlet introducing the Greek Orthodox seminary came into his hands, changing the course of his life forever.

In 1942, Agamemnon Papastephanou entered Holy Cross Greek Orthodox Seminary, at that time located in Pomfret Center, Connecticut. All classes were taught in Greek, at which he excelled. In 1946, Papastephanou's senior year, the campus of Holy Cross moved to Brookline, Massachusetts. Finishing his studies at Holy Cross in June 1947, he completed his Bachelor of Arts degree at the University of Michigan in the spring of 1948. The fall of the same year Papastephanou attended Nashotah House Seminary, a seminary of the Protestant Episcopal Church in Nashotah, Wisconsin, where he earned a Master of Sacred theology degree in June 1949. In fall of 1949 he travelled to New York City, attending General Theological Seminary, another Episcopal seminary, and earned a Doctor of Theology degree in June 1950. Following his time at General Theological Seminary, Papastephanou attended classes from fall of 1950 to spring of 1951 at St. Vladimir's Orthodox Theological Seminary. Newly established by the Russian Metropolia, St. Vladimir's rented facilities on the campus of Union Theological Seminary. He was especially impressed by lectures given by the imminent Orthodox theologian, Fr. Georges Florovsky. Florovsky's emphasis upon a "Patristic revival" greatly influenced Papastephanou own theology, as seen in his later writings and reflections.

In August 1950, Archbishop Michael of the Greek Orthodox Archdiocese tonsured Papastephanou a monk giving him the name Eusebius, which in Greek means "blessed." The newly tonsured Eusebius took the opportunity of the name change to also shorten his last name from

---

3. Alfeyev, *Worship and Liturgical Life,* 110. Prosphora is the specially baked bread used in the Divine Liturgy for Holy Communion in the Orthodox Church. The bread, in some cases up to five loaves, is usually baked, and accompanied by prayers, by a family in the parish and offered for use in the Liturgy. The bread is stamped on top with a special religious stamp and is given to the priest with a list of names of both the living and the dead who are to be prayed for. Particles are taken from the loaf for the name of each person commemorated and placed on the diskos, a liturgical dish, by the priest. Only the center section of the prosphora is used for communion. This section, called the "lamb" is consecrated by the invocation of the Holy Spirit upon the bread, by whose power the bread becomes the body of Christ. The remainder of the bread is cut up and offered to the priest and people following the Divine Liturgy and known as the "antidoron."

Papastephanou to Stephanou. The following month of September, Bishop Gerasimos, of Chicago, ordained Eusebius to the diaconate. Deacon Eusebius was assigned to serve at St. Eleftherius Greek Orthodox Church in New York, not far from General Theological Seminary. It was while serving at St. Eleftherius that Stephanou first came in contact with lay members of the "Brotherhood of the Zealots of Orthodoxy." This brotherhood followed the teachings of Greek Orthodox philosopher and theologian Apostolos Makrakis, who Stephanou had been introduced to while a student at Holy Cross. This was his first exposure, of which he was conscious, to Greek Orthodox laymen who zealously pursued the spiritual life and were active in the Church in more than in a perfunctory manner. The brotherhood met weekly in the basement of the Greek Orthodox Archdiocesan headquarters to study the Scriptures and Makrakis' commentaries.

Following Stephanou's studies at St. Vladimir's, he embarked upon a trip to Europe. Archbishop Michael provided him with a scholarship to study theology at the University of Athens, Greece. While in Greece Stephanou visited his father's ancestral home of Philatria, where on February 10, 1953, the feast of St. Charalampos the Hieromartyr, he was ordained a priest by Metropolitan Damascenos of Kyparissia who also elevated him to the rank of Archimandrite. Upon the completion of his studies at the University of Athens, where he was awarded a degree in theology, and before his return to the United States, he undertook a tour of the historical Orthodox patriarchates of Constantinople, Antioch, Jerusalem, and Alexandria. He believed that this travelling experience was the seal of his Orthodox education and the fitting completion of his studies in Greece and ordination to the priesthood.

Several months after his return to the United States in June of 1953, Stephanou received his first pastoral assignment which took him back to Ann Arbor, Michigan to the small parish of St. Nicholas. While serving St. Nicholas he completed further graduate studies at the University of Michigan in the area of philosophy. In 1956, three years into his pastoral work in Ann Arbor, he received a cable from Archbishop Michael informing him that he was appointed Sub-dean and Professor of Theology at Holy Cross Greek Orthodox Seminary in Brookline, Massachusetts.

It was while teaching at Holy Cross that Stephanou first came into conflict with his ideal of the Church and what he actually saw, or heard taking place. He saw a serious disconnect between the teachings of the Orthodox Church and what was being lived out, especially by the young men who were training to be pastors in the Church and whose confession he heard. This sense of dissatisfaction was certainly exacerbated by Stephanou's personality, which tended to be introverted and his demeanor austere and judgmental. In turn, this caused him to be isolated from the other faculty members. In his own words, Stephanou relates in the third person:

> . . . the sub-dean was by nature an introvert, uneasy, . . . with little, if any sense of humor, and not given to levity. Due to the circumstances of his childhood, strong self-discipline was his magnificent obsession. He unconsciously imposed the same loveless austerity upon his students that he dictated for himself.[4]

Because of Stephanou's experience at Holy Cross he found himself in a place of internal uneasiness, a recurring theme in Stephanou's life, which he again relates in the third person:

> The lack of meaningful relationships, a total lack of spiritual support or direction from superiors, and a sense of rejection was fast becoming a source of inner unrest. Feelings of anxiety and insecurity were mounting and bringing him virtually to an impasse.[5]

In 1959, Archbishop Michael died and was succeeded by Iakovos (Coucouzes). Stephanou claims that in his first meeting with the newly appointed Archbishop, Iakovos spoke to him of plans to elevate him to the episcopate. Stephanou further claims that he shared this information with friends and colleagues which angered Iakovos. As a result, Stephanou was never consecrated a bishop in the Greek Orthodox Church. One can deduce from Stephanou's reflection on this episode of his life that this was a constant source of tension between him and Archbishop Iakovos for years to come.[6]

On October 1, 1960, Stephanou took up his pastoral responsibilities at the newly assigned parish of St. Demetrius in Newton-Wellesley, Massachusetts only to receive another assignment in Venezuela to organize parishes for recent Greek immigrants to the city of Caracas. Almost as quickly as he was sent abroad he was recalled and assigned to pastor St. Charalampos parish in Canton, Ohio, which he served from 1960–61, from which he was assigned to Annunciation parish in Woburn, Massachusetts and reappointed to teach at Holy Cross through the fall of 1963. Again, a

---

4. Stethatos, *Voice of a Priest*, 32.

5. Ibid., 33.

6. Ibid., 35–36.

letter of transfer came from Archbishop Iakovos being assigned to Ss. Constantine and Helen Church in Chicago. At this time Stephanou writes that Iakovos again mentioned to him the probability that he would be called upon to serve the Church in the episcopacy.[7] However, during his time in Chicago Stephanou's relationship with parish council president and the diocesan bishop deteriorated. Stephanou's pastoral style and certain decisions made regarding admission of a black student to Sunday School accelerated the tensions. Added to this was a memorandum written to Archbishop Iakovos entitled, "Why English is Needed in the Scriptural Liturgical Readings." Stephanou had been using English in the Epistle and Gospel readings during the Liturgy which the Bishop of Chicago saw as a serious breech of traditional liturgical practice. All these together caused the Archbishop to once again remove Stephanou.

In 1964, the chancellor of the Greek Orthodox Archdiocese informed Stephanou that he would join the staff at the Archdiocesan offices in New York City; however, this assignment was canceled a few days later. The beleaguered priest's new appointment was to Uniontown, Pennsylvania. Here, at a run-down, five-acre estate, he was to establish a "Center for Theological and Patristic Studies" for the use of the Archdiocese. The deteriorated condition of the twenty-room house necessitated Fr. Eusebius to undertake a challenging and costly overhaul of the building and grounds. Lack of financial support for the project, as well as the isolation he felt, took its toll on Stephanou. During this time, he penned his first book, *Belief and Practice in the Orthodox Church*.[8] Fr. Eusebius never received any further support from the leadership of the Church in developing the Center. Stephanou in his own words writes, "Deep disillusionment set in. The caprice and indecision of the hierarchy became clear; the archbishop was not serious about the Uniontown appointment."[9] Stephanou resigned the post only to be succeeded by newly ordained priest Fr. Anthony Morefesis, who would himself become quite active in the Charismatic Movement in the Orthodox Church. Before the year's end plans for the Center were scraped by Archbishop Iakovos and it was sold to the Knights of Columbus.

Stephanou's disheartening experience in Uniontown caused his disillusionment with the Church and its leadership to increase. He took a short sabbatical during which time he visited family in the Midwest and also

7. Stethatos, *Voice of a Priest*, 37–38.

8. Stephanou, *Belief and Practice*.

9. Stethatos, *Voice of a Priest*, 45.

travelled to Moscow, Belgrade, and Istanbul. While in Istanbul, Fr. Eusebius visited with the Ecumenical Patriarch Athenagoras who appointed Stephanou an Orthodox observer to the Vatican II Council being held in Rome. The historic gathering of so many Roman Catholic bishops and priests impressed Stephanou while at the same time sparking in him a great concern for the spiritual renewal of his own Orthodox Church.

Stephanou's personal sabbatical came to an end in December 1966 when Bishop Gerasimos of Detroit called upon him to serve the small Holy Trinity Greek Orthodox parish in Fort Wayne for Nativity and Epiphany. Initially he turned down the bishop but then he changed his mind and accepted the temporary assignment. Nativity and Epiphany turned into Great Lent and Pascha and eventually Fr. Eusebius was appointed the permanent rector of the parish. In the summer of 1967 he received an invitation to teach in the Department of Theology at the University of Notre Dame. This venture in teaching however was short-lived and after a year he was informed that he would no longer be needed. In Stephanou's biography, he reflects once again in the third person,

> There was nothing to fill the free time created by Father Eusebius' departure from Notre Dame. His disappointment left him with an inner void and led to a new restlessness in his soul. He began to question the wisdom of serving in Fort Wayne. He found nothing to challenge or excite him; . . . his thoughts turned again to the general state of Orthodoxy on the national and world scene. He felt a need for a forum in which to express his views and convictions publicly on the spiritual decline in the church that grieved his spirit.[10]

This intellectual and spiritual unrest led Stephanou to pursue a totally different venture then he had ever embarked upon before. In January 1968, he decided to publish a magazine to promote the spiritual revitalization of the Orthodox Church in the United States and entitled the periodical *The Logos*.

The Beginning of *The Logos*

The run of the first issue of *The Logos* numbered 5,000 copies. A copy was sent to every known Orthodox parish in the United States. Under the prominent masthead, *The Logos,* were these words, "A Journal for Promoting

10. Stethatos, *Voice of a Priest*, 51.

Orthodox Re-awakening." Stephanou was joined in this publishing venture by Serbian Orthodox Charles Ashanin, PhD, a long-time friend of Stephanou and Associate Professor of Early Church History at Christian Theological Seminary in Indianapolis, Indiana.[11] Ashanin was listed as assistant editor and Andrew Copan, MA, as associate editor.[12] Later in the year Dr. Thomas Lelon and Katherine Valone joined the editorial staff. Copan, Lelon, and Valone were all in the parochial education programs at Ss. Constantine and Helen Greek Orthodox Church in Chicago.[13] Stephanou, in the initial editorial wrote that the objective of the *The Logos* was

> . . . neither theological scholarship nor ecclesiastical journalism. It comes, rather, to serve as a forum for instructive and constructive comment on the current happenings, trends, and issues in the life of the Orthodox Church. . . . There is a growing feeling that the Orthodox Church, including both laity and clergy, suffers today too much reticence. We witness to a sad lack of candor over the grave issues that confront the Church from within and without.[14]

The editor goes on to further explain the reasons behind his choice for the title of the new magazine,

> "The Logos" was selected as the name of this journal, because it aims at becoming a humble offering in the service of the Christ of Orthodoxy Who is the preexistent and consubstantial Logos of God. . . . We feel that there could be no more appropriate name than "The Logos" for such a publication whose purpose is Logical articulation of Logos-like truth. To be more Logos-minded is to be more Orthodox, because the Holy Orthodox Catholic and Apostolic Church of history remains the Church par excellence of the Logos. The Logos theology and Logos philosophy of the Church Fathers is Orthodoxy's cherished heritage . . . .[15]

In the first year of publication, *The Logos* dealt with several issues of particular interest to the Church in America. The close of the Vatican II Council in Rome, and the ensuing rapprochement between the Roman Catholic Church and mainline Protestant denominations, made the ecumenical movement a hot topic. The meetings of Ecumenical Patriarch

11. Ibid., 51–55.

12. *The Logos*, 1, no., 4.

13. Stethatos, *Voice of a Priest*, 57.

14. Stephanou, "A Self Introduction," 3.

15. Ibid., 3, 10.

Athenagoras and Pope Paul IV, their mutual lifting of the ancient excommunications and the subsequent ecumenical activities of Archbishop Iakavos in North America were constant sources of speculation and consternation. Reflections on the possibility of a unified "American" Orthodox Church and the nascent Civil Rights Movement were all topics covered. Many times, *The Logos* aired opinions and perspectives that were not in keeping with the prevailing views of the Greek Orthodox hierarchy. Readers responded positively to the publication, as can be seen by the letters printed in the second and third issues of the journal. Prominent Orthodox theologians such as Fr. Georges Florovsky, then teaching at Princeton University, and Dr. Constantine Cavarnos sent letters of support as did scores of other Orthodox priests and lay people of all Orthodox jurisdictions and ethnic backgrounds, even receiving responses from Greece.[16]

However, not all of Stephanou's readers applauded his efforts. As early as March 1968, Archbishop Iakavos expressed his displeasure with Stephanou and *The Logos*. In a letter to Stephanou the Archbishop writes:

> We received your periodical entitled "The Logos" and we express our regret that you are engaged in activities without the consent of the Holy Archdiocese and you pursue your old methods of self-projection and disseminate your own personal viewpoints and opinions.[17]

Archbishop Iakavos followed up with another letter dated August 26, which reads:

> It appears that for some time now you take pleasure in publishing articles as an "opposition party," as "censurer," or as the "conscience of others" without any censure from your priestly conscience. What has happened to it? We pray that you come to your senses as quickly as possible and rediscover your true self which you know better than anyone else. Compare yourself to God. It will do you good.[18]

In October 1968, Stephanou finally received a letter from the offices of the Greek Orthodox Archdiocese in New York City summoning him to

---

16. "Views of the Readers," *The Logos*, 1, no. 2, 2, 12 and "Views of Our Readers," *The Logos*, 1, no., 2, 16.

17. "A Glance at our First Year," *The Logos*, 2, no. 1, 10.

18. Ibid.

. . . appear before the tribunal on November 20 to answer to charges of "undermining and shaking ecclesiastical authority and generally the authority of the holy clergy of the Greek Orthodox Archdiocese, thus becoming a scandal to the conscience of the faithful."[19]

Timothy, Auxiliary Bishop of Chicago, presided over the tribunal that included Gerasimos, Auxiliary Bishop of Pittsburgh and Emilianos of Charlotte, North Carolina. Four passages from issues of *The Logos* had been lifted and were presented as evidence to support the charges against Stephanou. All four passages were critical of actions and attitudes shown by Archbishop Iakavos in his leadership of the Archdiocese. Stephanou was asked to recant and apologize for these published statements. To this the editor of *The Logos* replied:

> I would gladly recant what I have written and ask forgiveness if I had not spoken the truth. But for what I have regarded as truth I cannot in good conscience recant. [20]

As a result of Stephanou's refusal to retract his statements the episcopal tribunal suspended him from his priestly ministry for six months. In spite of the suspension *The Logos* continued to be published. The December 1968 issue gave special attention to the situation and details relating to the tribunal and resulting suspension of Stephanou. Stephanou himself believed that the Lord used the suspension to teach him a lesson. Writing in the third person he reflects:

> The suspension proved to be a blessing in disguise. It brought Father Eusebius to a place where he was compelled to come to grips with the reality of his inadequacy. It helped him to begin to recognize how limited his confidence in Jesus Christ really was.[21]

The time of the suspension passed and the circulation of *The Logos* continued to grow. Since Stephanou's suspension relieved him of his pastoral responsibilities at Holy Trinity parish in Fort Wayne, he accepted invitations to visit parishes and make presentations and lead retreats, especially throughout the Midwest. At the request of Stephanou Archbishop Iakavos appointed him an itinerant preacher for the Diocese of Chicago only to have it rescinded because of a disagreement with Bishop Timothy over

19. "Our Editor Suspended." *The Logos*, 1, no. 12, 2.

20. Stethatos, *Voice of a Priest*, 61–62.

21. Ibid., 71.

salary. Stephanou relates in his pseudonymously written autobiography that he was convinced that several of the auxiliary bishops of the Greek archdiocese, especially Silas of New Jersey, were jealous of him and were constantly working behind the scenes to sabotage any advancement that might be presented to him by the Archbishop. [22]

From 1969 to 1971 Stephanou continued to edit *The Logos* without being assigned or attached to an Orthodox parish. He continued to relentlessly confront the hierarchical leadership of the Church, especially of the Greek Archdiocese, while at the same time calling the priests to a more Christ-centered ministry and the laity to a more Christ-centered spiritual life. Letters addressed to the editor continued to come from all quarters of the Orthodox Church in the United States and abroad. Mostly of a commendatory and positive nature, Stephanou, however, was not hesitant to print letters of those who seriously disagreed with his opinion or analysis, or those of his co-writers, and in some cases who rebuked him soundly for what they perceived as a disrespectful attitude toward the hierarchical leadership of the Church. Articles addressing the challenges of the Ecumenical Movement continued to figure prominently as did the reoccurring themes of unity among the Orthodox jurisdictions in the United States and revitalization of the spiritual life of the laity.

Stephanou's Life Takes a Radical Turn

The power of a personal testimony to influence another life and even radically alter its course can never be underestimated. Such is the case with Fr. Eusebius Stephanou's encounter with Fr. Athanasius Emmert in the late summer of 1971. Stephanou states that one day he received a phone call from Emmert, who at that time was pastor of Holy Spirit Antiochian Orthodox parish in Huntington, West Virginia, asking to come and visit with him in Fort Wayne. Emmert had been a student at Holy Cross Seminary while Stephanou was there teaching. During Emmert's visit in Fort Wayne he related to his former teacher the spiritual crisis he faced and his planned suicide while pastoring St. George parish in Danbury, Connecticut. Emmert also testified of his baptism in the Holy Spirit and how it had radically changed his life and altered his priesthood. He further related how the Lord had called him to Huntington, with the blessing of his Metropolitan, Philip Saliba, to found Holy Spirit parish and how most of the members

22. Ibid., 82–83.

of the parish had themselves experienced the baptism of the Holy Spirit. This occurrence of the baptism of the Holy Spirit was being experienced by individuals throughout the Roman Catholic and Protestant churches and that this wave of the Holy Spirit was being called the Charismatic Movement or Renewal. Stephanou readily confesses that Emmert's testimony challenged much of his preconceived theology. Stephanou was further challenged when Emmert suggested that they pray, that is in extemporaneous fashion, together before he parted company.[23] In addition to this before Fr. Athanasius departed he invited Fr. Eusebius to come and visited him in Huntington and to see what was happening among the people of Holy Spirit Orthodox Church.

In September 1971, Stephanou responded to Emmert's invitation and travelled from Fort Wayne to Huntington to spend a weekend there. During their visit, Fr. Athanasios further educated Stephanou on the subject of the Charismatic Renewal, introducing him to such books as Howard Ervin's *These Are Not Drunken as Ye Suppose*[24] and audio tapes of many of the prominent teachers, including Kathryn Kuhlman as well as the ministry of the Full Gospel Business Men's Fellowship.

Sunday evenings were set aside for the weekly prayer meeting held in the nave of Holy Spirit Church. Stephanou accompanied Emmert to the meeting and once again was challenged by a new and unfamiliar experience. Stephanou describes the scene:

> Men and women were standing with their hands lifted up and singing hymns of praise. But this time the hymns were not liturgical hymns familiar to Father Eusebius. They had a Protestant ring to his ear. "I was somewhat uneasy because of my instinctively negative reaction to anything that was Protestant. Ordinarily I would have disapproved vigorously. However, I was retrained for I had to fully acknowledge that I was in an Orthodox temple of worship where a beautiful Liturgy had been celebrated in the morning of the same day and that the parishioners lived a Eucharistic life." . . . While the congregation sang the unfamiliar charismatic choruses, the visiting priest had a sense of the atmosphere was charged with the presence of the Lord in a very new way. The faces of everyone had a glow upon them and all appeared as though they were beholding Jesus right in front of them! They prayed and praised Jesus with a holy intimacy and warmth that,

23. Stethatos, *Voice of a Priest*, 91–94.
24. Ervin, *These Are Not Drunken*.

he had to admit, he had never seen before in any group of Orthodox Christians during worship. . . . Then there was a sudden interruption. Father Emmert, standing at the front, surprised his guest by asking him to come forward so that everyone could pray over him. He was puzzled by the request because he had not asked for prayer, least of all, from lay people. He was, after all, a priest, and was conditioned by years of training and experience as a priest to being the one who always blesses others with prayers. However, . . . he squeamishly consented without really knowing to what he was giving his consent. Father Emmert asked him to kneel in front of the podium. Then, to his astonishment, he felt many hands placed on his head and he heard a chorus of spontaneous prayer. Four people, including their priest, were praying in pentecostal fashion, with each person saying his own prayer but simultaneously with the others. They prayed that God would bestow a special infilling of the Holy Spirit upon their guest priest. He was struck not only by the choral style of diverse prayers but the enthusiasm and emotion with which they were all praying. He was deeply touched. . . . After the prayer was finished he rose to his feet. Everyone stared at him as if something was supposed to have happened to him as a result of their prayers, namely that God would have baptized him in the Holy Spirit.[25]

Stephanou further relates in his autobiography that he had no outstanding or unusual spiritual experience that evening. He was informed that he had indeed received the baptism of the Holy Spirit and it would be confirmed experientially sometime in the near future. However, one thing that changed Stephanou forever was the experience of having laymen and women pray for him. He had been taught that as an ordained priest *he* was the one to pray for other people and to give them his blessing. This prayer meeting was a spiritual experience in which he and the laity were on equal footing with a common commitment to Christ: "it was a lightning bolt of new awareness that lay men and women, as people of God, are active recipients of the gifts of the Holy Spirit and share in the royal priesthood."[26] This was a profound moment for Stephanou, who being raised in the home of an Orthodox priest, who himself was from a priestly family, and for the previous twenty years had been formed and educated in an atmosphere that could be fairly characterized as "clerical" in the extreme, was discovering for the first time in an experiential manner the common heritage of all Christians, the gift of the

25. Stethatos, *Voice of a Priest*, 96–98.
26. Ibid., 98.

Holy Spirit! This event set in motion a course of events that would radically alter the life and ministry of Eusebius Stephanou.

Instead of dismissing his experiences in Huntington as so much Protestant emotionalism, Stephanou returned to Fort Wayne with a heightened sense of expectation. Uncharacteristically Stephanou chose to put aside his theological misgivings for the time being and wait patiently to see what the Lord would do. He continued in this same frame of mind throughout the remainder of 1971 and into 1972. The only indication of any change in Stephanou's thought as a result of his visit to Huntington can be seen in an article he authored in the August-September issue of *The Logos* entitled "The Prospects for an Orthodox Awakening: Why Many are Members of the Orthodox Church 'Unto Damnation'. How a Rediscovery of the Charismatic Lay Ministry Can Spark a Revival." Stephanou speaks to the need of spiritual rebirth, of not quenching the Spirit, and of "repentance and confession [which] will then make possible a true awakening and the charismatic renewal in the Church."[27] This is the first mention of "charismatic renewal" in the pages of *The Logos*. The December issue of *The Logos* printed the first two letters relating incidents of Charismatic Renewal among Orthodox parishes and prayers groups.[28]

A New Direction for Stephanou and *The Logos*

The cover of the January 1972 issue of *The Logos* clearly announced to its readers that something new was taking place among the journal's editors. This fifth anniversary issue proclaimed the two main articles for the edition in bold letters. An article by E. A. Stephanou entitled, "The Mighty Outpouring of the Holy Spirit" and a second authored by A. Emmert with the provocative title, "The Need for the Power of the Holy Spirit in our Day." Both articles signaled a new direction for *The Logos*. While earlier issues had issued a call for a "reawakening" and "revitalization" of the Orthodox Church even clearly stating that:

> The Logos believes that rejuvenation can come to the Orthodox Church only with the repentance of our sins of disobedience and with a reconversion to Christ and a complete surrender to His will.

27. "The Prospects for an Orthodox Awakening: Why Many are Members of the Orthodox Church 'Unto Damnation'. How a Rediscovery of the Charismatic Lay Ministry Can Spark a Revival." *The Logos*, 4, no. 7, 3–4.

28. "Views of Our Readers." *The Logos*, 4, no. 10, 2.

The Logos holds that while other churches suffer from a crisis of theology and doctrine, Orthodoxy is undergoing a crisis of personal commitment and leadership.[29]

It is clear from these two articles that Stephanou desired to introduce the readers of *The Logos* to the Charismatic Movement and to inform them that there were many Orthodox Christians who had received the baptism of the Holy Spirit and spiritually benefited from the experience. Stephanou, however, does not sidestep the dilemma which this Movement present to the Orthodox Church. He writes:

> Countless men and women outside the Orthodox Church are crying out in anguish for deliverance and salvation. How can their prayers, tears and fasting be answered by God? The Church is not there to manifest God's love and mercy. Yet, the Church is the steward and dispenser of grace. We face a dilemma: Outside the Church is unmistakable evidence of spiritual awakening. In these last days we are witnessing to a remarkable revival of faith in Jesus Christ. There is the Jesus Movement among the youth and the charismatic revival involving older men and women both of whom reveal signs of genuine and earnest faith and self-surrender to the Lord. Lives are being miraculously transformed. The sick are being healed. Drug-addicts are finding spectacular deliverance. Churches and meeting rooms resound with the stirring testimonies of spiritual rebirth. Formerly nominal church members have gained a new awareness of Jesus as a source of inner vitality and zest for living unselfish lives. Jesus has become alive for countless men and women of all ages, single and married, among the professional, as well as the uneducated. A large-scale outpouring of the Holy Spirit is occurring among Protestants and Roman Catholics many of whom have been receiving the gifts of tongues, prophecy and healing. What does all this mean for the Orthodox who cherishes his conviction in the true Church? In my opinion we cannot afford to ignore this spiritual movement. I have had the opportunity to witness in person such charismatic prayer groups among both Orthodox and non-Orthodox. . . . Is God truly pouring out His Spirit upon all flesh . . . [o]r can it be a valid movement only among Orthodox . . . ?[30]

Stephanou goes on to further raise issues that are to this day of great theological and practical concern to Orthodox hierarchs, priests, and lay

29. "What the Logos Stands For." *The Logos*, 4, no. 9, 17.

30. Stephanou, "The Mighty Outpouring," 12–13.

people; issues and questions that still await a response and an answer by Orthodox theologians and Scripture exegetes:

> How can the non-Orthodox receive the gifts of the Holy Spirit outside the Orthodox Church which alone has valid sacraments? How can Orthodox speak of a baptism of the Holy Spirit happening several years after their original baptism? Is not their immersion into the baptismal font and the Chrismation that follows the only possible baptism of the Holy Spirit?[31]

The editor goes on in an attempt to answer some of the questions by raising the irregular nature of the initial Gentile reception of Holy Spirit prior to their water baptism as recorded in Acts 10. For Stephanou, the Charismatic Movement was a sovereign act of God outside the normative channels of the Church, just as the Gentile "Pentecost" was a sovereign move of God outside the normal channels of the young Apostolic Church.[32] He further comments:

> Could we Orthodox truly be witnessing a similar phenomenon today? Is God temporarily bypassing the divinely established institutions of His one Church because of the disobedience and prejudice of her pastors who are adverse to proclaiming His Word to the gentiles? Is God trying to tell us Orthodox something? Are men in the Church capable of frustrating God's purposes and preventing His infinite goodness and compassion from reaching those who in prayers, tears and fasting (like Cornelius) beseech Him for redemption, not knowing the Christ of Orthodoxy? . . . [E]ach Orthodox receives the Holy Spirit at the time of Chrismation . . . [b]ut the gifts of the Holy Spirit usually remain dormant and inactive with those baptized at infancy, or they are eventually banished because of little faith or personal sins. When an Orthodox later receives the "baptism of the Holy Spirit," his original baptismal initiation is existentially renewed and actualized.[33]

Fr. Athanasius Emmert's personal testimony followed Stephanou's article and confirmed experientially what the first article asserted. Emmert declared that while his priesthood was valid and he believed in the true faith of the Orthodox Church he still missed something and that something was *power*, the power of the Holy Spirit. He concurred with Stephanou that,

31. Ibid.
32. Ibid.
33. Ibid., 14.

As an Orthodox priest, I knew that I possessed the Holy Spirit, through water-baptism, Chrismation, and finally through Ordination, but why was my own ministry and the priesthood of so many of my fellow priests apparently lacking in the results that I read in the "Acts"? I knew that the Lord is the same "yesterday, today, and forever." The Holy Spirit abides with, and dwells in the Church forever, and as Lord, he does not change. After a long period of questioning and pondering, I gradually came to realize that perhaps the problem was not so much with the Lord, or a matter of church history, or of another "dispensation," but rather with me.[34]

The fifth anniversary editorial, written by associate editor Dr. Charles Ashanin, also brought the attention of readers to the "charismatic" element needed for the revitalization of the Orthodox Church. Ashanin's editorial struck at the heart of the perceived problem: clericalism.

The reason for Orthodox spiritual lethargy is a simple one. The Spirit of Christ among us is bound, for one charisma, that of the priesthood has "outlawed" all other charisms in the Church and denied their right to exist. In consequence of this *meaning* of the priestly charisma evades those who own it formally. They have become instead the captives of legalistic formalism which hurts them spiritually the most. The Church of Christ must help our priests to regain the spiritual meaning of the priesthood. This will not happen unless those endowed with other charisms come boldly and exercise them *in the Church*.[35]

The year 1972 also saw new names appear as contributing editors and authors to *The Logos*. Most of these new names were Orthodox priests and lay men and women who themselves had received a charismatic baptism of the Holy Spirit. Together with Fr. Athanasius Emmert, Fr. Constantine Monios of Holy Cross Greek Orthodox Church in Pittsburgh, Pennsylvania, Fr. Gregory A. E. Rowley, a priest of the Antiochian Orthodox Christian Archdiocese, and the young layman Jordan Bajis were added as writers. The editors seemed to take great care to place this new emphasis upon the Charismatic spiritual life within the context of the Orthodox spiritual tradition. Extracts from the writings of Apostolos Makrakis and "A Monk of the Orthodox Church" (aka, Fr. Lev Gillet) on Chrismation as well as numerous articles relating the Charismatic experience to the Orthodox Church's sacramental and liturgical life.

34. Ibid., 15.
35. Ashanin, "THE LOGOS," 3–4.

While it is clear from Stephanou's editorials and articles in the 1972 issues of *The Logos* he had embraced the message of the Charismatic Renewal he had not yet personally experienced the baptism of the Holy Spirit. In February 1972, six months after his trip to Huntington, Stephanou received an invitation to lead a Lenten Retreat in Phoenix, Arizona. Co-sponsored by Holy Trinity Greek Orthodox Church, pastored by Fr. James Tavlarides and St. George Antiochian Orthodox Church, pastored by Fr. David Buss, both Charismatic priests, also attended by Fr. Athanasius Emmert, the retreat became the catalyst for many to receive the baptism of the Holy Spirit. Stephanou once again, as well as Serbian Orthodox Dragon Philipovich, were both prayed for by Tavlarides, Buss, and Emmert to receive the baptism of the Holy Spirit.[36] At the conclusion of the retreat Fr. Andrew Kish of St. Michael's Serbian Orthodox Church in Tucson invited Stephanou to come and address his parish. Fr. Eusebius spoke on "No Substitute for Christ" and invited the listener to recommit their lives to Christ.[37]

It was at this time that Stephanou began to develop his methodology of calling Orthodox people, who attended his talks and sermons, to come forward and stand at the bottom of the solea[38] and to offer prayers of recommitment to Jesus Christ employing the form of repeating the initial prayers of the Orthodox Baptismal Rite.[39] The Priest Stephanou instructed the people to turn and face the back of the church, and then using these or similar words, he asked, "Do you renounce Satan, and all his works, and all his angels, and all his service, and all his pride?" The people were to respond, "I renounce them." Then Stephanou would ask this question three times and the people responded three times. Then he questioned the people, "Have you renounced Satan?" And, the people answered, "I have renounced him." As above this question is asked three times by Stephanou and the people responded in the affirmative three times. Then he instructed the people, "Blow upon him, and spit upon him." Stephanou encouraged the people to actually breathe outwardly and then to spit on the floor. This was dramatic in its effect! Then instructing the people to turn and face the

36. Stephanou, "How the Quickening," 3–5.

37. Stethatos, *Voice of a Priest*, 99–100.

38. Alefeyev, *Architecture, Icons and Music,* 79. The solea is the area directly in front of the iconostasis (icon screen) in a traditional Orthodox Church building. The solea is typically a raised area (platform) of one step, or more, above the floor of the nave of the church. Many times the homily is delivered from here.

39. Stephanou, "The Undying Flame of Pentecost," 14. Olekshy, Orest. 2009. Interview by author. Melville, Saskatchewan, Canada. June 27.

altar a new set of questions were asked. "Do you unite yourself to Christ?" Again, asked three times the people responded each times, "I unite myself to Christ." Then the people were asked to once again affirm that question by being asked three times, "Have you united yourself to Christ? To which again the people would respond three times, "I have united myself to Christ." To complete and seal the confession of the people a final question was asked, "Do you believe in Him? The final response was, "I believe in Him as King and God."[40] This method tied the entire experience of a personal renewal in Christ to the initiatory rite of baptism and became a routine part of Stephanou's presentation as he travelled from parish to parish leading retreats and seminars on spiritual renewal.

Stephanou's Personal Pentecost

In the January and April 1972 issues of *The Logos* Stephanou revealed to his readers his experiences at Holy Spirit Church in Huntington, West Virginia and at the Lenten Retreat held in Phoenix, Arizona. At both venues Stephanou received prayer and the laying on of hands by both layman and priests, for the baptism of the Holy Spirit. The June-July 1972 issues carried and article in which Stephanou testified to his own personal pentecostal baptism. He writes:

> Over the years I have felt that nothing extraordinary happened in my own spiritual life that would be worth sharing with other people. But the Holy Spirit is helping me understand that God's will and power is not always manifested in some startling manner, but rather is expressed in simple day-to-day decisions, thoughts and actions. . . . In recent months there have been remarkable signs in my life by which the Lord has been speaking His will to me and giving me a greater certainty about my ministry together with the resiliency to meet the demands. I have already given an account of my experience with the charismatic congregations of the Orthodox Churches in Huntington, West Virginia and Phoenix, Arizona. In recent weeks, however, two new stirrings of the Holy Spirit have renewed my life of faith in a more tangible way. During the past few years I had been praying for a greater infilling of the Holy Spirit in the cause of a bolder witness and with the same fervor I had been seeking that heavenly language by which to praise Jesus ineffably. If I have coveted the gift of tongues, it was

40. St. Tikhon's Monastery, *The Book of Needs*, 24–26.

only because I wanted everything God has to offer that would empower and strengthen me in meeting the demands of my calling. The testimonies of others who spoke in tongues and the perceptible difference it made to their lives of Christian praise prompted me to seek this gift only that I too might glorify Christ to a greater degree. I know it is given for self-edification, for "He who speaks in a tongue edifies himself" (1 Cor. 14:4). It is for private use and not for public display and confusion. But let me describe the first of the two experiences concerning the existential renewal of my baptism in the Holy Spirit. Ordinarily I take my meals alone at home. As I was offering thanksgiving on Tuesday of Holy Week, standing behind my chair at the kitchen table in the usual manner, an instantaneous feeling came over me of God's presence that seemed to fill the room and it overwhelmed me to the point where I began to weep uncontrollably. It resembled the experience I feel occasionally at the altar celebrating the Divine Liturgy. But this was more intense and lasted much longer. After several minutes of continued weeping, I finally realized that I had nothing to do with what was happening and I left the kitchen and moved into my study where I knelt and began simply accepting the impact of God's visitation. I remained under the power of the Holy Spirit in continuous weeping and sobbing for half hour. My reason stopped functioning. My thinking processes were suspended. My mind was unfruitful (1 Cor. 14.14). I found myself totally passive to the touch of the Holy Spirit. His presence was so comforting and refreshing. It was like a father's embrace had enveloped me in all tenderness and loving affection. The weeping stopped as suddenly as it had begun and I sensed a tremendous release. . . . I thanked God for this purifying and healing gift of tears and the catharsis of my soul from the burden of all my sins. A wonderful sense of peace and calm filled me. An exuberant gladness and reassurance surged through my whole being and I began praising and glorifying the Lord with a grateful heart. It was the following Paschal week when my tongue broke loose to express the gift of speaking in that heavenly language. . . . I was praising and magnifying the Lord one evening I caught myself saying the Greek word "niki" (which means victory) over and over again, until I broke out in a machine gun-like outburst of tongues, and since that moment I have been fully enjoying the experience of "praying in the Spirit, for the Spirit helps us in our weakness; for we do not know how to pray as we ought, but the Spirit himself intercedes for us with sighs too deep for words" (Rom. 8:26). Now

I could understand why St. Paul could say: "Now I want you all to speak in tongues" (1 Cor. 14: 4,5).[41]

Father Stephanou further relates his thoughts about this extraordinary spiritual event that became a defining moment for his priesthood, ministry and the remainder of his life:

> The Holy Spirit experience of April 1972 was not a passing spiritual "high." It was moment that literally revolutionized the life and priesthood of Father Eusebius. He finally could claim a personal experience of Pentecost. Such a life-changing experience of Christ was to have far-reaching consequences in the years ahead.[42]

This "baptism of the Holy Spirit" affected Stephanou's experience of prayer. "Prayer became more than just a religious routine, . . . a new intimacy with the Lord was now there."[43] He uses other words such as "joy" and "exuberance" in describing prayer. This Orthodox priest states that a "slavish reliance on the prayer book for every conceivable prayer need was broken."[44] His approach to holy Scripture also changed. Studying the Bible was no longer a "religious chore" and words were "quickened and every word on the page was now releasing Holy Spirit power for salvation, healing or deliverance."[45] Stephanou's approach to preaching was also altered. He testified to being more comfortable and confident in expounding the Scriptures. Written out sermons and prepared texts were no longer necessary because he was "speaking from the overflow of the heart."[46]

This experience likewise overflowed and affected Stephanou's entire relationship to the Orthodox Christian Faith. "The Orthodoxy of the dead letter that kills the soul now became the Orthodoxy of the Spirit that quickens the soul."[47] Stephanou's approach to Orthodox theology was no longer simply up in his head or "cerebral" but in keeping with the understanding of the Church Fathers where a true theologian is one who prays. The celebration of the Divine Liturgy and other Mysteries of the Church took on a new

---

41. Stephanou. "Rekindling the Gift," 17–18.
42. Stethatos, *Voice of a Priest*, 105.
43. Ibid.
44. Ibid.
45. Ibid.
46. Ibid.
47. Ibid.

depth. Stephanou writes "At one time, I knew *about* Jesus, the correct teach-ings on Christology and sound theology, but now I *know* Jesus."[48]

Charismatic Witness at the Greek Orthodox Clergy-Laity Congress

The October 1972 issue of *The Logos* related that the Charismatic Renewal in the Orthodox Church, encouraged by the magazine, was a topic of some discussion among priests and other delegates at the biennial Clergy-Laity Congress of the Greek Orthodox Archdiocese held in Houston, Texas. Stephanou, in the article "The Charismatic Witness at the Church Con-gress" related that on the first day of the congress a group of Charismatic priests and layman gathered in a hotel room and

> . . . held a prayer meeting and discussed how we might witness to the delegates at large. We could feel that the Holy Spirit was there with us. Two women spoke in other tongues, while others followed with the interpretation.[49]

The article continues to relate that another prayer meeting was called for the following evening and that an invitation had been given to many priests, who were thought to be open to spiritual renewal, to come and attend. Approximately thirty-five priests came and Father Constantine Mo-nios, pastor of Pittsburgh's Holy Cross Greek Orthodox parish shared his personal testimony of how the infilling of the Holy Spirit had transformed him and the parish. Laymen and women from Holy Cross and from Holy Trinity parish in Phoenix likewise shared their testimonies. Holy Trinity's pastor, Fr. James Tavlarides spoke on the need for repentance and spiritual renewal in the Greek Orthodox Church. Dr. John Zotos, a contributing author to *The Logos* and a professor at Boston's Northeastern University also shared with the group.

Many of the priests raised theological questions, uncomfortable with some of things being said about the Renewal. However, according to Stephanou, "the Lord did not leave us without the most convincing sign of His Spirit that evening." Earlier Fr. James Tavlarides had been discuss-ing the baptism of the Holy Spirit with one Fr. John Angelis. Fr. Tavlarides related to Fr. John that the baptism of the Holy Spirit "could be his just for

48. Ibid., 106.

49. Stephanou, "The Charismatic Witness," 22.

the receiving . . . he laid his hands on Father Angelis and prayed over him for the infilling. Immediately he felt the surge of the Spirit flooding his soul and passing throughout his whole body." Fr. Anthony Coniaris, pastor of St. Mary's Greek Orthodox Church and founder of Light and Life Publishing in Minneapolis, commented on the fact that Fr. Angelis' face was radiating a warm glow. Fr. Angelis arose from his chair and lifted his hands high in air and began walk in a circular fashion and looking toward the ceiling of the room as if we were seeing a vision kept repeating in a soft voice, "It's beautiful and overwhelming when you receive Him. I don't have to debate the reality of the Holy Spirit . . . ."[50] As the meeting broke up, one priest, Fr. Contantine Simonis of New London, Connecticut remained behind to be prayed over for the baptism of the Holy Spirit.[51]

In final paragraph of *The Logos*' article on the Clergy-Laity Congress, Stephanou reflects:

> Was the Charismatic witness felt at the congress? This was the question in all our minds. It is too premature to evaluate the re-sults of the efforts of the Charismatic presence. We are certain only of one thing: that ample seed was planted. The growth is not ours to achieve, but the Lord's. It is not what we can do, but what God can work through his instruments of clay. We can only wait and see what the Holy Spirit accomplished in Houston. "It is not by might nor by power, saith the Lord, but by my Spirit."[52]

Orthodox Charismatic Prayer Groups
and the Call for a Conference

The year 1972 appeared to be the year in which the Orthodox priests who had experienced Charismatic renewal in their own personal lives, discov-ered each other. The pages of *The Logos* reveal that Fr. Emmert and Fr. Stephanou "discovered" one another in 1971. During Great Lent of 1972, Fr. Stephanou made contact with Frs. Tavlarides and Buss in Phoenix as well as Frs. Philipovich and Kish. Fr. Constantine Monios, of Pitts-burgh wrote an account of the Renewal in his parish and Fr. Stephanou was in personal contact with Fr. Monios at the Clergy-Laity Congress in

50. Ibid., 23.
51. Ibid.
52. Ibid.

Houston. However, unlike the Charismatic Renewal in Roman Catholic and Protestant circles, in which those who were involved in the Renewal, clergy and laity, sought to organize themselves into Renewal fellowships, the Orthodox participants did not make any moves to create or form Charismatic fellowships beyond local parochial prayer groups. As early as the August-September 1972 issue, *The Logos* was floating the idea of an Orthodox Charismatic Conference:

> Closer ties of communication among persons involved in the Orthodox Charismatic Revival can serve a very important purpose. There is a growing feeling that there is a need for mutual acquaintance, joint prayer, fellowship and praise in the Spirit across parish lines and mutual spiritual support and cooperation wherever and whenever possible in the cause of Orthodox Christian awakening. Few, if any, of those who have experienced the charismatic renewal in the Holy Spirit would want to question such a need. Besides, who can dispute that personal transformation in the Spirit alone can resolve our inter-jurisdictional feuding? A consolidation and unity of charismatic witness on a national and even international scale has obvious advantages. The office of the Logos Foundation for Orthodox Awakening, Inc. has already received word from Orthodox charismatic circles as far away as France and even Australia. The sweep of the Holy Spirit is reaching every corner of world Orthodoxy. Praise the Lord![53]

The November 1972 issue also ran a short announcement calling for an Orthodox Charismatic Conference.[54] The December 1972 issue likewise ran a small, half-page call which also declared beyond a shadow of a doubt that *The Logos* believed that the spiritual renewal of the Orthodox Church would only be accomplished through "charismatic" renewal.

> The cry for renewal in the Orthodox Catholic Church is spreading. Dissatisfaction with the spiritual state of affairs among us is the result of thirsting for a deeper relationship with the Lord Jesus Christ. The feeling is growing that only the fresh stirring of the Holy Spirit can make the historical structures of the church come alive again. This means renewal has to be charismatic. Already charismatic prayer groups are springing up in many parishes and the power of God's Holy Spirit is being released in a mighty way. Spirit-filled believers whose lives have been changed in a new

53. "Time for an Orthodox Charismatic Conference?" *The Logos*, 5, no. 7, 9.
54. Stephanou, "The Proposed," 5.

surrender to Jesus are already in touch with each other in sharing and giving glory and praise to the Lord. Unlike the Roman Catholic Church in which the laity have taken initiative and now exercise leadership in charismatic circles, within American Orthodoxy the charismatic movement seems to be emerging along parish lines with parish priests leading all charismatic prayer groups. Insofar as we know they meet inside a church and usually in front of the altar. It is interesting to note that, unlike the Church of Greece in lay initiative in spiritual endeavors has been remarkably impressive and effective, here in America the laity (especially among the Greeks), though highly over-organized in secular and ethnic causes, are under-organized in the cause of Christ and Orthodoxy.[55]

In three consecutive issues of *The Logos* a solicitation was made to all those charismatically involved for thoughts on a possible Orthodox Charismatic Conference this summer, similar to those held annually by Roman Catholic charismatics.

> The Logos Foundation is serving as an *ad hoc* provisional communication center until such time as a conference can make final and authoritative decisions on questions of organization. In order for such a proposed Pan-Orthodox (inter-Orthodox) convocation to become a reality it will be necessary to speed up preparations. You can help by communicating your thoughts and sentiments as quickly as possible. A step of practical importance is verifying the number of charismatic prayer groups and their location. You can be helpful right now by providing us with the following information for compiling a directory: 1) Name of prayer group 2) Parish and jurisdiction 3) Day and time of the weekly meeting 4) Place of meeting 5) Name, address and phone number of contact person 6) Number in the group. Meanwhile, let us give thanks to God who gives us the victory through our Lord Jesus Christ and sonship through His Holy Spirit![56]

The year 1973 and Volume 6 of *The Logos* brought further changes to the periodical. *The Logos* went from a monthly journal to being released every other month. The January-February issue published a list of Orthodox Charismatic prayer groups throughout the United States. Twenty-five groups were listed, mostly of the Greek Orthodox Archdiocese, however

---

55. "To All Orthodox Charismatic Prayer Groups." *The Logos*, 5, no. 10, 4.
56. Ibid.

there were also groups meeting in Antiochian and other parishes of Slavic identity.[57]

The main editorial in the first issue of 1973 announced the convocation of the first Orthodox Charismatic Conference. The conference was slated for the weekend of July 4 in Ann Arbor, Michigan. The editorial also announced that a Steering Committee had been formed comprised of Fr. Constantine Monios, Fr. Athanasius Emmert, Fr. Nicholas Cracium, a Romanian Orthodox priest from Akron, Ohio,[58] Fr. Stephen Wallsteadt of Columbus, Indiana and Fr. Stephanou.[59] However, by the March-April 1972 issue the steering committee changed from five priests and no lay people to two priests and four laymen. The *Logos* did not give the names of the priests who no longer served on the steering committee or the names of the laymen who joined.[60]

The pages of *The Logos* carried news of speaking engagements conducted by Fr. Eusebius throughout the United States and Canada. In several issues announcements were placed informing readers that Fr. Stephanou was available to speak at parishes and retreats. As copies of *The Logos* were disseminated throughout the country, Orthodox clergy and laypeople became interested in hearing more about the Renewal, resulting in invitations for Fr. Eusebius to come and speak at different venues. The March-April issue carried a one-page synopsis of Stephanou's travels, just from January to early April 1973, complete with reproduced photos. On January 7, Fr. Stephanou preached in Grand Rapids and presided at the Liturgy at Holy Trinity Greek Orthodox Church. On January 28, he travelled to Chicago where he served and preached at St. Michael's, affiliated with the Orthodox Church in America. On February 12, he returned to the Chicago area to specifically speak on Charismatic Renewal at St. Nicholas Ukrainian Orthodox. It was at this engagement that Fr. Boris Zabrodsky, pastor of St. Nicholas, and his wife, Jaraslava, of whom more will be written later, came into contact with the message of the charismatic experience. The weekend of February 18, a Lenten retreat, was conducted by Stephanou at St. George Greek Orthodox Church in Rock Island, Illinois. He returned to his alma mater, Holy Cross Orthodox School of Theology in Brookline, Massachusetts, and lectured on the Renewal to a group of Orthodox clergymen. The

57. "Directory of Orthodox Charismatic Prayer Groups." *The Logos*, 6, no. 1, 24.

58. Stethatos, *Voice of a Priest,* 101.

59. Stephanou, "Preparing," 16.

60. Stephanou, "Priestly," 12.

following weekend, March 13, found Fr. Stephanou at St. Andrew's Greek Orthodox Church in South Bend, Indiana where spoke on the Book of Revelation. From Indiana, he travelled north to Winnipeg, Manitoba and St. Paul's College where he delivered a talk at the invitation of a group of Ukrainian and Russian Orthodox students. While in Winnipeg he officiated at the Liturgy and preached at St. Demetrius Greek Orthodox Church, and later delivered the sermon at the Sunday of Orthodoxy Vespers conducted at St. George Romanian Orthodox Church. Heading west into the Province of Saskatchewan he spoke to a group of Ukrainian Orthodox at the Peter Moghila Ukrainian Center in Saskatoon. While in Saskatoon, Fr. Stephanou made the acquaintance of Fr. Orest Olekshy and his wife Oksana, who became a leader of Orthodox Charismatic Renewal in western Canada. Heading to the southland of Texas, Fr. Eusebius conducted yet another Lenten retreat March 24–25. St. Michael's Antiochian Orthodox Church in Beaumont, pastored by Fr. Michael Graham, hosted the weekend retreat. Stephanou traveled to Reading, Pennsylvania and spoke at one more Lenten retreat at SS. Constantine and Helen Greek Orthodox Church, presiding and preaching at the Sunday Divine Liturgy.[61] As can be seen Fr. Stephanou allowed no moss to grow on him, but rather traveled extensively sharing the message of personal spiritual commitment to Christ and the charismatic experience of the baptism of the Holy Spirit.

The First Orthodox Charismatic Conference

Almost the entire July-August 1973 issue of *The Logos* was given over to coverage, both with words and photos, of the first Orthodox Conference. Held July 4–6, 1973 in Ann Arbor, Michigan approximately 100 attended the conference. Ten Orthodox priests, as well as one Roman Catholic and one Melkite priest, a Greek Pentecostal, and a Greek Evangelical pastor, attended part, or all, of the conference. Fr. Lazarus Moore, an Orthodox monk under the jurisdiction of the Russian Orthodox Church Abroad, originally from England, was also present. Fr. Lazarus spoke at later conferences and became a proponent of Charismatic Renewal in the Orthodox Church. Members of the Charismatic Roman Catholic Word of God Community opened their homes and provided hospitality to several of the Orthodox conferees. Word of God Community coordinators and Charismatic Catholic leaders, Ralph

---

61. "Where the Word of Awakening is Being Carried." *The Logos*, 5, no. 2, 21.

Martin, Steve Clark, and Jim Cavnar attended the conference and Cavnar presented a talk on the topic of prayer meetings.

Friday morning, July 6, the conference closed with the celebration of Divine Liturgy at St. Nicholas Greek Orthodox Church. Fr. Stephanou was joined by three priests of the Antiochian Archdiocese: Frs. Gregory Rowley, Paul Kleinschrodt, and Mark North, in concelebrating the service. Frs. Boris Zabrodsky and Gregory Rowley, as well as lay persons Darryl Jones of Fort Wayne, Indian and Mary Polopolos, wrote their personal impressions of the conference.

Fr. Anthony Morfessis

The July-August issue also introduced readers to another Greek Orthodox priest touched by the Renewal, Fr. Anthony Morfessis, pastor of Dormition Greek Orthodox Church in Morgantown, Pennsylvania. Fr. Morfessis, an immigrant from Greece, was purported to have the charismatic gift of healing. Over the years, the pages of *The Logos* were filled with letters and testimonies of Orthodox faithful who claimed to be miraculously healed at the prayers of Fr. Anthony. Fr. Morfessis wrote a short booklet entitled *God Made Me for His Plans*, about his childhood and youth, growing up on the Greek island of Ithica. While still in his mother's womb she tried to abort him by repeatedly throwing herself, stomach first, upon the ground. However, months later he was born healthy, was baptized, and given the name Pantelis. In his book, Fr. Anthony, in his unique homespun way, relates his personal experience of the baptism of the Holy Spirit:

> I had gone to Pittsburgh, Pennsylvania, and one evening I went to see a priest name Father Constantine, who was the priest of a large, spirit-filled church. It was Monday evening, and there were a lot of people in the church praying and imploring the Holy Spirit to come upon them. To tell you the truth, I was overcome by fear at this. I did not like the way these people were praying. At that time, I was still a strict traditionalist, and I felt they weren't praying in an orthodox manner. I felt the need to leave. Then, Father Monios approached me and said, "Come and pray with me to receive the Holy Spirit." It was a "little strange" to receive the Holy Spirit, he said. But I felt the leading to pray as he asked me to do, even though I did it with great reluctance, and I must admit, fear. At this point I cannot describe exactly what happened that evening, because the greatness of God is far beyond any earthly description.

I can only tell you that I was filled with an incredible spirit of joy, the likeness of which you yourself, must experience to understand. A few days later I was in another spirit-filled church, this time in Westover, West Virginia. I desired to experience this joy again. There must have been around 400 people praying in that church that particular evening. I was there with a certain Dr. Trifiatis, and I had gone to see "how these other Christians—'spirit-filled' Christians, prayed." My dear reader, as soon as I sat down, I felt a hot electric current throughout my body, and unconsciously I raised my hands. My body was burning to the point that I was afraid my clothes would catch on fire! Immediately I became a different person. In my left hand, many open sores appeared; then they disappeared completely. I looked around me. There were perhaps 400 people there that evening, and as nearly as I could see, I was the only one going through such an experience. Then, after I felt this intense heat, I began to feel as though cool water were being poured upon me, and I never felt so clean in my life! If I had the strength, I would have probably gone down on my knees, but instead, I had to sit down. I know now, that the "feeling that water was being poured on me" was the baptism, not of water, but of the Holy Spirit. From that moment on my life was changed.[62]

God Made Me for His Plans contains several pages of testimonies of various types of healings as a result of Morfessis' prayers. Moving from Morgantown to Johnstown, Pennsylvania, Fr. Anthony ministered to thousands who came from as far away as New York, New Jersey, Chicago and Canada, many times chartering busses to come and be prayed for healing and deliverance from demonic oppression.[63]

Hierarchical Opposition to Stephanou's Ministry

As noted above, not long after the inauguration of the first issue of *The Logos* Stephanou ran afoul of the hierarchy of the Greek Orthodox Archdiocese. Stephanou's first suspension from priestly duties came at the end of 1968 as a result of certain statements printed in the pages of *The Logos* that were less than flattering to the leadership of the Greek Archdiocese in general and to Archbishop Iakovos, the primate of the Archdiocese, in particular.

---

62. Morfessis, *God Made Me*, 1, 3, 23–24.
63. Stethatos, *Voice of a Priest*, 127–28.

None of the opposition at this time stemmed from Stephanou's Charismatic activities because he had not as yet become involved in the Movement.

In February 1979 Stephanou (referred to below as Papastephanou) received a letter from His Grace, Bishop (Draconakis) of the Greek Orthodox Diocese of Boston requesting he appear at Holy Cross Greek Orthodox Seminary in Brookline, Massachusetts, before a panel of professors and theologians. The letter stated:

> In view of the fact that complaints have been heard both from brother-priests and from the laity as to the correctness of certain points which you touch upon in your books, brochures and sermons, that they are contrary to Orthodox doctrine, you are hereby invited by command of the church to a theological dialogue to be attended by professors of the Theological Seminary, Father Stylianos Harakas, Theodore Stylianopoulos, John Zanetos and George Papademetriou in the presence of the titular Bishop of Diocleia . . . for the purpose having your status clarified once and for all.[64]

Below is the text of the letter dated June 18, 1979, addressed to His Eminence, Archbishop Iakavos, the ruling hierarch of the Greek Archdiocese, written by Bishop Anthimos, regarding the proceedings of the above meeting with Stephanou and their conclusions.

GREEK ORTHODOX ARCHDIOCESE
OF NORTH AND SOUTH AMERICA
THE DIOCESE OF BOSTON
1124 West Roxbury Parkway · Brookline, MA 02167
(617) 522–2471

18 June 1979

Your Eminence,

The February 12th letter gave me the order to call the Priest Eusebius Papastephanou to a theological dialogue, to form a committee under my chairmanship with a specific purpose to clear up certain ambiguities regarding the Orthodoxy of his positions, teachings, written and oral points of his preaching. This was executed as follows: The committee, consisting of:

---

64. Stethatos, *The Voice of a Priest*, 175–76.

The God-loving Bishop of Pittsburgh, Maximos
Respectful

      Pr. John Zanetos
      Pr. Stylianos Harakas
      Pr. George Papademetriou
      and Pr. Theodore Stylianopoulos

Initially convened, with all present, on 14 March (of this year) in my office and deliberated for two hours on our strategy and thematic positions as revealed during the meeting with the Pr. Papastephanou. It was recommended to the members of the committee to study the books, magazines and articles of the Pr. Papastephanou, so that if there are non-Orthodox arguments of teachings opposed to the true faith and traditions of our Holy Church or points that need clarification to be discussed with him and to ask his opinion.

On March 27th a meeting place with the Pr. Papastephanou in the Theological School, in this meeting all the above members (except the holy one from Pittsburgh) were present, and in the middle of meeting, at the request of your Eminence, were joined by Mr. I. Tsirpanis.

The meeting began with prayer and lasted over three hours. The Pr. Papastephanou tried to present himself as the victim often repeating: "Holy brothers, I teach what you teach." To all the questions, this needed exact and direct responses, with appropriate tactics he tried to convince the committee that all his preaching and conduct and behavior are absolutely in line with the teachings of the Church. When he was presented with excerpts from his texts questionable in their Orthodox stance, his answer was stereotypical: "Don't look at what I write, consider what I say" and the opposite, "Don't listen to what I say, look at what I write."

To the question as to clarifying the meaning and significance of that which is so overemphasized "Baptism of the Holy Spirit," again the response was ambiguous, different from the one he lets those who go to his gatherings and lectures assume. He talked about "re-kindling" more than baptism and he referred to a personal experience. To my own question, on the healing of the sick, which he advertises in self-promoting commercials in his gatherings how it is possible to predetermine the healing power and grace of the Lord <u>in advance</u> through his special prayer, his answer was ambiguous again. He systematically avoided the point: how can he take for granted the healing in advance" referring to those points in Holy Scriptures about the healing of the sick. In another one of my questions why he does not obey the order of the Church to accept a priestly position which he wanted the Archdiocese to give him, the response was perhaps rude: "The Church does not only have priestly positions but also positions for a preacher."

The Committee, Your Eminence, convened anew on May 29th, 1979 with the membership of the Pr. Haraka, Papademitriou and Stylianopoulos and from the whole conversation which took place with the Pr. Papastephanou (which is tape recorded and at our disposal) resulted in the conclusion that the Pr. Eusebius, although tactfully avoided to admit Protestant influences, however, all his teachings, especially in reference to expression, terminology and presentation is foreign to the Tradition of the Orthodox Church and undoubtedly influenced by the Pentecostal and Charismatic tendencies which he tries to base in Orthodox sources. He espoused the Pentecostal movement and he is trying to tailor it to Orthodox teachings. Of course, always, when asked especially by those in authority, he confesses Orthodoxy, but his whole demeanor and teaching and use of methods and terminology is foreign to our accepted truths, <u>creates confusion for our clergy/easily leading the congregation into heresy</u> (i.e. the continuous negative criticism of the clergy and the governing Church, as presented by the Pr. Papastephanou can very easily lead to the thought that "the Church nor the clergy is needed for the saving <u>of the soul</u>?).

In addition, he gives the impression to his audience or to his readers of his texts that he (and he alone) has been called specifically from God and has received "special orders" to preach what he preaches.

The Committee, Your Eminence, is of the opinion that if the Pr. Papastephanou had greater success he would not in the least be interested in the position of the Church; therefore, (the committee) humbly imports that Priesthood of the Holy Archdiocese, after judging whether the ministry of the Pr. Papastephanou, as he presents it now, is constructive or not (the committee, as mentioned above, without doubt evaluates that with the confusion it creates it is more probable that it creates damage) proceeds to the relevant act.

In the Committee's judgment, the whole issue and problem of the Pr. Papastephanou, is most likely Pastoral and Psychological rather than Theological.

He proposes and asks the Committee to give him a priestly position in some Parish so that it will be proven if he is indeed a responsible Orthodox priest obeying the order of the Church. In case of his refusal it is possible to take appropriate measures.

With this are sent individual reposts of the members of the Committee referring to particular and specific points of the teaching of the Pr. Papastephanou and the entire file remains with us. The holy one of Pittsburgh with whom we communicated again for the specific and responsible opinion of the professor of Dogma, he informed me that he has had direct communication with Your Eminence.

The studies of John Tsirpanis, Iliou Bourboutsi and George Christoulidi remain in our file.

With the deepest respect,

Anthimos of Boston[65]

Stephanou reported that the meeting was pleasant and that a spirit of openness pervaded the proceedings. He felt that he was able to clearly present his position on issues raised by the theological faculty. However, he never received any further communication from Bishop Anthimos or any member of the panel that had interviewed him regarding his Charismatic teachings. Instead of clarifying his status "once and for all" Stephanou writes that he felt his position in the Archdiocese was just as ambiguous as it had been before the meeting.[66]

October 1979 brought another suspension to Stephanou from the office of Archbishop Iakovos. Unlike his first suspension, which came to him via a telegram from the Greek Orthodox Archdiocese, Stephanou became informed of his suspension by reading the announcement in the pages of the *Orthodox Observer*, official newspaper of the Greek Archdiocese. Stephanou's suspension was recorded as a result of his failure to receive the Archbishop's permission to visit Kenya, Cyprus, and Australia earlier in 1979. Stephanou reasoned that this was not necessary since in 1976 he travelled outside of the country to preach and on his return had reported to the Archbishop on his activities and had not met with any negative

65. Letter to Archbishop Iakovos (Koukouzis) from Bishop Anthimos (Draconakis), June 18, 1979. Greek original provided by Fr. Theodore Stylianopoulos. English translation by Manuela George, Fr. Gregory Christakis and the author.

66. Ibid., 179.

comments or question about episcopal permission.[67] On March 7, 1980 Stephanou travelled to New York City to attend the Holy Synod meeting of the bishops of Greek Archdiocese of North America which were to deliberate on Stephanou's suspension. While he was not invited to attend the Synod meeting, on the advice of his Bishop he made an appearance.[68] In the September-October 1980 issue of *The Logos,* Stephanou reported that it was the one year anniversary of his suspension and offers a defense against the "non-canonical" nature of Archbishop Iakovos' decision.[69] None of the remaining issues of 1980 mention the lifting of the suspension. However, in the January-February issue of *The Logos* Stephanou mentions that he served the 1980 Christmas morning Divine Liturgy in the presence of His Grace, Bishop Timotheos of Detroit. From this information it can be ascertained that sometime between October and December of 1980 Stephanou's suspension was lifted by the Greek Orthodox Archdiocese.[70]

In December 1983, in reaction to Stephanou's preaching and teaching ministry among Greek Orthodox in the Washington, DC and New Jersey areas, Metropolitan Silas (Koskinas), Greek Orthodox Archbishop of the diocese of New Jersey sent a letter to all his clergy banning Stephanou from any ministry in his diocese, whether in parishes or even private homes, without the Metropolitan's written permission. Stephanou published a copy of Metropolitan Silas' letter in the pages of *The Logos.*[71] Stephanou also published an "open letter" to Metropolitan Silas and provided a form letter for Orthodox parishes to copy and send to the Metropolitan registering their protest of his actions.[72]

In November 1983, Stephanou, who at the time was under the authority of Greek Orthodox Bishop Maximos of Pittsburgh, was summoned to appear before the Bishop and answer questions regarding his theological positions on the Charismatic Movement. However, the meeting was postponed because of the funeral of eminent American Orthodox theologian, Rev. Dr. Alexander Schmemann, Dean of St. Vladimir's Orthodox

---

67. Stephanou, "Sharing in the Spirit," *The Logos,* 12, no. 6, (November-December 1979), 5–6.

68. Stephanou, "Sharing in the Spirit," *The Logos,* 13, no. 2, (March-April 1980), 4–5.

69. Stephanou, "Sharing in the Spirit," *The Logos,* 13, no. 5, (September-October 1980), 4–5.

70. Stephanou, "Sharing in the Spirit," *The Logos,* 14, no. 1, (January-February 1981), 5.

71. *The Logos,* 17, no. 1, (January-February 1984), 5.

72. Ibid., 6–7.

Theological Seminary in Crestwood, New York. Bishop Maximos attended Schmemann's funeral and reschedule the meeting with Stephanou for February 24, 1984. Six priests also attended the three-hour meeting placing many questions before Stephanou regarding his teachings. While there was not absolute agreement Stephanou felt he was able to address misunderstandings that were the result of hearsay. In *The Logos* Stephanou explained that this was the first opportunity in the seventeen years of his Charismatic ministry he had been given the chance to explain to Church leaders the content of his teaching.[73]

Once again, on March 31, 1986, Stephanou received a letter from the offices of Greek Orthodox Archdiocese in New York City. The letter succinctly stated that the Archdiocese was seeking to have Stephanou defrocked as a priest by appealing to the Ecumenical Patriarchate of Constantinople and that,

> Until such time the decision is issued, the Holy Eparchal Synod prohibits you from officiating and preaching in the holy temple of the Holy Archdiocese of North and South America.[74]

No reasons for this action were related to the stupefied priest. At no time had he been summoned to a spiritual court nor had he received any preliminary letter informing him of any canonical infractions that would lead to such a decision on the part of the Archdiocese. It was all a mystery. Needless to say, Stephanou protested the non-canonical manner in which this was handled, especially pointing out the fact that he had not even been given the chance to know the charges for which they were seeking to have him defrocked nor had he been afforded the opportunity to defend himself in a canonical spiritual court.[75]

Stephanou later reported that Bishop Maximos of Pittsburgh, in an interview in the June 8, 1986 issue of *Church Messenger,* the official newspaper of the Carpatho-Russyn Diocese, stated,

> The Patriarchate of Constantinople has deferred a decision on defrocking Stephanou in hopes that he will realize his mistake and return to the flock. . . . They don't want to make a martyr of him.

---

73. Stephanou, "Sharing in the Spirit" 17, no. 2, (March-April 1984), 3–4.

74. Stephanou, "Who is Really Troubling Israel," *The Logos,* 19, no. 3, (May-June 1986), 1.

75. Ibid., 1–2.

. . . They hope Fr. Stephanou will come to his senses and change his mind.[76]

In a later issue of *The Logos* Stephanou printed a letter from one of his readers who had visited the Ecumenical Patriarchate in Istanbul. The writer claimed to have spoken directly to Metropolitan Bartholomew, the personal secretary of the Ecumenical Patriarch Demetrios, regarding Stephanou's case. The writer claimed that the Metropolitan had stated that Stephanou was not defrocked because there was no reason to defrock him and that issue was between Archbishop Iakovos and Stephanou.[77]

Over the years Stephanou, beleaguered by the fluctuating attitude of the Greek Orthodox Archdiocese to his ministry, understandably came to distrust the hierarchy. Hard upon the heels of the Archdiocesan action to have him defrocked by the Ecumenical Patriarchate, which was obviously rejected by the authorities at the Phanar[78] in Istanbul and of which Stephanou had not been officially informed, came another letter inviting him to appear before a committee formed by the Eparchial Synod.[79] The letter, signed by Metropolitan Silas of New Jersey, stated that members of the Synod were concerned "that an opportunity was never given to you (Stephanou) to defend yourself and to answer charges which are being leveled at you."[80] The letter further asked him to appear before the committee at the offices of the Archdiocese in New York City on March 31, 1987. The letter closed with the ominous words, "If for any reason you cannot come on that day, please inform me about this in due time . . . because as you understand, your silence will not be to your benefit."[81]

The last day of March 1987 found Stephanou in New York City at the offices of the Greek Archdiocese. However, as he entered the meeting room instead of facing a gathering of the Synodal bishops he stood before three men; Metropolitan Silas, Bishop Philotheos (Karamitsos) and Fr. Demetrios

---

76. Stephanou, "An Exciting Discovery," *The Logos*, 19, no. 4, (July-August 1986), 2.

77. Paul Mastoridis, letter to the editor, *The Logos*, 19, no. 5 (September-October 1986), 7.

78. The name given to the compound of the Ecumenical Patriarchate of Constantinople of the Greek Orthodox Church located in Istanbul, Turkey.

79. The Eparchial Synod is a deliberative committee of the Greek Orthodox Archdiocese of North America comprised of the Archbishop and the Metropolitans of the several dioceses within the Archdiocese.

80. Stethatos, *Voice of a Priest*, 233–34.

81. Ibid.

Frangos. Instead of confronting Stephanou regarding his Charismatic writing, teaching, and preaching Metropolitan Silas offered him a pastoral assignment.[82] The meeting showed a complete about-face on the part of the Archdiocese regarding Stephanou. On April 14, 1987, Stephanou received a mailgram from Metropolitan Silas requesting him to serve the end of Holy Week at the Greek Orthodox parish in Lynchburg, Virginia. Stephanou was mystified.

The appeal to the Ecumenical Patriarchate was the last attempt by the Greek Archdiocese in North America to bring Stephanou to heel under the leadership of Archbishop Iakovos and to curb his Renewal activities. After the forced retirement of Archbishop Iakovos from his position as head of the Greek Orthodox Archdiocese of North America by the Ecumenical Patriarchate in 1996, Stephanou never again received any suspensions or censures from ecclesiastical authorities in the Greek Archdiocese. At this point he remains a presbyter/priest in good standing in the Greek Orthodox Metropolis of Atlanta.[83]

The Greek Orthodox Archdiocese Responds to the Charismatic Renewal

By the middle and late 1970s and early '80s the Charismatic Movement in the United States peeked. However, among Orthodox Christians it was just beginning to be noticed. As early as the July 1973 Clergy-Laity Congress of the Greek Orthodox Archdiocese of North American, called for a study of the issue of spiritual renewal in general and especially how the topic should be addressed among the Orthodox faithful. The Congress voted to establish an Archdiocesan Committee on Spiritual Renewal. Bishop Maximus (Aghiorgoussis) of Pittsburgh chaired the committee. On the heels of the formation of this committee Archbishop Iakovos declared 1974 a "Year of Spiritual Renewal." In a letter distributed to all priests, parish councils, youth members, church school teachers, choir members and laymen and lay women of the Greek Archdiocese, the encyclical read:

> One of the most meaningful and studied reprints of the recent Clergy-Laity Congress in Chicago was the report of the Committee on Spiritual Renewal. It offered direction and insight as to how

82. Ibid., 235–36.

83. "About Archbishop Iakovos," Greek Orthodox Archdiocese of America, http://www.goarch.org/archbishop/iakovos/archbishop_iakovos (accessed July 15, 2010).

we can expand our movement toward a renewal of ourselves as members of the Body of Christ.

In the age of uncertainty in which we live we are all faced with challenges and demands, both physical and moral that sometime even tests us to the limits of our human endurance. Yet in Christ we can always find strength and courage to advance beyond the borders of despair.

. . . As leaders and members of our Holy Greek Orthodox Church in the Americas we must also look more deeply into our own spiritual resources. All too often these are set aside for the more mundane concerns of everyday life. We must not forget that as children of God we have a sacred covenant with both God and our conscience, to which we owe obedience at all times. Spiritual renewal therefore should be our first priority.

The purpose of this encyclical is not to reiterate the Chicago Report, or repeat the suggestions offered in the Spiritual Renewal Syllabus sent to all the parishes last spring, but rather to officially proclaim the ecclesiastical year 1974–75 as "A YEAR OF SPIRI-TUAL RENEWAL" for the faithful comprising the Greek Ortho-dox Archdiocese of North and South America.

A theme has been chosen for this sacred proclamation, and it is taken from the text of the Communion Hymn of the Feastday of the Holy Transfiguration: "In the radiance of Thy countenance O Lord I shall walk forever." Following this spirit of illumination of the Holy Transfiguration of Our Lord, I pray that a dedicated and conscientious effort be made to that our life may truly mirror the radiance of His countenance in the beauty of which we are called to journey always.[84]

In 1978, another call for general spiritual renewal was issued at the Clergy-Laity Congress of the Greek Orthodox Archdiocese, held in Detroit. The following text, written by Fr. Theodore Stylianopoulos, professor of New Testament at Holy Cross Greek Orthodox School of Theology in Brookline, Massachusetts and a member of the editorial board of the *Greek Orthodox Theological Review*, was presented to the Congress:

Each person in his daily life frequently senses the difference be-tween **existing** and **living**. We want to **live** but often we merely **exist** as we deal with self, others, job, marriage, family, problems and responsibilities.

84. n.a., "Year of Spiritual Renewal Proclaimed by Archbishop Iakavos" *The Logos*, 7, no. 6 (November-December 1974) 7.

Christ said, "I came that they might have life, and have it abundantly" (John 10:10). Christ's words were not spoken only for the future of His Kingdom, but also for our daily lives. Christ completed His redemption work through His person, teachings, death and resurrection. Those who believe in Him can now enjoy the fruits of new life—true communion with God through the power of the Holy Spirit.

Both the Bible and Tradition assure Orthodox Christians that the new life in Christ is possible for us now, that it is meant for ordinary Christians, and that it is a sure gift flowing from the saving work of Christ. The Apostles, Martyrs, Church Fathers, Saints and countless Christians were empowered by this new life and testify to it as a dynamic reality which changed their lives.

How can this abundant life become part of our daily existence? According to Orthodox teaching, authentic Christian life is a **synergy**, a cooperation, between man and God. **Synergy** does not, of course mean that God does half of the work and man does the other half. Rather it means that while God does all of the saving work, man freely responds to God with his whole being.

For the majority of Orthodox Christians, the response to God begins at infancy with Baptism. Through Baptism, each Orthodox Christian receives Christ and the Holy Spirit **mystically** (mustikvs). The response to God is first made by one's parents and sponsor who **acknowledge** Christ and pledge to Him, as it were: **This young person is yours!**

After wards, the goal of Christian life is to become aware of Christ and the Holy Spirit **actively** and **consciously** (energvz). As the baptized Christian grows from child to adult, and participates in the sacramental life of the Church, his personal response to God becomes crucial. Each Christian must personally re-affirm the baptismal pledge and himself say by free choice to Christ: **Yes, I am yours!** Spiritual renewal comes from this adult commitment to Christ, sharing in the Eucharist, daily prayer, and sincere efforts to live the kind of life Christ lived and preached.

A genuine response to God involved faith, repentance, and obedience. **FAITH** is the acceptance of the Gospel, that is, acknowledgement of Christ as our Lord and Savior. **REPENTANCE** is a thorough conversion of the mind and heart to Christ, with sincere confess of sins, so that He may forgive them and reconcile us to God. **OBEDIENCE** is the willing use of one's total inner and outer resources toward the building up of a life worthy of Christ.

That we may stumble and fall does not so much matter because God lovingly forgives us and teaches us precious lessons through our shortcomings. What does matter is that we turn to Christ as often as we fall, tell Him everything about everything, trust Him for strength and guidance, and learn daily dependence on Him. As we keep our eyes on Him, and united with Him in prayer and sacrament, He renews our lives in the course of daily tasks and responsibilities by the power of the Holy Spirit.

Spiritual renewal is ordinary Christian life in its fullness— through Baptism, Chrismation, all the sacraments, corporate worship, daily prayer, study of God's Word and the teachings of the Holy Fathers, and authentic Christian living in the world. For the Orthodox Christian spiritual renewal is not something separate from the life of the Church, effectively lived, in all its sacramental, catechetical and pastoral ministries.

If God has through Christ granted new life to the world, why do many Christians not experience it more tangibly? If Christians are promised a life of joy and victory in Christ, why are so many baptized believers leading spiritually defeated lives marked by dissatisfaction, fear, boredom, or even by conflict, sin and guilt?

There are several answers to these difficult questions. First, the new life in Christ involves growth. Various persons are at various stages. People are different, with different experiences and different spiritual struggles. But the same Spirit is given to all. The same Lord is the Lord of all. Christian love does not permit comparisons, self-righteousness, and elitism. What is important is to hold onto the Orthodox Faith, to share fully the life of the Church, and to continue to grow in the new life granted us by God, each according to one's gifts and capacities.

But secondly, we must also consider that a Christian may not have let Christ truly reign in his heart. A Christian adult may not have consciously acknowledged Christ with genuine repentance and loving obedience. In that case, the believer is still self-centered, not Christ-centered; he remains inwardly unconverted, living on the basis of ego, rather than on the basis of baptismal grace. Another problem may be a particular unconfessed sin or the unwillingness to forgive someone who has wronged us.

In spiritual renewal Christ is the center of the Church and the believer. As we pray the Liturgy, we must "give ourselves and each other and our whole life to Christ," entrusting ourselves to Him and placing our lives in His hands. At the core of our being, where thoughts and feelings are born, where motivations and decisions have their root, we must trust Christ and let Him rule so that all we think, say and do is according to His love, not according to our self-will. When we ask Him to come into our hearts, a personal

relationship develops between Christ and the believer, as real as
that between two good friends or a husband and wife. Spiritual renewal is a deeper knowledge of Christ Himself. Christ comes alive
in us. As a Church Father has written: "For the believer, Christ is
all."[85]

This statement clearly summed up the definition of "Spiritual Renewal"
according to the understanding of the Greek Orthodox Archdiocese of
North America and was received by the Archdiocesan Congress, which
included the approbation of the primatial archbishop, hierarchs, clergy
and lay delegates representing the various parishes of the Greek Orthodox
Archdiocese.

The ministry of the Archdiocesan Committee on Spiritual Renewal
resulted in three spiritual renewal conferences; the first held in Pittsburgh,
the second in Chicago and the third in Denver. The first National Conference on Orthodox Spiritual Life gathered around the theme "New Life
in Christ." Hosted by the Greek Orthodox Diocese of Pittsburgh, this first
conference of its kind, over three hundred people met August 16–18, 1979,
on the campus of Duquesne University. Chaired by His Grace Bishop
Maximos (Aghiorgoussis), Fr. Alexander Veronis, pastor of Annunciation
Greek Orthodox Church in Lancaster, Pennsylvania served as master of
ceremonies. Other speakers included Fr. Stanley Harakas, then professor
at Holy Cross Greek Orthodox Seminary who spoke on the topic, "New
Life in Christ in the Liturgy" as well as Fr. Theodore Stylianopoulos, who
spoke on "New Life in Christ in the Bible." Further talks were given by
Fr. Demetrius Constantelos, professor of Byzantine and Church History,
who spoke on "New Life in Christ in Orthodox Tradition and History"
and Fr. Anthony Coniaris, pastor of St. Mary's Greek Orthodox Church in
Minneapolis, Minnesota and founder/director of Light and Life Orthodox
Publishing Company, who spoke in the final session of the conference on
the topic, "New Life in Christ in Prayer."[86] His Grace Bishop Maximus is
reported to have encouraged

> The participants . . . to be open to the Holy Spirit and His gifts
> . . . , inasmuch as they are authentic and not abused. . . . It is our
> hope that the fire of the Holy Spirit will consume our impurity and

85. Fr. Theodore Stylianopoulos, "Spiritual Renewal in the Orthodox Church," *Theosis*, 1, no. 5 (September 1978) 2–3.

86. n.a., "New Life in Christ National Conference on Orthodox Spiritual Life and
Renewal," *Theosis*, 2, no. 12 (December 1979) 5–6.

enlighten and warm us with the light and fire of His fiery tongues as in a new Pentecost. Please pray for these goals to be accomplished, to the benefit of our communicants, of the church, of the world in which we live and of[87] the glory of the Holy Name of God.

The second National Conference on Orthodox Spiritual Life and Renewal met August 21–23, 1980 in Chicago, Illinois at Concordia College. Hosted by the Greek Orthodox Diocese of Chicago, the conference theme was "Growing in Christ." Diocesan Chancellor, Fr. Isaiah Chronopoulos, later Bishop of the Greek Orthodox Metropolis of Denver, brought the greetings of Archbishop Iakavos and welcomed the conferees. As with the first conference, the Divine Liturgy was celebrated each morning and Vespers prayed each evening. In addition to Fr. Stanley Harakas, Fr. Thomas Hopko, Instructor of Dogmatic Theology at St. Vladimir's Orthodox Theological Seminary in Crestwood, New York spoke, as did Fr. Alkiviadis Calivas, Professor of Liturgics at Holy Cross, and Ernie Villas, Director of Lay Affairs for the Greek Archdiocese.[88]

The third, and final national conference sponsored by the Archdiocesan Committee on Spiritual Renewal convened July 9–11, 1981 at Hellenic College/Holy Cross Greek Orthodox School of Theology in Brookline, Massachusetts just outside of Boston. Attended by over two hundred faithful, the conference was hosted by Bishop Anthimos then bishop of the Greek Orthodox Diocese of Boston. Fr. Theodore Stylianopoulos opened the conference by expounding upon the theme, "Serving in Christ." In addition to the regular slate of speakers, Bishop Kallistos (Samaras), later "locum tenens" Bishop of Denver, addressed the conference on the topic of "Christ the Servant." John Douglas, Director of Communications for the Greek Orthodox Archdiocese spoke about "Serving Christ in a Secular World." Special guests at the conference were Gordon Walker and Dale Autry, then Bishops in the Evangelical Orthodox Church (EOC). They were asked to address the assembly regarding the EOC and the dialog that had been established with the Orthodox Church in America (OCA) in hopes of becoming communicants of the Orthodox Church.[89] At the conclusion

87. Ibid., 5.

88. n.a., "Growing in Christ Greek Archdiocese Conference on Spiritual Life and Renewal," *Theosis*, 4, no. 1 (January 1981) 7–8.

89. Peter Gillquist, *Becoming Orthodox* (Nashville, TN: Woglemuth & Hyatt, 1989). Formerly affiliated with Campus Crusade for Christ, the leadership of the EOC was eventually received, together with approximately two thousand laypeople, into the Orthodox Church through the Antiochian Orthodox Christian Archdiocese of North America.

of the conference Bishop Maximos announced that all future conferences would be held on a diocesan rather than a national level.

Several publications—*Christ is in our Midst: Spiritual Renewal in the Orthodox Church*,[90] on the general theme of spiritual renewal, an introduction to the Bible, [91] and a series of Bible studies based upon the Liturgical Year[92]—resulted from the work of Fr. Theodore Stylianopoulos with the Committee on Spiritual Renewal and published by the Greek Archdiocese Department of Religious Education, a few which are still in print and available.

It is reported that at a Clergy-Laity Congress subsequent to the last Spiritual Renewal Conference, Metropolitan Silas of New Jersey stood and in response to a report given to the Congress on the renewal conferences, stated that renewal conferences were not necessary and that all the spiritual renewal needed by the Greek Archdiocese was provided in the Divine Liturgy celebrated every Sunday morning in its several hundred parishes. The lukewarm support of the hierarchs, as typified by this statement attributed to Metropolitan Silas, for the ongoing work of the Archdiocesan Committee on Spiritual Renewal resulted in it disbanding and the issue of spiritual renewal ceased to be of any vital importance to the leadership of the Greek Orthodox Archdiocese.[93]

The Move to Florida and the Establishment of the Brotherhood

Since the inception of *The Logos* Fort Wayne, Indiana had served as the home of the Logos Ministry for Orthodox Renewal. After Stephanou's suspension in 1968 and his subsequent removal from priestly ministry at Holy Trinity Greek Orthodox parish, he remained in Fort Wayne. However, after the fateful meeting with Metropolitan Silas in New York City in March, 1986, and his offer for Stephanou to take a parish assignment, the parish-less

90. Stylianopoulos, *Christ is in our Midst: Spiritual Renewal in the Orthodox Church* (Brookline, MA: Greek Orthodox Archdiocese Department of Religious Education, 1981).

91. Stylianopoulos, *Bread for Life, Reading the Bible* (Brookline, MA: Greek Orthodox Archdiocese Department of Religious Education, 1980).

92. Stylianopoulos, *A Year of the Lord (Liturgical Bible Studies)*, 5 vols. (Brookline, MA: Greek Orthodox Archdiocese Department of Religious Education, 1985).

93. Fr. Alexander Veronis, telephone interview with author, July 28, 2010.

priest began to seriously consider the offer. In Stephanou's autobiography he recorded his anxiety over the dilemma of accepting a parish assignment or continuing on with the Renewal Ministry. The Charismatic Renewal Movement in the Orthodox parishes throughout the United States was beginning to wane and many once-strong Charismatic Orthodox prayer groups were disbanding. Stephanou felt like it might be time for a change. He made it known to the Archdiocese that he was interested in a small Greek Orthodox parish in Fort Walton Beach, Florida named St. Markella's. The chancellor of the Archdiocese, Bishop Isaiah (Chronopoulos), sent a letter to Bishop John (Kallos) of Atlanta informing him of Stephanou's status as a priest in good standing and should be given a parish assignment. In turn Bishop John wrote to the parish council of St. Markella's Church informing them of Stephanou's appointment as their new priest. In the meantime, Stephanou found a residence in nearby Destin, Florida and prepared to move. The Logos ministry property in Fort Wayne was put up for sale. However, the parish council of St. Markella's informed the bishop that they had no intention of accepting Stephanou as their priest. Archbishop Iakavos entered the fray and sent a letter informing the council that Stephanou was "an acknowledged theologian" and a "canonical priest" and that that coming Sunday Stephanou would be at St. Markella's to celebrate the Divine Liturgy.[94] However, the following Sunday Fr. Eusebius arrived at St. Markella's in Fort Walton Beach and found the church doors locked and no one to greet him. At 10:00 AM, when Liturgy was scheduled to begin, a few stragglers appeared at the front doors. Instead of leaving, Stephanou—from the front steps of the church—read the epistle and Gospel lections for the day, sang some hymns, gave a short sermon, and dismissed the people. Ironically, now that Stephanou's status with the Archdiocese was normalized he still was not to find a home serving in a parish. Never again did he ever seek a parish assignment in the Greek Archdiocese.

These events, however, led to a new chapter in Stephanou's ministry. Having relocated to Florida in anticipation of the new parish assignment, Stephanou cast his eyes about looking for an opportunity to preach and teach. In May 1988 Stephanou requested Archbishop Iakavos' permission to serve at the private chapel of St. John the Baptist in Destin, close to his new residence.[95] While serving with Bishop John of Atlanta at the annual

94. Stethatos, *Voice of a Priest*, 250.

95. Ibid., 258. The chapel of St. John had been built as private chapel by Cleo Marler, in memory of her Greek immigrant father, John Maltezos.

Feast of the Entry of the Theotokos held at the Malbis Memorial Chapel in Daphne, Alabama, Stephanou was asked to give the homily. Following the Liturgy at a gathering of the clergy, Stephanou announced that he planned to build an Orthodox chapel in Destin.[96] True to his word, in January, 1989, Stephanou purchased land east of Destin and hired a bankrupt Pentecostal builder to begin construction of the chapel. By late summer 1989 the chapel was completed and on Sunday, August 6, the Feast of the Transfiguration of Christ, the chapel, erected in honor of St. Symeon the New Theologian, was dedicated. Supporters of Stephanou's ministry came from all over the United States for the event. From that day on Divine Liturgy was celebrated each Sunday in the chapel. The first Florida Orthodox Renewal Conference was held the weekend of February 16–18, 1990. The conference services of prayer and worship were conducted in the chapel of St. Symeon while the teaching sessions and meals were held at the local Holiday Inn. Professor Charles Ashanin of Indianapolis and Canadian Ukrainian Orthodox priest Maxym Lysack were the featured speakers.[97]

What began with a chapel burgeoned into a retreat center. Over the next several years property adjacent to the chapel was purchased or donated. In addition to the chapel a fellowship hall, a ten-room dormitory, an outdoor pavilion, a library, and office building now grace the grounds of the retreat center. After the move from Indiana it became necessary for the ministry to reincorporate in Florida. On this occasion the board of trustees, at the direction of Stephanou, changed the name of the organization from The Logos Ministry for Orthodox Renewal to the Orthodox Brotherhood of St. Symeon the New Theologian. The complex was likewise rechristened The St. Symeon the New Theologian Orthodox Renewal Center.[98]

Throughout the remainder of the 1990s, Stephanou sponsored Renewal conferences in Destin on three separate weekends. The dates closest to March 12, the Feast of St. Symeon the New Theologian, were set aside for the winter conference; an Easter conference, which usually fell in May and a fall conference which corresponded to October 12, the secondary Feast day of St. Symeon.

Stephanou remained attached to the chapel of St. Symeon the New Theologian in Destin, Florida throughout the decade of the 90's and into the first decade of the new millennium. In spite of his advanced age, and

96. Ibid., 257.
97. Ibid., 265–66.
98. Ibid., 268, 274, 279, 324–25.

health issues, he continues serving the Divine Liturgy each Sunday, conducting Bible studies on Wednesday evenings, writing and editing articles for *The Evangelist* as well as publishing new books and booklets from time to time.[99] The Brotherhood continues to hold tri-annual conferences and sponsors a website.[100]

The Orthodox and Charismatic Theology of Stephanou

One of the most distinctive features of the Charismatic Renewal, setting it apart from the Pentecostal Movement of the early twentieth century, was its ability to be embraced by the Roman Catholic and many-faceted Protestant traditions alike and re-interpreted theologically in such a way as to find a home in almost all denominations. Many Roman Catholic and Protestant theologians embraced the Renewal and put their theological training to use in recasting and synthesizing Charismatic spirituality and experience with their respective traditions. Roman Catholics boasted such Charismatic theologians as Leon Cardinal Suenens, Yves Congar, Killian McDonnell, Francis Sullivan, Edward O'Connor, Donald Gelpi, Francis MacNutt, and Simon Tugwell. These men wrote excellent theological reflections and answered the challenges to the Movement presented by Roman Catholic hierarchs and non-Charismatic theologians alike. Their ability to articulate the Renewal in a clear and uniquely Roman Catholic idiom kept many thousands of Roman Catholic laymen and women within the Roman Catholic Church who otherwise may have left and defected to classical Pentecostal or independent Charismatic congregations.

Like their Roman Catholic counterparts Orthodox Charismatics also sought to communicate their newfound spiritual renewal experience in a language that was familiar to their fellow Orthodox Christians and consistent with the Orthodox spiritual tradition. Following Stephanou's introduction to the Charismatic Renewal in late 1971, and before his Baptism of the Holy Spirit in spring of 1972, the pages of *The Logos* printed several extensive quotes from Orthodox Church Fathers, saints, and theologians on the subject of the Holy Spirit. Following Stephanou's Baptism in the Holy Spirit however, he aggressively appropriated the life, writings, and spirituality of the eleventh-century Orthodox saint, Symeon the New Theologian. Stephanou's discovery of St. Symeon came very soon after his "Pentecost"

99. Eusebius Stephanou, telephone conversation with author, July 30, 2010.

100. www.stsymeon .org

experience and was understood by him as the definitive answer to his questions regarding the Orthodox nature of the Renewal. Stephanou states that he was in Chicago waiting to meet with Fr. Howard Sloan, a Ukrainian Orthodox priest involved in the Charismatic Movement. They were meeting at the University of Chicago Divinity School Library. Arriving early Stephanou began to peruse the section of volumes of Patristic works written in Greek. Coming across the multi-volume work *Sources Chretiennes*, which included a parallel French translation, he came across a volume of the writings of St. Symeon the New Theologian, edited by Orthodox theologian Basil Krivochene. Stephanou's discovery of St. Symeon' writings led him to draw analogous conclusions between St. Symeon's teaching on the "Baptism of the Holy Spirit" and the Charismatic Renewals teaching on the experience of the same name.[101]

In the November-December 1973 issue of *The Logos* Stephanou introduced his readers to the person and writings of St. Symeon the New Theologian for the first time. The article, entitled, "Orthodox Charismatics Listen to a Voice from the Past," sought to establish a direct link between the experiences of twentieth-century Charismatic Orthodox Christians and the eleventh-century monastic saint. The article presented a short biography of the saint taken from the pages of the classic Orthodox spiritual text the *Philokalia*.[102] In the remainder of the article Stephanou points out several parallels between the teachings of St. Symeon and the reactions of the monastics and hierarchy in the eleventh century and the present reactions of many Orthodox to the contemporary Charismatic Renewal. First, he states that rank and file Orthodox laymen have no sensory awareness of the presence of the Holy Spirit in their lives, yet they claim that by virtue of their water baptism and chrismation they have the gift of the Holy Spirit. Stephanou, making use of St. Symeon's words, challenges this presupposition by pointing out the great number of Orthodox Christians who are fearful of death and the last apocalyptic age. St. Symeon states that this is a sign that they are "unsealed," devoid of the Holy Spirit and the only remedy is for them to "Run!" and "make haste to be stamped with the seal of the Spirit."[103] Quoting St. Symeon's thoughts Stephanou challenges those

---

101. Stethatos, *The Voice of a Priest,* 109–10.

102. Kadloubovsky and Palmer, trans., *Writings from the Philokalia in the Prayer of the Heart,* 95–96.

103. Stephanou, "Orthodox Charismatics Listen to a Voice from the Past," *The Logos,* 6, no. 6 (November-December 1973) 12.

Orthodox who rest totally upon their baptismal certificate for their spiritual security,

> Let nobody say: "I received Christ when I received holy baptism." Such a person should learn that not all those who are baptized receive Christ through baptism, but only the *bebaiopistoi* (those who believe with assurance) and those who prepare themselves with perfect knowledge and previous catharsis. He who searches the scriptures will discover from apostolic words and deeds this fact, for it is written: After the apostles in Jerusalem heard . . . they laid hands upon them and they received the Holy Spirit.[104]

Stephanou's understanding of St. Symeon's words supports his personal experience. As an ordained priest in the Orthodox Church, the son of a priest, a graduate of America's preeminent Greek Orthodox seminary, and the recipient of degrees in higher theological education, who regularly, weekly celebrated the sacraments of the Orthodox Church, Stephanou claimed to be devoid of a personal, experiential encounter with the Holy Spirit and the spiritual power that results from such an encounter.

St. Symeon's approach to the spiritual life likewise incorporated many "charismatic" themes otherwise neglected by contemporary mainstream Orthodox sacramental theology. St. Symeon sees that it is possible to have truly and genuinely received the grace of salvation through the mysteries of baptism and chrismation in the Church, but through neglect, apathy, and sin, to have suppressed or even lost the grace of these mysteries. Therefore, in order to recover or renew the grace of baptism/chrismation the lapsed Orthodox Christian must receive a "Baptism of the Holy Spirit" once again in a concrete and experiential manner. This became the thrust of Stephanou's writings in the pages of *The Logos*, as well as the emphasis of his early itinerant ministry of preaching and teaching. The pages of *The Logos* contained numerous testimonies of Orthodox Christians from all ethnic backgrounds and jurisdictional parishes who echoed Stephanou's testimony.

After the initial introduction of the life and theology the St. Symeon the New Theologian to the readers of *The Logos* in the November-December, 1973, excerpts from the writings of the saint became a regular feature in the periodical. The length of the passages varied somewhat, and the titles given to the articles were intentionally "Charismatic" in tone. The January-February 1974 issue contained a fairly lengthy article entitled, "The Baptism of the Holy Spirit: as found in the writings of St. Symeon the New

104. Ibid., 14.

Theologian."[105] In this article Stephanou quotes extensively from the writings of the medieval saint of Constantinople. He opens the article with the bold assertion,

> If the Orthodox Church claims Pentecost as her birthday, then we have to believe that the fullness of the Pentecostal experience in not only a normal part of her life, but in fact normative for her members.[106]

Immediately following this statement however, he reports that some Orthodox "theologians and clergy" refuse to recognize the manifestations of the Holy Spirit and label them "as either foreign to the Orthodox traditions or as demonic signs to be carefully avoided."[107] Stephanou alleges to have received letters from Greece in which a priest stated that to claim to possess the gifts of the Holy Spirit was "presumptuous and arrogant" while others asserted that it was the result of "succumbing to Satanic deceit."[108] Stephanou responded that while it was important to "test the spirits" as commanded by the Apostle John, it was likewise as important not to outright reject every supernatural manifestation and attribute it to the working of the Evil One in order not to blaspheme the Holy Spirit. He quotes St. Symeon who in turn appealed to the writings of St. Basil the Great, regarding blaspheming the Holy Spirit.

> "Let us inquire as to what the blasphemy of the Holy Spirit is. Blasphemy against the Holy Spirit is attributing the working of the Spirit to the adverse Spirit as St. Basil states." (Catechesis 32 in "*Source Chrétiennes*.") This earlier church father teaches that "the person that blasphemes against the Holy Spirit is one who ascribes the energies and fruits of the Holy Spirit to the opposing spirit" (Shorter Rule, 273).[109]

Stephanou goes on to establish the connection between St, Symeon's day and the present situation among some Orthodox.

> Even in his own day many Orthodox (especially monks—believe it or not!) ascribed the spiritual charismata (gifts) to the Devil.

---

105. Stephanou, "The Baptism of the Holy Spirit as Found in the Writings of St. Symeon the New Theologian" *The Logos*, 7, no. 1, (January-February 1974) 12–5.

106. Ibid, 12.

107. Ibid.

108. Ibid.

109. Ibid.

Doesn't this sound familiar? Look at what St. Symeon says about such critics: "Whenever a miracle takes place by the virtue of the Holy Spirit, or when one observes a divine charisma in one of his brothers—contrition, tears, humbleness, divine knowledge or a word of wisdom from above or some other charism given by the Holy Spirit to those who love God—he contends that such a thing is of the Devil's deception."[110]

To the Orthodox hierarchs and priests who labeled the Charismatic movement among Orthodox Christians as heretical, Stephanou likewise turned to St. Symeon and let the words of the saint provide the rebuttal.

But I call heretics also those who say that in our own day and in our midst there is none who is able to observe the precepts of the Gospel and to become as were the holy Fathers. To begin with the most reliable and practical consideration of all is the fact that faith is demonstrated by means of works in becoming illuminated and receiving the Holy Spirit beholding the Son together with the Father. . . . Those who contend that this is impossible are guilty of not simply one particular heresy, but of all heresies, and if one can say, exceeding and surpassing then all in ungodliness and excessiveness of blasphemy.. . . Those who state such things close heaven which Christ opened to us, and they obstruct the ascent to Him which He Himself initiated. Standing at the gates of heaven, bending down, seen of believers and declaring through the Gospel, He invites: Come unto me, all ye who labor and are heavily burdened and I will give you rest, while the *antitheoi* (God-opposing one,) or rather, the antichrists cry out, This is impossible! Impossible![111]

One of the most controversial elements of Stephanou's interpretation of St. Symeon regards his insistence upon a personal and physical awareness of the presence of the Holy Spirit in the life of the Orthodox Christian. Stephanou pointed to the thousands of Orthodox Christians, who though baptized and chrismated as infants, and regular participants in the holy Eucharist, have no personal consciousness of the presence of Christ or the Holy Spirit in their lives. They have no spiritual desire, they do not pray, or read the Scriptures, they do not share their faith (they are ignorant of both the holy Scriptures and the Orthodox faith), and in many cases there is no action on their part to distinguish them morally or ethically from non-Christians or pagans. Stephanou, throughout the years of his writings both

110. Ibid.
111. Ibid., 13.

in *The Logos* and in his books, decries this as *the* most devastating weakness within the Orthodox Church. Once again, he turns to the thoughts of St. Symeon,

> He who lacks an awareness of his baptism (if he was baptized in infancy), and does not understand what it means to be baptized, but who accepts it merely on faith and has obliterated it by countless sins, and has renounced the second baptism—I mean the baptism of the Spirit, given from above by love of God to those who seek it through repentance—how can he possibly be saved? In no way whatsoever![112]

The writings of Stephanou regarding St. Symeon the New Theologian leave no doubt; in the mind of this Greek Orthodox priest, St. Symeon the New Theologian was the "Forerunner of Charismatic Renewal."[113] Stephanou sees many parallels between the Orthodox Church of eleventh-century Constantinople and twentieth-century America. He equates the experience of the Baptism of the Holy Spirit, subsequent to infant baptism, mentioned in St. Symeon's writings with the same experience claimed by many Orthodox Christian of all ethnic backgrounds. Likewise, the resistance experienced by St. Symeon from his fellow monks and hierarchs in the eleventh century is the same opposition suffered by Stephanou and other Charismatic Orthodox Christians in the twentieth century. For Fr. Eusebius Stephanou, St. Symeon the New Theologian was an eleventh-century prophetic voice speaking clearly into the twentieth century. In the May/June issue of *The Logos*, Stephanou summarized the rationale behind his constant appeal to the writings of St. Symeon.

> You be wondering why I have been using St. Symeon the New Theologian with such frequency in my articles—almost to the exclusion of other Church Fathers. There are at least three reasons for this. . . . Firstly St. Symeon towers over most of the other Church Fathers in authority and excellence of theology. Suffice it to remember that he stands third in line after St. John the Evangelist and St. Gregory of Nazianzus as "theologians," a distinction that of itself demonstrates unquestionably his unique authority on the doctrine of the Godhead.
>
> Moreover, St. Symeon, like St. John of Damascus, serves to recapitulate the theology of the Fathers of previous generations. He not only digests and expounds the teachings of the church for the

112. Ibid.

113. Stephanou, "Orthodox Charismatics Listen to a Voice from the Past," 12.

first thousand years, restates them dynamically in the Spirit, and he reaffirms the contemplative and spiritual approach to theology that was almost lost from the eighth century under Aristotelian influence.

Thirdly, St. Symeon, we must admit, is virtually a new discovery. He had been omitted from classical editions of the patristic writings, due partly to the Aristotelian bias of the Roman Church that viewed his works as suspect because of their mystical emphasis. Then there is the factor of his being unpopular with the Patriarchate of Constantinople that had him removed from his monastery and exiled to a remote island.

From all this we can see how easy it was for St. Symeon to fall into oblivion and to remain, to all intents and purposes, unknown and ignored even by the Orthodox. The Greek originals of his writings even to in our own day are difficult to find . . . .

The profuse use, therefore, of St Symeon is corrective, for one thing. It meets a real need. Most important of all—his devotional approach to the doctrine of the Holy Spirit is fresh and timely as the Charismatic Renewal grows in the Orthodox Church. The prophetic character of his theology also meets a practical need in a church that today is paralyzed with spiritual superficiality and barren formalism.[114]

Stephanou's theology of the "Baptism of the Holy Spirit," at least on the surface, echoes the assumptions of classical Pentecostal theology on the same subject. In all probability this is why many of Stephanou's detractors labeled him a "Protestant." However, they did not take the time to look beyond the surface and see the nuances of his thinking and how seriously it departs from classical Pentecostal thought on the Baptism of the Holy Spirit. According to classical Pentecostal theology, there are "stages" to the Christian life; first one is "born again" or "saved" then followed by the "Baptism of the Holy Spirit, which is initially, physically evidenced by speaking in tongues.[115] The main and most important difference between classical Pentecostalism and Stephanou's theology is the sacramental component. Stephanou nowhere in his writings denies the spiritual legitimacy or

114. Stephanou, "Sharing in the Spirit," *The Logos*, 11, no. 3, (May-June 1978) 4.

115. Reed, *"In Jesus' Name"* 87–94. The Wesleyan branch of classical Pentecostalism, represented by the Pentecostal-Holiness Church, the Church of God (Cleveland, TN) and the Church of God in Christ, officially holds to a "three stage" *ordo salutis* in which one is first "saved" or "born-again," second they are "sanctified," in which their heart is cleansed from the inbred sin "nature," which then makes them a "fit vessel" to receive the baptism of the Holy Spirit.

efficacy of the sacraments (mysteries) celebrated in the Orthodox Church. However, what he does question is the continuing effects of the grace received in those sacraments in the life of many Orthodox Christians who received those sacramental ministrations in infancy or childhood. Unlike classical Pentecostals, Stephanou argued that infants or adults baptized in the Orthodox Church are truly "born-again" or "saved". In one essay, under the heading, "Water Baptism is Regenerative," Stephanou writes,

> When you deliberately deny that trine immersion into the baptismal font is regenerative, you are in effect saying that you have simply received the baptism of water for repentance. You are merely a dry sinner before, and after baptism, you are a wet sinner. . . . You are not born again until you receive the baptism of water, the baptism of the Holy Spirit, and finally the Body and Blood of Jesus Christ in Communion. "Unless a man is born of water and the Spirit, he cannot enter the kingdom of heaven" (John 3:5), and "Unless ye eat the flesh of the Son of Man and drink his blood, ye have no life in you" (John 6:53).[116]

In another essay he again affirms his belief in the salvific character of water baptism,

> In the baptism of water, the Holy Spirit baptizes the believer in Jesus Christ. He is cleansed of both Adam's condemnation and his own personal sins. He is grafted as a new member into the Body of Christ. He becomes a vessel: cleansed, justified, forgiven through the blood of Jesus.[117]

In keeping with the traditional teaching of St. Symeon the New Theologian on the relationship between water baptism and personal experience, Stephanou quotes Russian Archbishop Basil Krivochene:

> Symeon does not deny the efficacy of infant baptism, although he recognizes that as "small babes," we are sanctified "without having awareness of it," but he insists on the necessity of being marked again with the "seal of Christ," since we have soiled our baptism by sin. It is always the same persistence on the conscience nature of grace.[118]

---

116. Stephanou, *Desolation and Restoration*, 64–65.

117. Ibid., 81.

118. Stephanou, *Pathway to Orthodox Renewal*, 66.

However, because of spiritual neglect, apathy and ignorance, the grace of salvation, truly an authentically received, in the mystery of Baptism, becomes dormant at best and lost at worst. Therefore, as a result most Orthodox Christians need to be "born-again" *again*. Since they have come to an age of awareness and understanding they must re-affirm their baptism in order to be "born-again" again. The grace of salvation, genuinely receive in holy Baptism, must be recovered, renewed and restored.

A regular feature of Stephanou's itinerant preaching ministry was to visit Orthodox parishes and after teaching on this subject he would issue an "altar call," inviting Orthodox Christians who had not affirmed their baptism as conscious adults to come forward to the solea, in front of the altar. He would then lead them verbally through the initiatory prayers of baptism, i.e., renunciation of Satan, complete with spitting on the Devil, unification with Christ, acknowledgment of His Lordship and dedication to live the Orthodox Christian life.[119] This effectively tied the sacrament of baptism to a public verbal action of committing oneself to Christ.

The first part of the Sacraments of Baptism and Chrismation is the "Prayers at the Reception of Catechumens." In the early days of the Church, before the baptism of infants became the common practice, adults were still leaving their pagan backgrounds and confessing Christ. So the text of the service presupposes that the candidates can speak for themselves. However, after many centuries and adult baptisms were less common, godparents or sponsors were asked to answer and speak for the child who in most cases could not speak for themselves. Following several exorcism prayers the candidate for the Catechumenate is then asked the following questions:

> PRIEST: Dost thou renounce Satan, and all his Angels, and all his works, and all his service, and all his pride?
>
> SPONSOR: (replies for the Child): I do.
>
> *The above question and answer are repeated thrice.*
>
> PRIEST: Hast thou renounced Satan?
>
> SPONSOR: I have.
>
> *The above question and answer are also repeated thrice.*
>
> PRIEST: Breathe and spit upon him.

119

The Sponsor, holding the Child, then turns to face the East (to-ward the Altar); as does the Priest.

PRIEST: Dost thou unite thyself to Christ?

SPONSOR: I do.

The above question and answer are repeated thrice.

PRIEST: Hast thou united thyself to Christ?

SPONSOR: I have.

The above question and answer are also repeated thrice.

PRIEST: Dost thou believe in Him?

SPONSOR: I believe in Him as King and God.[120]

Following the renunciations and unification then the sponsor, or the adult catechumen is asked to confess the Orthodox Christian Faith in the form of the Nicene-Constantinopolitan Creed. Following the confession of the Creed the catechumen is asked once again:

PRIEST: Hast thou united thyself to Christ?

SPONSOR: I have.

The above question and answer are also repeated thrice.

PRIEST: Bow down also before Him.

SPONSOR: (*bows and says):* I bow down before the Father, and the Son, and the Holy Spirit: the Trinity one in Essence and undivided.[121]

It was in these encounters that hundreds of Orthodox Christians claimed to be "born-again" or "saved" and testified to a life-changing encounter with Jesus Christ. These testimonies were printed by the thousands in the pages of *The Logos.* In many cases, Orthodox priests and laymen saw this as *Protestant* methodology similar to the "altar calls" given by Evangelist Billy Graham at his crusades, or the practices of other Evangelical Protestant churches.[122]

120. Antiochian Orthodox Christian Archdiocese of North America, *Service Book of the Holy Eastern Orthodox Catholic Church,* 148–50.

121. Ibid., 150.

122. Douglas A. Sweeney and Mark C. Rodgers, *"Walk the Aisle," Christianity Today,*

Also similar to classical Pentecostal theology was Stephanou's teaching that the newly "saved" or renewed Orthodox Christian becomes a candidate for receiving the "Baptism of the Holy Spirit" for the empowerment of being witnesses and for the reception of charismatic gifts, such as prophecy, healing, or tongues, etc. Again, the main, and most important, difference between classical Pentecostalism and Stephanou's emphasis is sacramental in nature. Stephanou would declare that in the sacrament of Chrismation, the completion of the baptismal rite, the infant truly receives the "seal of the gift of the Holy Spirit" and the grace of Pentecost. Nonetheless, just as in the case of the neglect and loss of the baptismal grace of salvation, the infant likewise loses the grace of Holy Spirit empowerment through sin and neglect and needs to renew and restore the lost grace of Pentecost through a personal "Baptism of the Holy Spirit." Stephanou refers to this as "Rekindling the Gift of the Holy Spirit".

> Child of God, you probably received the Holy Spirit when you were baptized at infancy. But a lot of time has elapsed since then. Sin banishes the Holy Spirit. You should seek to rekindle that heavenly gift with a new infilling. Be sealed all over again—not by getting anointed again with visible Unction at the hand of the priest, but by repenting and confessing your sins, by weeping and worthily receiving the Bread of Life and by seeking the Lord for a closer walk with Him. Some charismatically renewed people call this spiritual rekindling being "baptized in the Holy Spirit," though that originally took place at the time of chrismation. This expression need not disturb those of us who believe that there can only be one baptism in the Spirit.... It is not a repetition of the sacrament, but a reactivating of the baptism of the Holy Spirit initially received. There is one Holy Spirit baptism, but many infillings.[123]

Stephanou believed that this is exactly what St. Symeon referred to in his own writings about the loss of baptismal/chrismational grace and the need for an its experiential restoration or renewal of these sacraments in the personal life of the Orthodox Christian.

> St. Symeon does not explain what happens to that initial baptism of the Spirit received in infancy, that is, whether it is dormant and needs rekindling, or is totally effaced by personal sins and requires a new baptism of the Spirit. He does not speak in technical terms

October 22, 2008. http://www.christianitytoday.com/ch/thepastinthepresent/storybehind/walktheaisle.html (accessed August 4, 2010).

123. Stephanou, *Desolation and Restoration,* 64.

about the fate of that initial sacramental action. What really concerns him is the lack of evidence if the Holy Spirit in the actual life of adult baptized believers.[124]

Stephanou clearly departs from classical Pentecostal theology regarding the sign of the Baptism of the Holy Spirit. As stated above a great majority of classical Pentecostal denominations insist that the "initial, physical evidence of the baptism of the Holy Spirit" is speaking in tongues.[125] This is the unique and defining theological position of Pentecostalism.[126] While Stephanou claimed to have received the gift of tongues,[127] as many within the Charismatic Movement did, and believed that it is available to Spirit-filled Christians today as in Apostolic times, and because of the overwhelming interest in it by those outside the Charismatic Movement, gives attention to the subject in his writings, at no time does he articulate a belief that the gift of speaking in tongues is the evidential sign of the Baptism of the Holy Spirit, nor of its superiority to any of the other charismata. The only place in Stephanou's writing where it could possibly be construed that he holds to any theology that would suggest that speaking in tongues is an "evidence" that one has received the Baptism of the Holy Spirit is in his booklet on the mystery of Chrismation,

> We can thank God that there is a growing number of persons in the Orthodox Church today experiencing a life-changing infilling of the Holy Spirit, indeed with the *evidence* of the speaking in tongues. This means that definitely the Charismatic Renewal has ignited the flame of awakening in our own church and that the Spirit has already touched the lives of many Orthodox in a most extraordinary way.[128] *(emphasis mine)*

In Stephanou's 80-page book, *100 Questions and Answers on the Charismatic Renewal in the Orthodox Church,* there are only two questions that directly address the topic of speaking in tongues. Both questions and the answers together take up less than one and a quarter pages.[129] In a collection of Stephanou's essays, published in the book, *Desolation and Restoration in*

124. Stephanou, *Pathway to Orthodox Renewal*, 65.

125. Alton Garrison, "Baptism in the Holy Spirit," *Pentecostal Evangel* No. 5014, (June 13, 2010) 21.

126. Flower, "The Birth of the Pentecostal Movement," 3.

127. Stethatos, *Voice of a Priest,* 103.

128. Stephanou, *Chrismation: The Hidden Sacrament,* 64.

129. Stephanou, *100 Questions and Answers,* 11–12.

the Orthodox Church, he refers to the gift of tongues in several places, usually quoting passages in the Acts of the Apostles which mention this gift, but no in-depth treatment of the subject is found.[130] Throughout the pages of *The Logos,* during the years of it circulation, testimonies of hundreds and perhaps thousands of Orthodox Christians of different genders, ages, and ethnic background, were printed. Many of these men and women claimed to have received the gift of tongues, yet at no time were any claims made that the reception of this spiritual gift entitled them to spiritual superiority in comparison to other Orthodox Christians.

Of all the issues relating to the Charismatic Movement the most controversial was, and continues to be, the topic of speaking in tongues. As stated above the primary leaders of the Charismatic Movement in the Orthodox Church never embraced the doctrinal stance of classical Pentecostalism which insisted that the "initial, physical, sign" that one has received the baptism of the Holy Spirit is speaking in tongues, while at the same time claiming that they themselves received this gift in association with their baptism/release of the Spirit. Some Orthodox writers refused to even acknowledge that such a spiritual gift existed today and that Orthodox Christians might be able to receive it. Others, quoting certain Church Fathers, asserted that the gift of tongues was no longer available to the Church.

> It is quite noteworthy that there is a conspicuous absence of *glossolalia* in the spiritual writers of the Christian East throughout the centuries. But what should we make of this present-day situation in which most Pentecostal are sincere followers of Christ, and sincerely believe their "tongues" are from God? Many Church Fathers believe that tongues are no longer necessary in the Church. However, Bishop Ware agrees that although they are not necessary, they may not have disappeared altogether. He offers strong counsel that discernment is always needed; hence the importance in Orthodoxy of seeking the help of an experienced spiritual guide. Discernment, he warns is even more necessary in the case of tongues, and cautions that often it is not the Spirit of God that is speaking through tongues, but the all-too-human spirit of auto-suggestion and mass hysteria, and there may even be occasions when "speaking in tongues" is a form of demonic possession. As St. John the Evangelist states, we must not trust every spirit, "but test the spirits to see whether they are from God" (1 John 4:1).[131]

130. Stephanou, *Desolation and Restoration,* 42, 67–8, 84–6, 110–13, 128, 130.

131. Tibbs," "Pentecost and Speaking in Tongues: An Orthodox View of Glossolalia," 68.

Orthodox theologians were clear to point out that the importance of *glossolalia,* assigned to it by the classical Pentecostals or mainstream Charismatics was certainly not on the same level as that given by Orthodox spiritual life. In most early Orthodox literature, previous to the twentieth century, the gift of speaking in tongues was always related to the experience of the Apostles on the Day of Pentecost in which tongues was definitely a known language *(xenoglossy)* given for the sole purpose of proclaiming the gospel in the numerous languages of the *Ecumene,* a reversal of the curse of Babel.[132] Since the advent of Pentecostalism and the Charismatic Movement some Orthodox scholars ventured to suggest that there were two types of the gift of tongues, one evidenced on the Day of Pentecost and another manifested among the Corinthian Christians. One such theologian, Fr. Thomas Hopko, then Dean and Professor of Theology at St. Vladimir's Orthodox Theological Seminary, writes:

> In his first letter to the Corinthians the Apostle Paul speaks of a special kind of prayer in the Spirit. It is the spiritual gift of "speaking in tongues." With this particular gift the person praises God in a language he cannot understand. His "spirit prays" with ecstatic utterances, but his "mind remains unfruitful." According to the apostle, who himself had this gift and says that it should not be forbidden, such prayer in the Spirit is without benefit to man unless it is accompanied with "some revelation or knowledge or prophecy (i.e. the directly inspired Word of God) or teaching." He says that it should not be done in the public gathering of the church unless there be some interpretation and that even then there should be **"only two, or at most three,"** and that those who are **"eager for manifestations of the Spirit should strive to excel in building up the church"** and should "not be children in their thinking . . . but in thinking be mature." He says that all should seek rather to prophesy, i.e. to speak the Word of God clearly and plainly so that those who observe Christians would declare "that God is really among" them and not consider them mad." He says finally that "all things should be done decently and in order." (*cf. I Corinthians 12–14*)
>
> It is apparent that the gift of praying in the Spirit with tongues was the cause of no small confusion and disorder in the Corinthian Church, and that those having this gift of ecstatic prayer were disturbing and dividing the community by considering themselves more spiritual than others. St. Paul insists that not all have

132. Ibid., 64.

the same gifts, and that tongues are but one of the gifts, the last of those mentioned, to serve as a sign not for those who already believe, but **"for unbelievers."** (*I Corinthians 14:22*) In general it is clear that the sole purpose of the apostle's extended discussion of the spiritual gifts, and his insistence on giving up "childish ways" in the pursuit of perfection when one becomes mature, was to rebuke the members of the Corinthian Church for their misuse and abuse of the spiritual gift of tongues.

There is no evidence in the spiritual tradition of the church that any of the saints had the gift of praying in tongues or that such kind of prayer was ever a part of the liturgy of the church. The only mention that can be found of it, to our knowledge, was at the baptism of Montanus, a third-century heretic who left the Church to found his own spiritualist sect. If any of the saints or spiritual masters had this gift, they did not write about it or propagate it openly. It was unknown, for example, to Saint John Chrysostom by his own report, (*cf. Commentary on Corinthians*) Since a number of believers have this gift in our time, and since there are persons who seek it, it is critically important that this method of prayer be understood according to the counsels of Saint Paul and in the light of the teaching of the spiritual masters on prayer.[133]

Topics, in many ways peripheral to the core theology of the Charismatic Movement, likewise became points of contention between Stephanou and his detractors. Space does not allow a thorough treatment of this specific subject here but suffice it to say that Stephanou's label as a "Protestant" was not helped by his views on eschatology. Briefly stated, three points that were of concern to Orthodox leaders and theologians were Stephanou's acceptance of the doctrine of the "Rapture" as held by most Evangelical Protestants;[134] acknowledgment that the modern political State of Israel was the fulfillment of biblical prophecy in contemporary times which set the stage for the second advent of Jesus Christ;[135] and his embrace of the dogma of a literal "millennium" or chiliasm, which was condemned by the early Church.[136]

133. Hopko, *Spirituality.* Vol. IV of *The Orthodox Church*, 143–45.

134. Stephanou, "The Coming Deluge of Fire According to Bible Prophecy," *The Logos* 13, no. 4, (July-August 1980) 13–5.

135. Stephanou, *World Orthodoxy in Crisis*, 142–60.

136. Stephanou, *Sound the Trumpet*, 186–90.

CHAPTER 7

The Wind Blows in Chicago

Fr. Boris Zabrodsky

FR. JOHN MEYENDORFF, FORMER Dean of St. Vladimir's Orthodox Theological Seminary, once quipped, "The Ukrainians are the garbage-pail of Orthodoxy" referring to the colorful history of the Orthodox Church among Ukrainians.[1] However, Ukrainian-American priest Fr. Boris Zabrodsky would not agree with that characterization. Boris was born January 9, 1933 in Lansing, Michigan, to a family with four other siblings. Zabrodsky's mother, Anastasia Kudryk, came with her family to Canada from Ukraine in 1903. His father, Theodore, emigrated from Ukraine to the United States in 1913. Theodore and Anastasia met in Lansing, were married and there raised their two sons and three daughters. Boris was not raised in church as a young child because there was no Ukrainian Orthodox Church in the Lansing area. However, once or twice a year, at Pascha and Christmas, the family would travel ninety miles east to Detroit to attend the Ukrainian Orthodox Church in the Motor City. Zabrodsky reminisced that his mother did her best to teach him the fundamentals of the Orthodox Christian faith and to train him how to pray in the Ukrainian language, which was the only language spoken in their home.[2]

Zabrodsky received his formative education in the Lansing public school system and went on to Michigan State University (MSU) to earn a degree in Metallurgical Engineering. While attending a Pan-Orthodox Students' Association (POSA) meeting at MSU, Boris met Jaraslava Boychuk. They were introduced by Fr. Photios Francis Donahue, pastor of St.

1. Personal conversation of the author with Fr. John Meyendorff, Crestwood, NY, Spring, 1987.

2. Fr. Boris Zabrodsky. 2009. Interview by author. Country Club Hills, Illinois, June 4.

Andrew's, the English language Ukrainian parish. Boris and Slavka, as she is known to her friends, were married in 1956 while both were students.

While a sophomore at MSU Zabrodsky served as the president of POSA. During this time he relates that he received a definite call from God to the priesthood. A group of POSA members were in the home of one of their compatriots in Pontiac, Michigan drinking beer together and were joking around about some of the male members entering the priesthood. Pete Pappas, one of the students, began to play-act the part of a priest and began to chant in Greek and standing he began to circle around Boris continuing to chant and act as if he was swinging a censer, censing Boris. Zabrodsky reflects upon the event by stating:

> I don't know if I "died to self" at that time, and exited into Christ. Something happened. I have read where saints have come to Christ and into the Church by playing the roles of a priest and that is the closest I can come to explaining what happened. . . . I went back seeing things in a different way, I became active in the Church. . . . [R]emember I come from a totally unchurched background, smells and bells don't mean a hoot, the only thing I'm familiar with is Jesus Christ and a relationship in Christ. . . . This is something I got from Fr. Donahue, he was totally Christocentric.[3]

Boris graduated from MSU in 1957 and Slavka went on to earn a degree in Psychology. Fr. Boris commented that the family and friends always said that, "Slavka graduated with honors while it was an honor for Boris to graduate."[4]

Fr. Photios Donahue was the engine behind the formation of the Eastern Orthodox Catechetical Association, the first organization that published and distributed Orthodox catechetical materials in English. On Saturdays student members of POSA at MSU travelled forty miles south to Jackson, Michigan to attend catechetical lectures in English. While there they mimeographed, collated, stapled, and stuffed envelopes of catechetical materials that were then mailed off to parishes. The next Saturday the students returned to Jackson and began the process over again. This work, and the Church's need for it, profoundly affected Zabrodsky spiritually. Boris began to serve in the altar at St. Andrew's and came under the more direct spiritual tutelage of Fr. Photios. Fr. Donahue emphasized frequent confession and communion, which were both unusual practices at that time in

3. Ibid.
4. Ibid.

the Orthodox Churches in United States. Zabrodsky sensed a spiritual call and the need for theological training and left Lansing and studied from 1957–58 at St. Andrew's Ukrainian Orthodox Theological Seminary in Winnipeg, Manitoba, Canada. He returned to Detroit where Slavka, and their children, were living with her parents.

Zabrodsky travelled to New York City and met with the Ukrainian Orthodox Metropolitan Bohdan Spilka who blessed him to serve as a sub-deacon and sent him to Detroit to prepare for ordination to the diaconate and the priesthood. Area priests trained and mentored Zabrodsky in preparation for his ordination. Ordained a deacon in 1959 and later a priest on June 26, 1960 by Archbishop Volodymyr Maletz, Zabrodsky served his first liturgy at St. Mary's Ukrainian Orthodox Cathedral, Slavka's home parish. The newly organized St. Nicholas Ukrainian Orthodox Church, Harvey, Illinois became Fr. Boris' first and only parish. Thirteen attended his first Divine Liturgy and the following Sunday the parish grew to eighteen. For the first two months Fr. Boris served the liturgy in Ukrainian then instituted a second liturgy celebrated in English. Over time attendance at the Ukrainian language liturgy waned until it was finally discontinued and St. Nicholas' worship was conducted in English. Fr. Boris' salary in these early days was $50 a week and St. Nicholas grew to over a hundred parishioners, mostly converts from Roman Catholic and Protestant churches, which was unique at this time. Metropolitan John Theodorovitch once attended a banquet at St. Nicholas where he praised St. Nicholas as a "parish of the future." Unfortunately, this incited many of the local Ukrainian Orthodox communities to become jealous of Fr. Boris and St. Nicholas and some began a concerted effort to steal parishioners from the Harvey church.[5] While St. Nicholas never grew into an overly large Orthodox parish it has over the years produced a large number of men who are presently serving as priests and deacons in many of the Orthodox jurisdictions in the United States. St. Nicholas outgrew its home in Harvey and Fr. Boris and Slavka's family grew to one girl and four boys and in 1976 the parish erected a new church temple in Homewood, Illinois, where it remains today.

During the 1960s and 70s Zabrodsky worked full time as a metallurgical engineer at Wyman-Gordon, a metal-forging company, while also pastoring St. Nicholas Church. Fr. Boris characterizes St. Nicholas, at that time, as a "spiritually alive and active parish."[6] Since Zabrodsky worked a

5. Ibid.
6. Ibid.

full-time job as well as pastoring St. Nicholas, he relied heavily upon lay ministry and initiative. The "tent-making" priest states that he was not influenced by any outside Evangelical or Charismatic teachers or writings. His spirituality was totally formed and sustained from within the Orthodox tradition. One of the laymen at St. Nicholas approached Fr. Boris and inquired about inviting Fr. Eusebius Stephanou to come and address the parish. Zabrodsky had always held a very open policy about having guest priests come and visit his parish. He reflected:

> I have never been afraid of having a priest come in and talk to my people. Because if he is good I feel that people will say he hangs around with good people, and if he is bad it makes me look better the following week. It's a win-win situation![7]

Fr. Eusebius Stephanou, who at the time was living in Fort Wayne, Indiana came and preached at St. Nicholas in 1974. Fr. Boris vaguely remembers Stephanou's initial visit. The Greek-American priest was out-going, confident, and his message was Christ-centered and received warmly by all the members of St. Nicholas. However, Fr. Boris remembers nothing specific about Stephanou other than that Stephanou's preaching definitely added to the parish's spiritual thirst and hunger. That autumn Fr. Stephanou sponsored an Orthodox Charismatic conference in Ann Arbor, Michigan which Fr. Boris and Slavka, with twenty other parishioners of St. Nicholas attended. The Zabrodsky's were not put off or uncomfortable with their experience at this conference. This was, in Fr. Boris' words, "Our maiden voyage into Orthodox Renewal." Yet, they were open to being exposed to other spiritual expressions of the Orthodox Church. What they saw was a part of the Church; it was scriptural and not inconsistent with Orthodoxy so they had no fear. Returning to St. Nicholas, Fr. Boris established a weekly parish prayer group that met in different parishioners' homes. They prayed, sang Scripture choruses and songs that they learned at the conference in Ann Arbor and studied Scripture. For the Zabrodsky's and the parishioners of St. Nicholas it was not so much "Charismatic" Renewal as it was Spiritual Renewal. As a result of the weekly prayer meetings, Fr. Boris stated that those who attended developed

> . . . a greater thirst, . . . a greater awareness of God in their normal lives. . . . [I]n ourselves we began to notice spiritual changes . . . and in others. Give you an example, Margaret. Margaret came

7. Ibid.

because of one of our teenagers invited her. And at one of the first meetings someone told me that Margaret was drunker than a skunk. Well, it didn't bother any of us; she sat there and was quiet. Where better for a drunk to be than at a prayer meeting! She remained with us and later on she converted to Orthodoxy from the Roman Catholic Church. She went to her priest and told him she was converting to Orthodoxy and he proceeded to tell her she was going straight to hell. God has a sense of humor. Pascha was approaching and Margaret was at the midnight service, but she came early and was sitting in a pew and she looks up and there is her former pastor at St. Nicholas. He walked into the sacristy and asked me if I'd hear his confession, and my first reaction, for about five seconds was, do you know what you're asking? And then the answer came right away, well yes, you're here. . . . [S]o Margaret is sitting in the pew and she looks and there is her priest going to confession to an Orthodox priest. She remained with us the rest of her life, she was a great joy.[8]

A parish healing service began to be held on a monthly basis. A testimony of the power of the Spirit relates to the healing of Mrs. Jean Freeman, who attended St. Nicholas.[9] Fr. Boris relates the story that

Jean had been playing volley ball on the Southside of Chicago with her family. . . . [S]he went up to block a shot and came down on her ankle and shattered it. She ended up in surgery, she ended up in a wheel chair, she ended up on crutches and finally with a cane. She was in constant pain. One day we had a board meeting at the rectory . . . and we were sharing what had brought us to St. Nicholas. When we came to Jean she just started to cry, and the women ministered to her. When the meeting was concluded . . . I approached Jean and I said, "You know we have not really had an opportunity to pray." She was scheduled for more surgery because the doctors didn't know what to do . . . so she said "ok" and we went down to the office and we had a prayer. The prayer was five minutes long. I believe God hears and you go directly to Him, without any long ceremonious approach. She shared with me the reason she was crying was that she had had a dream and she was being plagued by a demon of death. She had one daughter . . . twelve years old, and the dream was that she was being suck into this vortex and she was going to die. . . . [I]t was real and it was bothering her 'cause she was going to orphan her daughter and leave her with Bill. And I

8. Ibid.

9. Freeman, "Encountering," 7.

said, "We'll pray for that at the same time, and we're going to pray for healing." So we had an exorcism for the death. In all the prayer didn't last more than five minutes, and it was extemporaneous, it wasn't a book prayer. She went back and joined the people and they took her home. Next morning I'm at the office and I could hardly wait to get on the telephone to call her to find out if she'd had that dream and find out about the healing. I called her, well; she didn't mention the dream whatsoever. She mentioned that she got home and she sat on the sofa for a little bit and she fell asleep, which was very abnormal. In the morning she woke up for the first time without pain, the swelling in her ankle gone down . . . and I wanted to know about the dream, because that was the thing that was an attack on her by a satanic force. She said the dream was gone. The next Sunday she came into church wearing heels. Did that make me a believer? Amen![10]

The parishioners of St. Nicholas were exposed to other elements of the Charismatic Movement by visiting local Roman Catholic Charismatic prayer groups and reading literature as well as meeting other Orthodox participants in the Charismatic Movement. Such Charismatic Orthodox luminaries as Fr. Lazarus Moore, monastic priest, author and translator of several books and member of the Russian Orthodox Church Abroad and Fr. Athanasios Emmert visited St. Nicholas.

The Hieromonk Lazarus Moore

Fr. Lazarus Moore made a very deep impression on Zabrodsky. Even though Fr. Lazarus was the author and translator of several books, Fr. Boris said he never heard him mention these accomplishments.[11] He relates this story:

My entry into this [the charismatic experience] was we had a very spiritual man come into our life; . . . he was on his way from the Himalayan Mountains, where he had spent time, on his way to Australia and he was in Canada and he called me one day and

10. Fr. Boris Zabrodsky. 2009. Interview by author.

11. Moore *St. John Climacus* and *The Psalter* (Brookline, MA: Holy Transfiguration Monastery), from the Greek Septuagint. He also translated from the Russian St. Ignatius Branchninov's *The Arena: An Offering to Contemporary Monasticism.* (Jordanville, NY: Holy Trinity Monastery, 1982). Likewise, Moore wrote a biography of *St. Seraphim of Sarov* (Blanco, Texas: New Sarov Press, 1994) and at least two other booklets entitled, *Sacred Tradition in the Orthodox Church* (Minneapolis: Light & Life, n.d) and *Baptism as Thirty Celebrations.* (Minneapolis: Light & Life, n.d.).

said, "Hey, can I come down and spend some time with you." So
he came down and spent a couple of weeks. I remember one night
I pawned him off on Fr. Howard, and I said, "Take him to the Roman Catholic prayer meeting because I need to make a guinea pig
cage for my daughter tonight because I need to do something with
my children." So off he went and he became friends with Ron Lee,
the spiritual leader of a very large Roman Catholic group. . . . They
made plans the next day to get together and I was the chauffer,
so I took them and their talking about "tongues" and "multiple
tongues." . . . [F]inally they said they're going to go and pray. So
I'm sitting there and they look at me and say, "Aren't you coming
along? . . . So we go and we pray . . . and I was blessed with going
over that threshold and getting over my reluctance that we many
times have. . . . There was a reluctance to surrender.[12]

Fr. Boris further relates that as Fr. Lazarus and Ron Lee were praying they began to pray in tongues, a phenomenon that Fr. Boris heard
many times at the prayer meetings in the homes of his parishioners, but
had not personally experienced. However, as Moore and Lee were praying Zabrodsky also began to pray in tongues, the first time he exercised
this gift. Whereas many Charismatics would claim a distinct and definitive
experience of the baptism of the Holy Spirit, in which speaking in tongues
many times accompanies the experience, Zabrodsky claims never to have
had such an experience, nonetheless he did, from this moment on, practice
the gift of praying in tongues.[13]

Fr. Lazarus' time with the people of St. Nicholas was spiritually formative for Fr. Boris, Slavka and the entire community. Before his departure
he spoke several times to the parish prayer group as well as concelebrate
with Fr. Boris and preach at the Divine Liturgy. Zabrodsky and the people
of St. Nicholas continued to be influenced by Fr. Stephanou through *The
Logos* and through its pages were introduced to the larger Charismatic
Movement in the Roman Catholic and Protestant churches. The impact of
the Charismatic Renewal on St. Nicholas extended beyond experiences of
personal conversion, healing and deliverance. It also effected how Fr. Boris
and the parish celebrated the liturgical services of the Orthodox Church.
Fr. Boris relates that the Renewal brought "joy" and "life" into the services,
which in many cases before had been performed by rote. The congregation
became more physically involved in the liturgy through the lifting of their

12. Fr. Boris Zabrodsky. 2009. Interview by author.
13. Ibid.

hands in worship as well as singing along with the choir. Occasionally non-liturgical hymns and Scripture songs appropriate to the service were also incorporated into the liturgy.

Zabrodsky comments that he was never castigated by any of his brother priests over his or St. Nicholas' involvement in the Charismatic Renewal. Likewise, he was never reprimanded by his bishop. At this time, St. Nicholas was under the authority of Bishop Andrei Kuschak of the Ukrainian Orthodox Church of America. Fr. Boris always informed Bishop Andrei of his attendance at or involvement in any Charismatic conference or gathering.

Born on October 18, 1902 in Swindon, England, Edgar Moore, as Fr. Lazarus was known before his conversion to the Orthodox Church, moved to Alberta, Canada at the age of eighteen. He worked as a ranch hand or "cowboy" as he related to one acquaintance.[14] While in Alberta, Moore sensed a call to missionary work so he returned to England and studied at St. Augustine's in Canterbury, a college for Anglican missionary training. In 1930, Moore was ordained deacon in the Church of England and then a priest in 1931, assigned to missionary work in India, where he travelled and joined "Christa Seva Sangha," an Anglo-Indian religious brotherhood which maintained an ashram in Poona.[15]

Moore's interest in the Orthodox Church led him to travel, in either 1934 or 1935, to Palestine and Mount Athos, the center of Orthodox Christian monasticism, and then to Serbia, where he was received into the Russian Orthodox Church Outside Russia (ROCOR) by Metropolitan Anthony Khrapovitsky. ROCOR's headquartered was centered that time in Sremsky Karlovsky, near Belgrade. Moore made his profession as a monk at Mikovo Monastery, and given the name Lazarus before being ordained a priest in January 1936 by ROCOR Archbishop Feofan.

Fr. Lazarus was assigned to the Russian Ecclesiastical Mission in Jerusalem, where he worked closely with fellow Anglican converts, Abbess Mary Robinson and Mother Mary Sprott, at the Russian Orthodox Convent of St Mary Magdalene located near the Garden of Gethsemane. While there he also taught at the school in Bethany which was operated by the Russian Ecclesiastical Mission. However, following the Arab-Israeli war of 1948, and the formation of the Jewish State of Israel, the new government handed over the properties of the Russian Ecclesiastical Mission to the Soviet Union, effectively severing the connection between the Mission and

14. https://orthodoxwiki.org/Lazarus_(Moore).

15. Winslow, *Christa Seva Sangha*.

ROCOR, which had maintained the property since the fall of Czarist Russia to the Bolsheviks. Fr Lazarus then served as priest to the Russian Orthodox Convent in Ain Karim, in which approximately 100 nuns resided and to the Orthodox Christians throughout the area of the Transjordan.

In 1952, Fr. Lazarus was asked by the leadership of ROCOR to return to India. ROCOR received a request from a group of non-Chalcedonian Syrian Orthodox in Malabar, South India, asking to be reunited to Chalcedonian Orthodoxy, and Moore was assigned to assist in their transition, which never materialized. However, Fr. Lazarus stayed in India for the next twenty years, doing missionary work for the Orthodox Church. During this period, much of his translation work was done and published. While in India this time, he met Mother Gabrielia Papayannis, a Greek Orthodox nun and charismatic personality in her own right, whom he consulted in his translations of the Fathers and of the Psalter.[16]

In 1972, Archimandrite Lazarus was called to Greece, where he contemplated settling; but in 1974, he was called to Australia. In Australia, Archimandrite Lazarus developed contacts with Pentecostalism and the Charismatic movement, which he viewed in a positive light. In this Archimandrite Lazarus' views diverged widely from his ROCOR bishop, leading the Archimandrite to write to his bishop, seeking canonical release. His bishop never replied to the letter, but nonetheless Archimandrite Lazarus transferred to the jurisdiction of the Patriarchate of Antioch, which was somewhat more amenable to the Charismatic Renewal.

Moore was a featured speaker at the Orthodox Charismatic Conferences held in East Lansing, Michigan. There is an anecdotal story told about his attendance at one such conference which was held in a hotel. One of the maids came by his room to clean and change the bed sheets and towels. She knocked but no answer was given. She assumed the room was empty and opened the door. She was frightened by the fact that the room appeared to be on fire, flames were everywhere. She quickly left the room and returned to the front desk to report the fire. The desk manager said that according to the hotel monitoring equipment there was no fire. The maid insisted that she had seen what she had seen and convinced the manager to check out the room. They returned to Moore's room and opened the door. There was no fire, however, Fr. Lazarus was in the corner of the room with his hands uplifted in prayer.

16. Gavrilia, *Mother Gavrilia*.

In 1983, being invited by Fr. Peter Gillquist, then presiding bishop of the Evangelical Orthodox Church (EOC), Archimandrite Lazarus, relocated to California to assist in the incorporation of the communities of the Evangelical Orthodox Church into the canonical Orthodox Church. This missionary endeavor proved to be very successful when the EOC was received into the Orthodox Church by the Antiochian Orthodox Archdiocese in 1987.[17] In 1989, Moore moved to St John's Cathedral in Eagle River, Alaska, a large community original established by the EOC, and continued this work of helping the EOC's communities' integration into canonical Orthodoxy. Shortly before his death, on November 27, 1992, he was visited by a ROCOR priest who reconciled him to ROCOR. Archimandrite Lazarus died from cancer and was buried in the cemetery at St John's Cathedral.

Service Committee for Orthodox Spiritual Renewal (SCOCR) and *Theosis*

Fr. Boris was instrumental in founding the Service Committee for Orthodox Charismatic Renewal (SCOCR). Zabrodsky believed that Stephanou was too combative in the pages of *The Logos* and wanted to take a more positive position towards the Church and hierarchy regarding the Charismatic Renewal. SCOCR launched a monthly magazine entitled *Theosis*. In the first issue, which came out in May 1978, *Theosis* introduced SCOCR to its readers:

> Very early in 1977, the Lord moved several men involved in the Renewal to join hands as a Committee and offer themselves in service to Orthodox charismatics and the Orthodox Church. This is how the Service Committee for Orthodox Charismatic Renewal (SCOCR) first began, the men united to form SCOCR include Father Boris Zabrodsky, pastor of St. Nicholas Orthodox Church in Homewood, Illinois, Father Howard Sloan, also of St. Nicholas, Gregory Gavrilides and Jordan Bajis, who both are members of Holy Trinity Greek Orthodox Church in Lansing, Michigan. Gavrilides and Bajis also serve as coordinators (pastoral leaders) in an ecumenical Christian Community in Lansing-East Lansing, Michigan called The Work of Christ Community.[18] Father Boris Zabrodsky serves as president of the committee. . . . The essen-

17. Gilquist, *Becoming Orthodox.*

18. The Work of Christ Community still exists in East Lansing, Michigan and is led by Greek Orthodox laymen, Gerald Munk. See http://www.workofchrist.com/

tial thrust of SCOCR is service. The Committee does not claim a position of delegated leadership for the Charismatic Renewal in the Orthodox Church, but rather a position of service for those who wish to use it. The stated purpose of SCOCR is "to serve the Charismatic renewal in the Orthodox Church at large, serving in the area of administration, coordination, communication, and in whatever ways the Charismatic Renewal could be fostered within the entire Orthodox Church, not limited to one particular jurisdiction." The actual work of SCOCR is quite varied, including the publication of Theosis, planning conferences, providing information to clergy and lay people in the Church, developing printed and taped materials on aspects of Charismatic Renewal, liaison functions with the official Church as requested, communicating with other charismatic organizations, and numerous other functions. The desire of SCOCR is to faithfully serve its Orthodox brethren and the Orthodox Church. The men comprising the Committee are committed to prayer and unity as they seek to follow the Lord together. The prayers of the faithful are needed and actively solicited. Indeed, the Committee looks forward with excitement to the work ahead, rejoicing in the opportunity to yield to the Holy Spirit as charismatic renewal progresses in the Orthodox Church.[19]

In later years, as the term Charismatic began to carry with it many negative connotations, SCOCR changed its name to The Service Committee for Orthodox Spiritual Renewal (SCOSR).

As one peruses the articles it is clear that the editors of Theosis' chose a more complimentary tone towards the institutional Orthodox Church. While most of the articles in The Logos were penned by Stephanou, Theosis' articles were by a variety of authors, some of who would not identify themselves as Charismatic or Orthodox, for that matter. As a result, Theosis was received with more openness among Orthodox Christians. This can be seen by the numerous names of Orthodox priests and even a few hierarchs who wrote positively about Theosis. The length of Theosis grew shorter and shorter as the years passed. SCOCR not only sponsored Orthodox Charismatic conferences and printed Theosis, they also published a small booklet entitled Orthodox Prayers as well as an edition of The Akathist Hymn to Our Lord Jesus Christ.

In June 1980, Greg Gavrilides, Jordan Bajis, and Demetrius Nicoloudakis, members of the Service Committee took a trip to Europe and the

19. "The Service Committee for Orthodox Charismatic Renewal," Theosis, Vol. 1 No. 1, 5–6.

Middle East "with the purpose of assessing the spiritual climate there and seeing the renewal that is or could be taking place there."[20] Traveling to Brussels they met with European lay leaders of the Renewal and also met with the abbot of the Roman Catholic Monastery of Chevatongne. They were met by Steve Clark, a lay leader in the Charismatic Renewal in the Catholic Church back in the United States, who travelled with them to Constantinople. There they met with His Holiness, Patriarch Demetrios, the Ecumenical Patriarch, presenting him with bound copies of *Theosis* and discussing with him the issue of spiritual renewal in the Orthodox Church. While in Constantinople they toured the Church of Agia Sophia.

From Turkey they flew to Beirut, Lebanon, where they met with Archbishop Georges Khodre of Mount Lebanon, who himself was an early leader in the Orthodox Youth Movement, a spiritual renewal movement among students in the Patriarchate of Antioch. They latter travelled to Cairo and then to Athens, meeting with Orthodox hierarchs, theologians and lay leaders and informing them of the work of renewal in the Church in America and the ministry of SCOCR.[21]

The last issue of *Theosis* was released September 1987 with the lead article entitled, "Charism and Institution."[22] The last two pages featured letters from readers. One readers letter was so typical of many Orthodox Christians' misunderstanding of the Charismatic Renewal in the Orthodox Church, "Dear Editor, Orthodox and Charismatic are mutually exclusive terms. Please to not send your Protestant periodical to me. Alexis S. San Diego, California." Editor Gerald Munk responded by writing,

> The term "charismatic" simply means inspired by the Holy Spirit. It is often used to refer to the miraculous gifts of the Spirit poured out upon the Apostles and others in the days following the ascension of Jesus Christ into heaven: gifts of knowledge, supernatural healing, speaking in unknown languages, prophecy and more. These same gifts can be seen emerging again and again throughout the extensive history of the Orthodox Church (see previous articles on the charismatic gifts). They are in no way a modern or Protestant phenomenon. To say that Orthodox and charismatic are mutually exclusive terms reveals a lack of honor and appreciation for the gifts God has given His bride, His people, His Church.

20. "Orthodoxy, Renewal and the Middle East: Service Committee Report on Trip to the Middle East." *Theosis*, November 1980, 5–8.

21. Ibid.

22. Jim Scully, "Charism and Institution," *Theosis*, September 1987, 1–5.

One can always debate appropriate application of spiritual gifts in the Church. We could also criticize the work and personal lives of certain "charismatic" ministers (and there has been no lack of that in recent months). It would also be proper to note that some teaching and some practice of some "charismatic" group is not in harmony with Orthodoxy. But, to say that Orthodox (correct belief) and charismatic (spiritual gifts) are mutually exclusive, is just wrong! The gifts of the Holy Spirit belong to the Church and should be experienced regularly in Her life. This is the clear message of Holy scripture; this is the teaching of the church fathers; this is the consistent witness of history; and this is the clear position of our publication. For this I make no apology.

These were the last words of the last issue of *Theosis* magazine. Very appropriate it would seem.

CHAPTER 8

The Wind of the Spirit on the Canadian Plains

Fr. Orest Olekshy

FR. EUSEBIUS STEPHANOU'S CHARISMATIC ministry was far reaching. Not only did it span the United States, Greece, and Kenya, but also went north of the border into Canada. As early as 1973 Stephanou made forays into Canada speaking in several provinces, from Ontario to Manitoba and Saskatchewan. In March 1973, after preaching and leading a Lenten Retreat in Winnipeg, Manitoba, Fr. Eusebius traveled west to Saskatoon, Saskatchewan and addressed a group of Ukrainian Orthodox Christians who were meeting at the Peter Moghila Center on the campus of the University of Saskatchewan. A new parish of the Ukrainian Orthodox Church of Canada, All Saints, was meeting at the Moghila Center and a young student, Martin Zip, had read several copies of *The Logos* and was impressed with what he read. At a meeting of the students with their priest, Fr. Orest Olekshy, Zip suggested that the new parish sponsor some lectures, in order to draw new people to the congregation. It was suggested to have a special speaker following the Vespers of the Sunday of Orthodoxy, which in 1973 fell on March 19. Zip suggested that they invite Stephanou and based upon his recommendation Olekshy and the group agreed. They contacted Stephanou and he informed them that he was committed to speak at the Sunday of Orthodoxy Vespers at St. George Romanian Orthodox Church in Winnipeg but that he could come the next day and speak on Monday for a gathering at the Moghila Center.[1] This was agreeable to the group. On Monday, March 20, 1973, Fr. Orest Olekshy and a delegation from All

---

1. "Where the Word of Awakening is Being Carried." *The Logos*, 5, no. 2, 21.

Saints greeted Fr. Stephanou at the airport. When Stephanou disembarked from the plane, he greeted them with a hearty "Praise the Lord"; the priest Orest Olekshy's life, and many of those of All Saints Ukrainian Orthodox Church, would never be the same.[2]

Orest Olekshy was born on April 11, 1939, in Edmonton, Alberta, Canada to Stefan and Evdokia (Fhur) Olekshy. Both Orest's paternal and maternal grandparents were pioneers on the plains of Alberta. His maternal grandparents, Theodore and Anna Fhur, were the first Ukrainians to own land in Alberta. Theodore Fhur's family were part of Russian Tsarina Catherine the Great's program to relocate ethnic Germans in Ukraine. The Fhurs fully assimilated into their adopted Ukrainian culture.[3]

The borderlands of Germany, Poland, and Ukraine were settled with thousands of Uniates. Historically Orthodox Christians, over the years Roman Catholic political leaders and missionaries sought to convert them to Roman Catholicism and met with little success. As a result, Rome took a different tack by creating a "union" or "unia" between the Roman Catholic Church and the Orthodox allowing them to retain their liturgical, hymnographic, and religious traditions while requiring them to swear allegiance to the Pope of Rome; hence the term Uniates. In many cases, however, after the union was agreed upon, the more politically and materially powerful Roman Catholic Church foisted certain "Latin" customs upon the Uniates. The Uniates became "second-class" Catholics to their Latin-Rite comrades and despised as renegades and traitors by the Orthodox. While a Uniate, Theodore Fhur was educated for his time and social position and he was aware of the truth about the relationship between the Uniates and the Roman Catholic Church. An outspoken young man, Fhur attempted to convince his Uniate neighbors that they should return to the Orthodox Church. This finally led to Fhur's encounter with the local authorities. As a result, he packed up his wife, children and mother and fled Ukraine for Canada. When Fhur arrived in the Leduke/Edmonton area of Canada he immediately began to do what had gotten him in trouble in the old country. He invited his neighbors to classes at which he taught them about the history and faith of the Orthodox Church and converted them from the Uniate Catholic Church to Orthodoxy. Hundreds and thousands of Uniates

2. Vasil Szalasznyz. 2009. Interview by author. Saskatoon, Saskatchewan, Canada. July 7.

3. Orest Olekshy. 2009. Interview by author. Melville, Saskatchewan, Canada. June 27.

came to the Orthodox Church through Fhur's teaching ministry. He erected a small chapel on his property and the Orthodox clergy who travelled to western Canada ministered in Fhur's chapel. Because he was such a spiritual and well-respected man many Orthodox bishops sought to ordain him as a deacon or priest but in every case he refused. Yet he continued to hold weekly services in the chapel, reading the liturgy and the gospel, baptizing the babies in the community and awaiting the visit of an Orthodox bishop or priest to seal the marriages and consecrate the graves of the Orthodox departed. However, when the closest Uniate community of Nisku, which was about a mile from Fhur's chapel, all converted to Orthodoxy, he closed his chapel and those who worshipped with him began to attend the now Orthodox Church at Nisku. In a personal interview Fr. Orest relates an incident from his mother's childhood.[4]

> It came to the place that grandfather decided to close down his chapel now that they had the buildings of the Catholic parish, and my mother remembered as a girl St. Arseny[5] giving her an icon to carry, and all the Orthodox that had already been converted in years prior to that in my grandfather's chapel started walking with banners and crosses and icons and the Catholics who were ready to get converted left their church with banners and crosses . . . and my mother often said she could not understand why it was such a powerful thing but she said she just thought that this was a historical event, . . . she knew it. And they met in the middle of the field and all she could remember was that scriptures were read and then everyone started crying and embracing and from that point where they met they all continued back to the Catholic church and that established a much larger community which is still St. Mary's in Nisku.[6]

Olekshy's father Stephan was from the same village in Ukraine from which the Fhur's came and like the Fhurs when they came to Canada were Uniates. However, at the age of fourteen Stephan was excommunicated from the Uniate Church. Young Stephan loved to read and copies of the

4. Ibid.

5. Applegate, "The Orthodox Church Process," 1–34. St. Arseny (Chagovstov), 1866–1945, established a monastery in Canada and a theological school in Swifton. He was shot by a Catholic layman while serving liturgy in Canorra, which resulted in poor health, so he relocated to St. Tikhon's Monastery in PA and died there. St. Tikhon (Bellavin), later Patriarch of Moscow, stayed at the Fhur's home and baby-sat Fr. Olekshy's mother Evdokia and Aunt Anastasia while their parents attended to farming chores.

6. Orest Olekshy. 2009. Interview by author.

early Ukrainian nationalist magazines such as *The Ukrainian Voice* that was published in Winnipeg by an Orthodox priest, came into his possession. The *Ukrainian Voice* was stridently anti-Catholic and constantly called for the Ukrainian Uniates to return to the Orthodox Church. Most of Stephan's neighbors were illiterate and interested in any news would gather at the Olekshy house in the evening to listen to Stephan read from the latest issue of the *Ukrainian Voice*. The Uniate priest got wind of Stefan's activities and when the young boy went to church to confession the priest severely scolded him. Stefan questioned the priest asking him what was sinful about reading historical facts, to which the priest responded by forbidding Stefan to read these newspapers again. When Stefan questioned the priest's authority to forbid him to read certain newspapers the priest then issued a ban of excommunication barring Stefan from receiving Holy Communion in the church. Stefan never returned to the Uniate Church after that point and refrained from receiving communion until he married Evdokia Fhur in the Russian Orthodox Church that she attended. Evdokia was very influential in establishing the first Ukrainian Orthodox Church in her community. The Russian Orthodox Church she attended conducted all of its services in Church Slavonic which she did not understand. As a result, she gathered together a group of her Ukrainian compatriots who desired to worship and hear the Scriptures read in her native language. Unfortunately, this added one more point of tension to an already contentious situation in the Fhur–Olekshy family which was made up of Uniate Ukrainian Catholics and Russian Orthodox who refused to recognize the historical separate existence of the Ukrainian people apart from Russia, and the division among the Russians who were loyal to the Patriarch of Moscow (and thought to be collaborators with the Communists) and the Russian Church in exile (rabidly anti-Communist). It made for interesting family reunions.[7]

Orest Olekshy was very active in the Orthodox Church from his youth. His family gathered for prayers at the family icon corner and read the Scriptures together every day. The local priest served several parishes and only could get to the Olekshy's parish once a month. On the off weeks Orest's father drove the family to Edmonton to St. John's Cathedral for liturgy. If the roads were bad because of foul weather, on Saturdays Stefan would drag the car by tractor two miles through muddy roads and leave the car there close to a major road that was paved. On Sunday morning, after completing the farm chores, the family would travel the two miles

7. Ibid.

by tractor to the car and then complete the trip to church in Edmonton. If they were unable to attend the liturgy at church they would still assemble at home and read the Epistle and Gospel lessons, on which his father would then comment, pray through the service, and sing hymns. This also took place on the special feast days throughout the Church Year. In this way Olekshy's spirituality was soundly formed by a living Orthodox Christian faith practiced at Church and home. Young Olekshy received his foundational education in the Calmar, Alberta public school system.[8]

From his earliest recollections Orest wanted to be a priest. While his parents happily supported his call at the same time they wanted him to be properly prepared. Upon his graduation from high school in 1958, he wanted to go directly to the seminary to study. However, his parents forbade him and wanted him to have a break for at least a year before entering seminary. Orest however was not totally unfamiliar with seminary life. The two summers previous to his graduation he attended intensive six-week courses on Ukrainian language at the seminary. Therefore, Orest worked in a local bank for the following year and then went off to seminary at St. Andrew's College in Winnipeg, Manitoba.[9]

Olekshy's experience at St. Andrew was not positive. While there he encountered seminarians whose energies were consumed with Ukrainian nationalism and radical politics. Other seminarians entertained prostitutes in their dorm rooms. Even though many of these seminarians attended all the Church services they lacked any true Christian spirituality. Olekshy would have left the seminary except for one student, Fr. Myron Klysh, who befriended Orest and constantly reminded him that he was at St. Andrew's to fulfill the call that the Lord had place upon him and not to look at others and their behavior, scandalous though it may be. Ironically, from the outset Olekshy was sure that he would be expelled from the seminary because the administration would quickly discern that he did not have the moral fiber needed to qualify for a priestly vocation. His expectations that the seminary would be filled with holy people who would look down upon him for his worldliness proved to be false and it was difficult for him to adjust to the reality he encountered. Never had Olekshy faced such hypocrisy in his youth.[10]

8. Ibid.

9. Ibid.

10. Ibid.

This blew my mind! Because I was so sure and I told all of my friends, I'm probably going to be back because there is no way this place when they find out who I am they're going to realize that I am not material to be a priest and I'm probably going to get kicked out. And my only fear was how are my parents going to handle that, but I so desperately wanted that but I just didn't think I was worthy and expecting therefore to have to live with very holy, holy people and how am I going to become holy enough to even live there, and your first week you're seeing things that . . . —it's like catching your mother with some lover behind your father— . . . I didn't know what hit me. Then I got angry . . . and first there was denial and then there was anger and then I was leaving and I didn't know how to tell my parents. Because I thought, my God, they'll leave the Church. And Klysh somehow saw my dilemma and put his arm around me, "What's going on?" And I started crying and told him and he said, "You're not here to observe others, you're here to get to know Christ, and focus on your studies. Never mind what somebody else is doing." And I though what the hell are you talking about, I'm not in a bar, I'm at seminary! But he kept harping at me and gently and gently . . . and when I'd get angry over other things, he would father me. . . . I thought I needed so much growing. . . . I'd never experienced that much hypocrisy in my Christian upbringing.[11]

Olekshy completed his studies at St. Andrew's and graduated in 1964. He continued to work at St. Andrew's, lived on campus, and attended further classes at the University of Winnipeg. While at St. Andrew's, Myron Kylsh introduced Orest to Oksana Onufrychuk. Onufrychuk, was from a Ukrainian family of the intelligentsia who fled from the Bolsheviks to Canada. The Communists sought to execute the more educated Ukrainians and the Onufrychuk's fled in wagons covered by hay until they reached a train by which they would be spirited out of the country to Germany. American army intelligence received wrong information that the train carried ammunition and therefore bombed the train. Oksana's father, fearing for the child's life, bundled her up and reasoned that if he threw the child from the train she would survive and be found by someone and if he survived then he would find her. The remaining Onufrychuk's jumped off the train as did fellow travelers Boris Yakokevitch, later consecrated a bishop of the Ukrainian Orthodox Church of Canada, and Mystslav Skrypnik, later Ukrainian

11. Ibid.

Orthodox Patriarch of Kiev. Unfortunately, Yakokevitch's wife and daughter perished in the train before they were able to jump to safety.[12]

When Olekshy met Oksana Onufrychuk, she was studying interior design and a highly trained opera singer. At the time Orest asked her to marry him she was in the process of planning a trip to Europe where she was to make her opera debut in Milan, Italy. Realizing that interior design might not be the best career for the wife of a priest she changed her major to library science. On September 4, 1964, they were married and Orest worked for the youth department of the Ukrainian Orthodox Church of Canada (UOCC) which took him across Canada. At the time two feuding groups were vying for power of the UOCC; the newly immigrant Ukrainians who considered themselves well educated and refined and the older Ukrainians who had been in Canada since the turn of the century and were from peasant stock. These Ukrainian factions also cut along political lines and caused great stress in the UOCC, demanding priests to serve them who also shared their same political views. The leadership of UOCC believed that Olekshy could somehow bridge these factions. Olekshy, who considered himself a "prairie boy" from Alberta, found himself in the hotbed of this rivalry in the eastern provinces. While visiting in Toronto a group of Ukrainian leaders told Olekshy that they would sit around him and protect him, and the local police had been alerted, because they had been told that there was a death threat issued for Olekshy by one of the other Ukrainian political factions. Olekshy sought to bridge the gap and used his own family situation as an example. He was a prairie Ukrainian of the peasant stock whose family had come early to Canada while his wife Oksana had been a part of the more recent immigration. They were happy together and the different factions could be also and for a time Olekshy saw results in his work.[13]

Ordained a deacon and then priest in 1965 by Metropolitan Ilarion Ohienko, Ohienko, influenced Olekshy in a profound manner. A famous Ukrainian philologist and scholar, Ohienko was the minister of education at the first attempt of Ukrainian independence after the fall of Czarist Russia. He translated all of the Russian Orthodox liturgical texts into modern Ukrainian for the new nation and because of his proficiency in classical languages the British Bible Society commissioned Ohienko to translate the Bible into modern Ukrainian. With the fall of Ukraine to the Communists he fled and the Orthodox Church of Constantinople through the Orthodox

12. Ibid.
13. Ibid.

Church of Poland tapped Ohienko and he was ordained, within a span of two weeks, deacon, priest, and then bishop. The strong political faction of the UOCC brought him to Canada hoping that his reputation would help them solidify their power in the Church. Instead Ohienko fought them to establish true spiritual order in the Church and won. He set the UOCC in order liturgically and organizationally and brought it into conformity with the spiritual traditions of the wider Orthodox Church. Ohienko believed that the only way this could be done was to bring the UOCC under the episcopal leadership of the Patriarchate of Constantinople.[14]

Olekshy served as Ohienko's subdeacon and deacon and became quite close to him. Olekshy relates that in the later years of Ohienko's life, at a time when he was ill, he was sitting with him in his hospital room in the early morning hours reading an Orthodox Youth magazine published by the U.S. Metropolia in the English language.[15] The ailing Metropolitan woke up in the middle of the might from sleep and asked his room attendant what he was reading. Olekshy replied that he was reading a magazine. The Metropolitan inquired what kind of magazine to which Olekshy replied a religious magazine. Again, the aged bishop asked what sort of religion to which young Olekshy replied he was reading an article by Alexander Schmemann. When Ohienko heard this, he suggested that Olekshy read everything by Schmemann he could. The Metropolitan went on to relate that Schmemann had been one of his best students, and an outstanding man and that Olekshy would learn much from his writings. Then Olekshy questioned the Metropolitan, "Does it matter if I am reading it in English?" To which the aging hierarch responded, "We fell a little too much in love with the Ukrainian language. I think we've harmed ourselves."[16]

Eventually Fr. Orest was assigned to the Ukrainian Orthodox Cathedral in Winnipeg where he proceeded to get himself into trouble. The Ukrainian Orthodox Church of Canada (UOCC) at that time was mired down in Ukrainian nationalism. The Church centered much more on the preservation and perpetuation of the Ukrainian language and culture and the Orthodox Christian faith was secondary. Olekshy was well aware of the

14. Ibid.

15. Stokoe and Kishkosky, *Orthodox Christians*, 55–67. The Metropolia was the name of the old Russian Orthodox Greek Catholic Church in America which was left without foreign oversight by the Moscow Patriarchate after the fall of Russia to the Bolsheviks in 1917. In 1970, the Metropolia was given autocephaly (independence) from the Moscow Patriarchate and renamed The Orthodox Church in America.

16. Orest Olekshy. 2009. Interview by author.

spiritual malaise in the UOCC that resulted from this emphasis and was willing to discuss his concerns with those who wanted to talk. However, the senior priest at the Cathedral was not of the same frame of mind and refused to entertain any conversation regarding the need for spiritual renewal in the UOCC. A small group in the Cathedral challenged Olekshy to introduce English into the Liturgy by simply presenting a short two or three-minute homily in English. The parish board president was a judge and the secretary was a world-famous geneticist and they were convinced that something had to be done in order to bring change to the UOCC. However, the more recent immigrants were violently against any use of any other language in the Liturgy than Ukrainian and as a result of their protests Olekshy resigned as priest at the Cathedral.

Olekshy's reputation spread and he was contacted by the leaders of an eleven-point parish in Willingdon, Alberta who needed a priest and was open to introducing English into the Liturgy.[17] Therefore in 1968 Olekshy and his wife Oksana left Winnipeg and headed west to Orest's home province of Alberta. While in Willingdon the Olekshy's welcomed their first and only child Ilaria. Olekshy served the Willingdon parishes for three years when All Saints UOCC parish in Saskatoon, Saskatchewan contacted him. The people of All Saints decided that the sermon at the Sunday Divine Liturgy was to be in English and with Fr. Orest's history they felt he was the man to be their priest.

In 1971, the Olekshy's were transferred to Saskatoon to pastor All Saints Ukrainian Orthodox Church. All Saints met in the Peter Moghila Center on the campus of the University of Saskatchewan. Built with funds donated from the UOCC, the Moghila Center served as a dorm and student center for Ukrainian Orthodox students studying at the University. The center had a wing for female students and a wing for male students separated by a large common room. At the end of the common room was the altar area of All Saints parish. A curtain covered the iconostasis during the week. Part of Fr. Orest's ministry at All Saints was to interact with the

17. There are hundreds of Orthodox parish communities scattered throughout rural Canada. Because of the younger generations relocating to the cities and leaving the rural communities, many smaller Orthodox parishes are without full-time priests. Therefore, many priests will serve many more than one parish and travel from community to community serving Liturgy at a different parish each week. In some cases, parishes will only hold Liturgy in their building once or twice a year, usually on the parish feast day. In this case Fr. Orest was responsible for eleven different parish communities scattered around the Willingdon, Alberta area.

students and many times he would come and visit with the students in the common area and talk about whatever came up in conversation. Several professors and students invited Fr. Orest and Oksana to dinner one evening and during the course of the meal raised a very serious question; does the Orthodox Faith really contained anything that was relevant to their lives or was the church only a social club. They informed him that if there was no relevance of Orthodoxy to their everyday lives then they were leaving the church. If, however, there was something relevant then they wanted to study the Orthodox faith and find out how to apply it to their lives. Fr. Orest was overjoyed by their desire to study, learn and truly encounter the faith. It was from these sorts of informal conversations that a weekly Bible study group developed in the Olekshy's home in addition to the Divine Liturgy held in the center on Sundays.

Olekshy's home Bible studies were not well received by all the members of All Saints. Since the study was held in the Olekshy home, instead of the Moghila Center, some suspected the purpose of the meeting. The new Ukrainian immigrants complained that he was not teaching classes in Ukrainian history, language, or culture. Others investigated Olekshy's background and believed that his mother was Russian and accused him of being a closet Russian, and therefore a Soviet Communist sympathizer, which played into all the fears and prejudices of the newer Ukrainian immigrants. However, in spite of these complaints the Bible studies continued and grew, attended by some of the "cream" of the young Ukrainian intellectuals and future leaders.[18]

Stephanou Visits Canada

During Great Lent, 1973, it was suggested by members of All Saints, who ironically were opposed to the weekly Bible studies, that Fr. Orest invite a special speaker to come and address the members of All Saints, many who considered themselves intellectuals. Martin Zip, a student, who was aware of Fr. Eusebius Stephanou through reading *The Logos*, suggested

18. Telephone conversation with the author on July 20, 2009, Fr. Orest Olekshy stated that some of the more prominent members who attended the weekly Bible studies were Yars Lozowchuk, well-known Canadian sociologist and his wife Olenka, Gerald Luciuk, an agriculturalist for the Canadian government, John Styrnik, Crown Prosecutor in Prince Albert, Raya Lewicki, Kathy Daneluk, Vasil Szalasznyj, Betty Gulatzan, Martin Zip, and Barbara Kolabab (wife of OCA priest Philip Ericson) who provided guitar accompaniment for the meetings.

that the Greek priest be invited to come and speak on some informative subject. Neither Olekshy nor any of the others were aware of Stephanou, other than his impressive academic credentials and experience, but agreed to invite him based solely on Martin Zip's recommendation.[19] Olekshy, reflecting on this, says:

> So, we got all excited, we're bringing in this intelligent guy who's going to really flatter us by giving us a mini thesis, and make us all feel very good about ourselves, we didn't understand it but we were there.[20]

Preparations were made for the event, the Greek Orthodox were invited as well as Anglicans and other prominent ecumenical dignitaries.

Stephanou arrived in Saskatoon on March 20, 1973. Fr. Olekshy, Martin Zip and Yars Lozowchuk met Stephanou at the airport and immediately Fr. Orest was perplexed by the visiting priest's behavior:

> . . . we see this monk-looking guy coming off the plane, the plane parks out on the runway, and he gets off and he goes "Praise the Lord!" [loudly] And we looked at each other, "Oh my God, was he drinking?" He comes into the airport and starts carrying on like a typical charismatic, well here we are, nice little farm Orthodox boys and, oh, what is this?[21]

Olekshy, Zip and Lozowchuk took Fr. Stephanou out to lunch in the hope that they might be able to figure out the odd behavior of their guest from the United States and if need be cancel the evening's event! Once in the restaurant Olekshy relates that Stephanou said, "Well, Fr. Orest you're the priest here, what do you want me to do tonight?" To which Fr. Orest replied, "Just give a talk." Stephanou quipped, "What kind of a talk? Do you want me to ask God to open the heavens and send the angels down, or do you want just a boring little talk?" Olekshy thought to himself,

> What did he just say? I was sitting there and looking at these guys, and I'm looking at Martin like, "Who did you invite? You said you know his writings, you should have known this about him! But, you know, it was too late." And I said [to Stephanou], "Well, maybe, kind of a little bit of both."[22]

19. Orest Olekshy. 2009. Interview by author.
20. Ibid.
21. Ibid.
22. Ibid.

Fr. Olekshy brought Fr. Stephanou to his home where Oksana had prepared supper. After eating Fr. Orest excused himself to go and prepare things at the church for the evening meeting. Approximately two hours later he returned to pick up his wife and Fr. Stephanou. Once in the house, Oksana motioned for her husband to come into the bedroom. In the bedroom, she expressed great concern over what Fr. Stephanou had mentioned would be a part of the evening's program: "he's talking about an altar call," she said. "My faith is very personal; I'm not going make some kind of idiot of myself." Fr. Orest responded, "What do you mean altar call, we don't have altar calls in the Orthodox Church." Oksana said, "Well he's talking about an altar call and he's talking about weird things." "Well how weird?" Fr. Orest replied. "Well, I don't know they're kind of interesting but weird," she responded. However, it was only a half hour before the service and Fr. Orest was very nervous. The Moghila Center was packed when they arrived. The diverse crowd included professors and students from the university, members of other Orthodox parishes, as well a large contingency of hippie-type Jesus People, who had somehow heard about the meeting. When Oksana arrived at the center she took Stephanou's hat, coat, and suitcase and, wary of what might take place, defensively anchored herself in a back corner. Stephanou's address was simple. Olekshy remembers the theme,

> You know, you cheer for your hockey team, your football team, when have you cheered for Christ, your Lord and Savior? What's your personal relationship? Yeah, maybe your godparents said they believe in Christ, do you? Have you ever said it? . . . And he said, "We're going to have an altar call, and it's time that we actually said to him, thank you for your love and we love you. And what we're going to do is the first part of the baptism service where we renounce Satan and confess Jesus. So who's prepared this evening to do that?" And I am totally, I am ready to faint, I'm so scared. What is he doing? And I hear a crash at the back and I looked and this chair fell over and my wife is running, crawling over people. People from all over, crawling all over each other, because it was so packed out, trying to get to the front. And I thought, I must be having a nightmare. This does not happen. And all kinds of people, university professors, the head engineer of Sinusaskatoon, who were fanatic Ukrainians, who were only in the church, and they told me, because it's a Ukrainian organization, where we can promote the Ukrainian nationalism, they're all responding! And I knew I wanted to respond, but you know, priests don't do this, but in the end I had to go up. So I was in [among] all these people lined

up [in front] . . . of him and I was one of the last ones and the [parish] president was a psychologist who was just beet red with anger, and he was in the first row. And I squeezed in right in front of him facing Stephanou. So, Stephanou says, "First we're going to turn around and we're going to renounce Satan and in Orthodox tradition we're going to spit at him. And I mean spit!" I turned around, I'm touching my president's nose, who's furious, and I knew he was furious, and Stephanou is screaming, "Spit. Spit! And then turn around." And he led us into confessing Christ as our Lord and God and Savior. And people were stumbling away as if they got drunk. I didn't know what was happening. Why were people so excited? Well, why didn't I do this, it would've been neat, but you know [I was] very confused. Then he, Stephanou, comes along and he says, "Orest, when we were having supper, I think your wife has demonic influence." He says, "When the stuff she went through, I think her headaches and things are caused by that. She was a newborn infant, the war was on, there was shooting and screaming, running . . . and her parents probably could not protect her, and I believe something happened at that time, Satan is always ready to enter a new, fresh vessel and I think we should have prayers." Well I said, "Does she want prayers?" And he said, "I'm going to talk to her." Well he went to her, and she's marching right behind him and he said, "Let's go into the altar area." By this time it was coffee break and that whole group; you had your charismatics that came there, these Jesus People that were just elated, all the people who went up for the altar call were just . . . wow, and the others were, "What the hell is this? This [is] some kind of top-notch, psychological brain washing, this is hypnotism!" Our president, who was a psychiatrist, is screaming this and his brother-in-law, the engineer of city hall, was one that ran up, he's [his brother the psychiatrist] trying to deprogram them. Then we're [Stephanou, Oksana, and Fr. Orest] praying and of course he's not using an Orthodox book, so I can't help or follow or anything and he's doing something, pleading some kind of blood of Jesus on Oksana and us all, and while we're praying and I'm thinking, "What is this, uh, what do I know?" . . . so I thought it was Orthodox. And he's just praying, talking to Satan, saying that he has no right to be messing up Oksana's life and I'm still kind of like, why are you degrading my wife, she's this beautiful, spiritual person, way more spiritual than I ever will be. I mean what are you talking about, demons and Satan? And suddenly Oksana started throwing up and going through all kinds of, almost convulsions, and at that point I knew something was happening that was not human; it was supernatural and I really sensed that it was divine, of God. And that blew my mind! And that was my initiation, apart from having to go to that altar call. That was the sign. Then there was another one that followed shortly after. Oksana was always nagging me to stop smoking and the next day when we got up and I had to drive Oksana around to the university to work, she was kind of like giddy . . . and as we were leaving the house and I was grabbing his [Stephanou's] bags and my cigarettes were lying on the coffee table and he said, "By the way Father, those are not good for you. I'm going to pray that God takes that away." . . . But not in any way connecting it with any kind of reality that might take place. So, I drove him to the airport and got him off, and then, wow, I've got to go and figure out what all happened here last night. Half of these people that went up for this altar call, piled into our house, and we sat up till about 3 and he [Stephanou] was trying to get us to sing and pray spontaneously, well there was no way you could hold a gun to our head and do these things. But I got him off to airport and my first thought was, oh, I just can't wait to have a cigarette. So, I dashed home, flopped down on the chesterfield[23] and grabbed the cigarettes, lit one up, and it was like sticking manure in my mouth. And I thought what the heck? My first thought was, Oksana, what do you think you're doing, you can't doctor up my cigarettes and cause me to stop. . . . I'll stop when I feel like stopping. So, I jumped in the car, drove down to the corner store, grabbed a package, got into the car and lit one up, and the same thing, I almost threw up. And it hit me that God did something. And I thought, God you're so big, you can also be this petty, this small . . . ? But driving home, I thought, why are those trees all so different and why is this whole city . . . like it was more vibrant . . . it was like I went on a holiday to the Riviera or someplace, it wasn't my city, it wasn't my street, it was and it wasn't. All of this was going on and at that point I realized something had happened and that God was so real that he probably was interested in my health and smoking cigarettes and that just blew me apart. So that was kind of the beginning.[24]

23. A British expression used by Canadians of an older generation, refers to a couch or sofa.

24. Orest Olekshy. 2009. Interview by author.

Results of Charismatic Renewal in Saskatoon

The results of that special service at the Moghila Center were varied. Many people at All Saints were confused and it led to a major split in the parish. Olekshy believes that much of the problem lay with the spiritually renewed members of All Saints, because they kept to themselves and did not speak openly of their charismatic experiences with other members of the parish and seek to explain to them their newfound fervency of faith in Christ. As a result, many in the parish felt that the charismatics were secretive and cliquish, which isolated them from each other.[25] The Ukrainian national-ists at All Saints felt that those who were spiritually renewed were psycho-logically duped and therefore tried to deprogram them, which led to even greater confusion. Those renewed knew they had experienced something deep and meaningful while their fellow parishioners were telling them it was wrong and the product of mass hypnotism. During this Fr. Orest made no attempt to defend or explain what had taken place.

The weekly study group developed into a charismatic prayer group. At Oksana Olekshy's suggestion the weekly prayer group began using the Bill Gaither Trio's album *Alleluia* as a guide for teach them how to sing and worship. Each week the album was put on the player and the group would sing along until the entire recording was finished. The group continued to meet while opposition continued to mount among the members of All Saints. Fr. Olekshy's concern for the welfare of the members of the prayer group increased and he sought outside advice. He served on a committee with a woman, who was preparing to become the first ordained Anglican clergyperson in Saskatoon, which Olekshy thought quite strange. None-theless, he approached her and asked her if she had ever heard of "charis-matics." She replied that she was familiar with a local Anglican cardiologist involved in the Charismatic Movement, Dr. John Merriman and his wife, Hope. Fr. Orest went immediately to the hospital, located Dr. Merriman's office and asked to speak with him. Merriman brought Olekshy into his office and asked him, "Are you here to talk about medicine or to talk about our Lord and Savior Jesus Christ?" Olekshy replied sheepishly, "Well, I guess about the Lord."[26] Olekshy began to weep and related how confused he was about the recent events at All Saints and stated that he needed help and guidance. Merriman grabbed the phone, called his wife, and

25. Ibid.
26. Ibid.

told her to expect an Orthodox priest and his wife for dinner. Fr. Orest and Oksana's dinner with the Merriman's went a long way to dispel the confusion. The couples talked at length about their mutual charismatic experience and the Merriman's assured the Olekshy's and embraced them warmly. Dr. Merriman informed them of the upcoming visit of Fr. Dennis and Rita Bennett, who were being brought to Saskatoon by two Anglican parishes, and encouraged them to attend. Ironically, the Merriman's lived next door to the president of All Saints' parish council, the psychiatrist. Dr. Merriman informed them that his neighbor thought he was a "crackpot" because of his involvement in the Charismatic Movement. In the future, in order to avoid any confrontation with All Saints' parish council president, whenever the Olekshy's visited the Merriman's they snuck down the back alley and entered their house by the back entrance.

The Bennett's arrived in Saskatoon and the Olekshy's attended their presentations as well as dinned with them at the Merriman's home. These opportunities helped answer many more of the questions that Fr. Orest and Oksana had regarding the charismatic life and how they should handle matters at All Saints. During one of the Bennett's talks, Fr. Orest and Oksana went forward for prayer. The local Pentecostal ministers responded immediately and laid hands on Fr. Orest and prayed in typical Pentecostal fashion, massaging his shoulders and praying loudly, which made him very uncomfortable. Rita Bennett however, saw his predicament and came to his rescue, shooing the Pentecostal ministers away from Fr. Orest, embracing him and assuring him of God's love for him. Both Fr. Orest and Oksana received the gift of praying in tongues that evening.

The situation at All Saints parish continued to deteriorate. The *Ukrainian Voice*, the same newspaper that had gotten Olekshy's father into trouble as a teenage boy, splashed headlines across its cover, "Olekshy in Saskatoon Invites Moscow Agent Who Rides into His Church on a Trojan Horse to Destroy the Ukrainian Culture." As a result, those who opposed spiritual renewal at All Saints convinced the central church authorities to remove Fr. Orest from his position at All Saints. Officials of the UOCC wrote Olekshy and informed him that he was being transferred from All Saints to Brandon, Manitoba. However, after much prayer and after being fortified by the support of those who looked to Fr. Olekshy for spiritual guidance and leadership, he notified the office of the Metropolitan that he had not requested a transfer. Metropolitan Ohienko was very ill at this time and the affairs of the UOCC were being run by a high-ranking priest. Fr.

Olekshy and Fr. John Stinka, then the priest of the UOCC in Moose Jaw, Saskatchewan, were summoned to a spiritual court before the consistory. At Olekshy's trial he was charged with bizarre offenses. He was accused of allowing his wife, Oksana, to enter the altar area, reserved for the ordained clergy, kiss the holy table, and turn around and spit on Ukraine and the Ukrainian culture. When Fr. Orest denied this charge, he was accused of being a liar. He was also accused of abandoning his parish on the day that they set aside to honor Ukrainian literary figure Taras Shevchenko, instead travelling to Pike Lake, Saskatchewan in order to preach to 300 Pentecostals. Olekshy responded that the commemoration of Shevchenko had been sponsored by Fr. Orest and Oksana, was celebrated the entire day following the liturgy, during which Oksana had prepared the children of the parish to present a concert and art was collected for a display table. At the conclusion of the day the Olekshy's stayed after everyone else went home and they cleaned and swept the hall. Again, the tribunal accused him of contradicting the testimony of his parishioners, to which Olekshy responded, "Well if one of your priests can gather 300 Pentecostals, shouldn't that be a feather in his cap?" The court was outraged at his words, charging him with disrespect. Further inane accusations were made throughout the remainder of the trial, which continued for days. Olekshy felt that he was powerless to defend himself against such lies and falsehood. It also shook his confidence in the Church and its leadership. After a long deliberation, the tribunal called Olekshy in for one final session. Archbishop Andre Metiuk addressed the accused, "We have one question, if you answer this correctly, then maybe we can still continue our relationship." Metiuk then held up the constitution of the Ukrainian Self-Reliance League of Canada and asked, "Do you accept this as what guides us?" Olekshy sat there stupefied and stunned by the fact that a bishop of the church was holding up the constitution of a social organization, and not a Bible, or even some other Orthodox document. The Archbishop pressed him and asked the question more emphatically, "Fr. Orest, do you accept this?" Olekshy stated that he accepted it because it existed as a document, all the while confused over what this constitution had to do with why he was on trial. "Then everything is OK," the spokesman for the court responded, "Go home."

Olekshy returned to Saskatoon and continued to hold weekly prayer meetings as well as visit other charismatic gatherings. Because there was a vacuum of guidance from fellow Orthodox priests or oversight from an Orthodox bishop, Olekshy turned to Pentecostal and Charismatic pastors in Saskatoon that he trusted for fellowship and guidance. Many of these men tried to convert Olekshy and convince him to leave the Orthodox faith since he had now received the baptism of the Holy Spirit and spoke in tongues. However, he would always respond with the question, "Why would I drop all of that? That's who I am. I just entered into a relationship with the Lord and Savior that I didn't really realize I could have. I'm enjoying being an Orthodox priest that much more now."[27]

Again, the UOCC tried to move Olekshy to another parish and again he refused to go. However, after the ordeal of the spiritual court he realized he could not continue to be a part of the UOCC. He felt that it had changed so drastically from the spiritual home that had nurtured his parents and family when he was a child. It had devolved into an institution which worshipped Ukrainian culture instead of Christ. Olekshy's refusal to move resulted in his suspension as a priest by the UOCC for disobedience. Ironically, the page of the church periodical that pictured Fr. Orest and announced his suspension, also gratefully acknowledged yet another $500 gift from Mrs. Eve Olekshy, his mother, to St. Andrew's College, the seminary of the UOCC.

Olekshy, and the tight-knit group gathered around him, prayed and sought God's guidance and direction for the right response to his suspension by the UOCC. These prayer meetings were marked by many tears, deep sighing, repentance, and acknowledgments that they were trusting in the Lord and submitting themselves to him, unworthy though they were, for him to use them however he saw fit. In spite of Olekshy's suspension the group continued to meet for prayer. Fr. Orest and Oksana were turned out of the parish rectory onto the streets. Members of the prayer group heard that a mobile home was for sale at a cheap price and they collected money to purchase it for the Olekshy's to live in and for the group to continue to meet for prayer. The weekly prayer group continued to grow, however, not with Orthodox members. Young people involved in the occult and other cultic religions, as well as drug addicts, prostitutes, and hippies visited the group. The Olekshy's were given a love for these young people and wanted to help them, but many times they did not know where to begin. However, these needy young people were prayed for and many of them experienced deliverance from drugs and demonic possession. Fr. Orest at times however, asked himself:

27. Orest Olekshy. 2009. Interview by author.

Where are these Ukrainians that I understand, I would know how to deal with them? I don't know how to deal with prostitutes and someone who was in a satanic cult. But, you learn fast, because you're doing it, and you sense somehow that God is saying, "At this moment this is what you need to do."[28]

Olekshy and his prayer group developed a close relationship with Mt. Zion church, a community of young people who were a product of the Jesus People movement sweeping North America at that time. Mt. Zion's two young pastors David Roberts and Bill Kellers were inexperienced in ministry and looked to Olekshy for spiritual guidance and oversight.[29] Nonetheless, the people who surrounded Fr. Orest were Orthodox and wanted to be a part of the Orthodox Church, in spite of how the UOCC responded to them. Fr. Boris Zabrodsky in Chicago heard of Fr. Orest's plight and contacted him and told him that a meeting with U.S. Ukrainian Bishop Metropolitan Andrei Kuschak in New York City had already been arranged and that he would receive him as a priest under his omophorion, nullifying his suspension by the UOCC. Dave Roberts, of the Mt. Zion Jesus People, offered to travel with Olekshy to New York and act as his guide. They flew to New York and Roberts, wearing his usual cotton flannel shirt, blue jeans, and cowboy boots escorted Fr. Orest to the bishop's residence in Jamaica, Queens. Metropolitan Andrei received them warmly and did not appear to be taken aback by Robert's attire. Metropolitan Andrei owned a large china cabinet in which he had placed the numerous gold, silver, and jeweled crosses and *panaghias* that he had received in his travels.[30] Roberts was so taken by the glitter and beauty of the objects, he inquired, "Wow! What's all this?" To which the Metropolitan responded, "O, just junk. It's going to rot just like this body is going to rot." Olekshy was surprised by the Metropolitan's detached response, which was a new experience for the beleaguered priest. The Metropolitan patiently listened to Fr. Orest's story and at the conclusion enthusiastically offered him spiritual oversight and encouraged him to organize a parish back in Saskatoon. In addition, the

28. Ibid.

29. James R. Davis, July 25, 2009, e-mail message to author.

30. Alfeyev. *Architecture, Icons, and Music,* 103. It is not uncommon that when a bishop makes an official visit to the bishop of another diocese, especially if it is in a foreign country, the host bishop, metropolitan or patriarch will present his guest with a gift which many times is a silver or gold cross inlaid with jewels or a *panaghia*, which is Greek for "All Holy" and refers to an oval medallion on which is painted an icon of the Virgin Mary holding the Christ child.

bishop counseled him, "You're going to have all kinds of difficulty and I'm all the way here in New York, don't waste your time phoning me or writing letters because that's just difficult. When you have a problem, ask the Holy Spirit what to do, He'll tell you." While these words were a confirmation of the spiritual direction that Olekshy sensed God was leading the community back in Saskatoon, at the same time he desired a bishop that would give him strong direction. In many ways, Metropolitan Andrei's laze-faire approach to the Saskatoon community was a double-edged sword; on the one hand Fr. Orest was given complete freedom in developing Holy Resurrection parish, the name taken by the community, and on the other hand they felt spiritually orphaned.

The charismatic nature of Holy Resurrection showed itself not only in the Wednesday Bible study and prayer meetings but also in the Sunday Divine Liturgy. Hymns and Scripture choruses typical of Charismatic churches and fellowships found a home alongside the traditional Orthodox liturgical hymns. If a certain Scripture song referred to the Gospel or Epistle reading of the day it was sung before the reading. Likewise, during the communion of the faithful theologically sound, but non-liturgical hymns were sung. In its formative years, Holy Resurrection was sensitive to the hundreds of non-Orthodox that were drawn to its services. Very quickly the Ukrainian "cradle" Orthodox were outnumbered by those who came from Mennonite, Baptist, and Pentecostal churches, as well as the unchurched "Jesus People." Olekshy sought to pastorally bring them little by little into the Orthodox Faith. He felt that if a "full-blown" Orthodox liturgy was served they would be overwhelmed and be "put-off." Instead, the use of traditional Orthodox, as well as familiar Charismatic choruses, helped bridge the spiritually immature over to Orthodoxy. While the Eucharistic Canon of the liturgy was strictly preserved, other musical innovations assisted the newcomers, who were either from Protestant backgrounds or completely unchurched, to become comfortable with liturgical and sacramental worship.[31] Olekshy likened this to the mistake made by the Greeks in the tenth century who refused to "baptize" certain Ukrainian customs and condemned them outright, while the Greeks themselves retained certain practices from their pre-Christian culture. He felt that as long as the Evangelical-style hymns and choruses contained no heresy they were essentially Orthodox in content and should be employed. In one instance Olekshy recalls asking Archbishop Seraphim's pastoral advice regarding the

31. Maxym Lysack. 2009. Telephone interview by author. August 6.

content of the hymnal compiled for use at Holy Resurrection.[32] Archbishop Seraphim, who was the episcopal overseer of Holy Resurrection once it entered the Orthodox Church of America, gave his blessing for hymns and choruses to be used as long as Christ was invoked and worshipped. However, he discouraged the use of those songs which only addressed the Father and or the Holy Spirit. In describing the overall focus of Holy Resurrection Church Fr. Orest states:

> I think we just became very Christ-centered, if I dare say that, Christ may not agree, but I thought we became a very Christ-centered Orthodox church. . . . Scriptures were very important . . . it wasn't just something that you carried around with a gold cover. We actually started reading them on a daily basis.[33]

Over the years Metropolitan Andrei's health declined and with it his ability to administer the diocese. In the late 1980s Fr. Orest felt it was time to find another bishop to oversee Holy Resurrection. During this time Olekshy came into contact with Metropolitan Theodosius Lazar, primate of the Orthodox Church in America (OCA). Fr. Orest and the community of Holy Resurrection shared the same vision of the OCA for an "American" Orthodox Church, especially after their negative relationship with the ethnic-driven Ukrainian Orthodox Church of Canada. Olekshy and several other Canadian Orthodox priests formed the organization "Concerned Orthodox Christians of Canada" (COCC) to address the scandal of disunity among the various ethnic Orthodox jurisdictions in Canada. These priests, individually and corporately, petitioned their bishops to begin to address the issue of Orthodox unity in order to reverse the negative image of the Canadian Orthodox Church as a splintered and fractured church. Metropolitan Theodosius invited himself to a COCC meeting and made a $500 contribution of his personal funds to the work of the organization. In preparation for the Metropolitan's visit to Holy Resurrection the question was raised about dropping all of the "charismatic" music from the Liturgy. Olekshy responded by asserting that Metropolitan Theodosius needed to experience them as they truly were and that if he felt their way of worshipping was unorthodox he would correct them. True to their practice Holy Resurrection inserted several "charismatic" hymns and

---

32. Archbishop Seraphim (Storheim), former ruling hierarch of the Archdiocese of Canada of the Orthodox Church in America.

33. Orest Olekshy. 2009. Interview by author.

choruses in the pontifical liturgy celebrated by Metropolitan Theodosius at the parish. Fr. Orest remembers:

> The day the Metropolitan left and flew to Montreal, Fr. John Tkeachuk phoned and said, "What the heck did you do? This Metropolitan cannot stop raving about you guys and about these Protestant hymns that you incorporate into the liturgy and he claims it even works."[34]

Holy Resurrection Orthodox Church became the "mother" church of Charismatic Renewal among Orthodox Christians in Canada. Holy Resurrection provided the spiritual atmosphere in which several men answered a call to ordained sacramental ministry. Dennis Pihatch, Maxym Lysak, Rodion Lusiuk, Philip Ericson, and Robert Polson were ordained priests and are presently serving parishes throughout Canada and Alaska. Dennis Pihatch, later elevated to the rank of Archimandrite, served as the pastor of the OCA's Metochian in Moscow until his death in 2016.[35] Several others serve as deacons in different parish communities. As Holy Resurrection grew and matured, especially after its entrance into the OCA, it evolved and conformed more and more to traditional Orthodox practices and worship.

The weekly prayer group and Bible study continued on into the middle 1980s. Fr. Orest and Oksana came under the influence of world-renowned Charismatic teacher and pastor, Dr. Paul Yonggi Cho, attending conferences led by Cho both in New York and Minneapolis.[36] Cho pastors the world's largest church, Yoido Full Gospel Church in Seoul, South Korea, with an active membership of over 800,000.[37] Yoido Full Gospel Church has over the years been able to maintain close Christian community and foster personal discipleship of new believers, in spite of its large size, because of its emphasis on small-group meetings within their huge church. The 800,000-member church is divided into thousands of small cell groups of a dozen or more members. The cell group may be formed around those who live in a certain geographical area or based upon the time the members are free to meet during the week. The cell groups meet

34. Ibid. Fr. John Tkeachuk was the chancellor of the Archdiocese of Canada of the Orthodox Church in America.

35. A Metochian serves as a religious embassy between self-headed Orthodox Churches.

36. Wilson, "Cho, David," 521–22.

37. www.fgtv.com.

on a weekly basis and gather in someone's home or other agreed upon location for the purpose of group worship, prayer, Scripture study and mutual edification. The leader, usually a layman or woman, is given special training in providing pastoral leadership for members of the cell group.[38] Cho's teaching on small cell groups rapidly spread throughout the entire international church. Many large Pentecostal and Charismatic churches throughout the world adopted Cho's methodology of cell groups and saw increased spiritual and numerical growth in their congregations as well as a strengthening of the spirit of Christian community. Holy Resurrection likewise organized itself into six or seven cell groups. Fr. Orest led the cell group comprised of older Ukrainians in which they sang Ukrainian Church hymns and read and studies the Scriptures in Ukrainian. Other cell group adapted to their specific needs. However, over a period of time trouble began to surface in a few of the groups. One cell group leader fell into sexual sin while another group devolved into a weekly "gripe session" about what were perceived as problems in the parish. As a result, the cell groups were dissolved. A year or so later Fr. Olekshy met with Archbishop Seraphim and expressed his bewilderment at why the cell groups had not succeed. The Archbishop gave his opinion:

> I'll tell you Fr. Orest why it didn't work. You have no business running one of the cell groups. You have to be the priest going from group to group overseeing it. If you want to start it again then that is a healthy thing but you can't be the head of a cell group.[39]

Unfortunately, Fr. Orest and the leadership at Holy Resurrection had not taken the positive teaching on cell groups and adapted it for use in the Orthodox Church setting, taking into consideration the unique place of the priest in the parochial setting and his position as pastor.

At no time during this spiritual journey did Fr. Olekshy question the compatibility of his charismatic experiences with the theology and spirituality taught by the Orthodox Church. To the contrary, at every turn he found his experience confirmed in the Scriptures and the writings of the Church Fathers and the lives of the saints. Olekshy maintained close ties with Charismatic and Pentecostal pastors throughout Saskatoon, many who tried to convince him to forsake the Orthodox Church and its use of icons and vestments; however, he could never be persuaded to leave the

38. Cho and Hostetler, *Successful*.
39. Orest Olekshy. 2009. Interview by author.

Church. Conversely, many of these pastors eventually embraced the Orthodox faith. As a matter of fact, Olekshy felt that he was more spiritually protected then his fellow ministers, due to his submission to an Orthodox bishop and the protection of the Church's 2,000-year tradition. His fellow Charismatic pastors, many who were independent, had no spiritual covering or theological moorings. As a result, Olekshy believed they were much more susceptible to the faddism and extremism that so easily dogged the wider Charismatic Movement in the 1980s.

Olekshy continued as the senior pastor of Holy Resurrection until 2005, when he was given the title "Priest Emeritus." On March 2, 1997, his wife Oksana passed away after a prolonged illness. Oksana's death took an emotional toll on Fr. Orest and finally he retired from full-time priestly ministry. He served as a supply priest to the outlying Romanian Orthodox parishes of St. Elijah in Lennard, Manitoba, St. John in Shell Valley, Manitoba and Holy Trinity in MacNutt, Saskatchewan after his retirement.[40] He passed away March 28, 2017.[41]

---

40. Fr. Orest Olekshy, telephone interview by author, July 26, 2010.

41. http://www.legacy.com/obituaries/thestarphoenix/obituary.aspx?pid= 184787250.

CHAPTER 9

The Charismatic Renewal

A "Non-Movement" among the Orthodox

WAS THERE A GENUINE Charismatic "Movement" in the Orthodox Church? The answer to that question is both "yes" and "no." When one looks at the Charismatic Movement among Roman Catholics, Episcopalians, or United Methodists, and compares the numbers of clergy and lay people who openly participated in, or were directly and personally affected by, the Movement within those denominations, with the numbers of people affected in the Orthodox Church, there was no *Movement*. Whereas Charismatics in the Roman Catholic and mainstream Protestant Churches organized conferences that drew thousands and even tens of thousands of participants, Orthodox Charismatic conferences barely drew a hundred or more people. Entire publishing companies, such as Logos International Publishing, Servant, and Creation House, to name only a few, produced hundreds and thousands of periodicals and audiotapes, serving the Catholic and Protestant Charismatic Movements. In comparison, only two magazines served those Orthodox Christians involved in Renewal and only Stephanou published any of significance.[1] In the same vein, thousands of Roman Catholic priests and Protestant clergymen, including bishops, became directly involved in the Charismatic Renewal. At least five Popes—Paul IV, John Paul I, John Paul II, Benedict XIII, and Francis—endorsed the Movement. The Renewal was sanctioned and leadership provided by members of the episcopacy in the Roman Catholic, Anglican, Lutheran and United Methodist churches. While a handful of Orthodox priests became involved in the Charismatic Renewal, not one

1. Unlike the books and tapes published by Roman Catholic and Protestant Charismatics, which crossed over denominational lines, Stephanou's books were read almost exclusively by Orthodox Christians.

single Orthodox bishop in North America openly supported the Renewal and in most instances condemned it as a "Protestant" aberration.

The leadership of the Roman Catholic and Protestant Churches felt that the Charismatic Renewal was of such vital importance that most of them undertook official theological studies of the Movement and publicly published their findings.[2] In contrast, none of the North American Orthodox jurisdictions took the time or energy to investigate the claims of the Movement in any depth or give it any serious theological consideration as a possibly genuine renewal of the Holy Spirit among Christians.[3] In most cases, the Movement was simply ignored and in some situations Orthodox priests and laypeople who claimed to be a part of the Movement or to have benefited positively from it were harassed or marginalized.[4]

In spite of the general negative attitude of the hierarchy there can be no doubt that thousands of Orthodox Christians, clergy and laity alike, were influenced, directly or peripherally, by the Renewal ministries of Frs. Monios, Emmert, Stephanou, Zabrodsky, Moore, Morfessis, and Olekshy, and countless other Orthodox laity were touched by the Charismatic Renewal in general.[5] The pages of *The Logos* and *Theosis* are replete with the testimonies of many laymen and women in the United States and Canada who considered themselves a part of the Movement. Whether they embraced all the aspects of the Movement, such as claiming an experience of

2. McDonnell, *Presence, Power and Praise*. In these volumes, Fr. McDonnell collected most of the official published studies of the Roman Catholic Church in various countries/dioceses and among various Protestant denominations, regarding the Charismatic Movement.

3. While the Greek Orthodox Archdiocese released a brief statement dealing with the issue of spiritual renewal and made allusions to the Charismatic Movement, it did not interact with those theological issues raised by the Movement. Likewise, the Synod of Bishops of the Orthodox Church in America (OCA) addressed the topic of generic spiritual renewal it did not specifically answer the claims of the Charismatic Movement.

4. Stephanou, "Sharing in the Spirit," 3. Stephanou announced in this editorial that Maximos, Greek Orthodox Bishop of Pittsburgh, issued an order banning Fr. Morfessis from holding a charismatic prayer group in his church which had been meeting weekly in the parish hall.

5. Fr. John Chakos, telephone interview with author, March 28, 2009. One case in point is the testimony of Fr. John Chakos, pastor of his childhood parish, Holy Cross Greek Orthodox Church in Pittsburgh, who unabashedly claims that because of his pastor's (Fr. Constantine Monios) involvement in the Charismatic Movement, he sensed a call to the priestly vocation and that the spiritual atmosphere of the parish to this day is Christ-centered because of the many laypeople affected positively by the Movement in the 1970s and 80s.

the "baptism of the Holy Spirit," which many did, or speaking in tongues, which some testified to, or attending a weekly Charismatic prayer meeting, which took places in several parishes, cannot be ascertained, but many of them do testify clearly and unequivocally to being "renewed" in their faith in Jesus Christ and their love and dedication to the Orthodox Church.

Why the Orthodox Church Failed to Embrace the Charismatic Movement

While the official Orthodox Churches in North America, speaking through their various synods of bishops, did not outright denounce the Charismatic Movement by name, they did forcefully warn the Orthodox faithful about the perceived perils of the Movement, though many in the Orthodox Church called for overall spiritual renewal.

So, what was it about the Charismatic Movement that was viewed as spiritually dangerous to the Orthodox people?

First and foremost, the Charismatic Renewal was believed to be a "Protestant" spiritual movement. While initially a theological split from the Roman Catholic Church in the sixteenth century, based upon Martin Luther's protest of ninety-five specific theological points, Protestantism quickly proliferated into some 20,000-plus sects and denominations, all claiming to base their beliefs directly upon the Bible. The "magisterial" Protestant denominations (i.e., Lutheran, Reformed, and Anglican) all claimed to honor the Ecumenical Councils of the undivided Church and give a modicum of authority to the Church Fathers; other denominations that trace their roots to the Anabaptist, Zwinglian, and Pietistic strains of Protestantism totally rejected these previously held authorities. While the Orthodox Church in the twentieth and twenty-first centuries, through such official ecumenical agencies as the National Council of Churches and the World Council of Churches, maintained cordial relations with the historic mainline Protestant denominations, such as the Episcopal, Lutheran, Presbyterian, and United Methodist churches, its relationship with Evangelical and Fundamentalist denominations has been a bit more strained. The reason for this appears to be rooted in the fact that the historic Protestant denominations are not as committed to aggressive evangelization and therefore, unlike the Evangelical/Fundamentalist denominations, are less likely to target individual Orthodox Church members with the goal of getting them "saved" and then become members of some Protestant denomination or organization. The historic Protestant denominations accept the Orthodox Church as a "sister" church and therefore do not consciously seek to convert members of the Orthodox Church or to aggressively challenge them doctrinally.

As shown in an earlier section of this work, certain strains of the Charismatic Movement trace certain of their theological presuppositions through Pentecostalism of the early twentieth century, the Holiness (Wesleyan) Movement of the eighteenth and nineteenth centuries back to sixteenth- and seventeenth-century Pietism. Even though Emmert, Stephanou, Zabrodsky, Olekshy, and other leaders of the Charismatic Renewal within the Orthodox Church, attempted to ground the Renewal solidly within the framework and tradition of Orthodox theology and spirituality, they failed to convince the hierarchy, as well as many of the clergy and laity, that the Charismatic Movement was fully compatible with, and actually inherent in, Orthodox Christianity.[6] One Orthodox writer commented on Stephanou's attempts:

> With a commendable view of encouraging spiritual renewal among Orthodox people, and drawing upon Orthodox saints such as St. Symeon the New Theologian and liturgical rites of the Orthodox Church, this writer, in my opinion, re-interprets them very much from within a Protestant charismatic perspective rather than from a thorough rootedness in Orthodox Tradition, and also takes only certain things from their teachings, and those out of the context needed for their proper understanding in the full teaching of such saints. . . . These criticisms are not intended to discourage a thorough quest for the fullness of the Holy Spirit's working in our lives, but to guard against confusion and distortion of teaching on this matter in Orthodox Tradition.[7]

Even the voice of such a well-respected theologian as Bishop Kalistos Ware admitted that there was a serious need for spiritual renewal in the Orthodox Church. However, he raised the same issue as many other Orthodox leaders regarding the methodology of spiritual renewal embraced by Charismatic Orthodox believers:[8]

> Certainly the need for an Orthodox re-awakening in the *diaspora* can scarcely be denied. For all too many Orthodox in the west,

6. Munk, "The Charismatic Experience in Orthodox Tradition," 1–3.

7. Estabrooks. "A Continuing Pentecost," 10–1.

8. Ware, "Orthodoxy and the Charismatic Movement," 185.

their Church is a link with the mother-country rather than with God; ethnic identity comes before Orthodox Catholicity. They are Orthodox because they are Greeks, Russians or Serbs, not because they have made any deep and conscious act of personal commitment to God. With its rich liturgical inheritance and its profound sense of continuity with the past, Orthodoxy is always in danger of degenerating into ritualistic formalism. But, granted that a renewal is needed, should this "Orthodox re-awakening" necessarily assume the form envisaged by Fr. Eusebius Stephanou? Should it not draw more fully on the Orthodox tradition and less on Protestant revivalism?

While the Charismatic Movement was not endorsed, at no time did the leadership of the Orthodox Church ever deny that the Orthodox Church was "charismatic" by nature. However, what they could not bring themselves to accept was that the same Holy Spirit, who had over the centuries inspired and empowered myriads of saintly Orthodox men and women—martyrs, wonderworkers, theologians, monastics, and spiritual Fathers and Mothers—was the same Holy Spirit that originated and animated the Charismatic Movement of contemporary times within the Roman Catholic and Protestant churches. For some Orthodox it was precisely *because* the Movement was present within and embraced by the Roman Catholic and Protestant churches that it was spiritually suspect.

As early as Priestmonk Seraphim Rose's *Orthodoxy and the Religion of the Future* and Fr. John Morris' article, and later booklet, *The Charismatic Movement: An Orthodox Evaluation,* the Movement had become identified as the historical and spiritual offspring of Protestantism. Rose was virulent in his rejection of the non-Orthodox sources of the renewal, while at the same time giving a back-handed compliment to Catholics and Protestants, he wrote:

> But what is it that those outside the Church of Christ are capable of teaching Orthodox Christians? It is certainly true (no conscious Orthodox person will deny it) that Orthodox Christians are sometimes put to shame by the fervor and zeal of some Roman Catholics and Protestants for church attendance, missionary activities, praying together, reading the Scriptures and the like. Fervent non-Orthodox persons can shame the Orthodox, even in the error of their beliefs. . . . Are we to believe that the Church is now to be superceded *(sic)* by some "new revelation" capable of transmitting grace outside the Church, among any group of people who may happen to believe in Christ but have no knowledge or experience

of the Mysteries (Sacraments) which Christ instituted and no contact with the Apostles and their successors who He appointed to
administer the Mysteries? No: it is as certain today as it was in the
first century that *the gifts of the Holy Spirit are not revealed in those
outside the Church.*[9]

Likewise, throughout many articles in *The Logos,* Stephanou constantly attempted to answer the challenge that his views were "Protestant." As
shown above, Anthimos, Greek Orthodox Bishop of Boston, in his report,
dated June 18, 1979, sent to Archbishop Iakovos, primate of the Greek Orthodox Archdiocese of North America, stated that Stephanou

> . . . tactfully avoided to admit Protestant influence, however, all his
> teachings, especially in reference to expression, terminology and
> presentation is foreign to the Tradition of the Orthodox Church
> and undoubtedly influenced by the Pentecostal and Charismatic
> tendencies which he tries to base in Orthodox sources.[10]

Some have questioned why the Catholic and Anglican churches,
which are sacramental, liturgical, and hierarchical, and therefore similar
to the Orthodox Church, at least on the surface, so readily embraced the
Charismatic Renewal, while the Orthodox Church ignored or shunned
the Movement. The answer lies not in the sacramental, liturgical, or hierarchical nature of the Roman Catholic and Anglican churches, but rather
their ecumenical outlook and self-identity among the other churches. The
Roman Catholic Church in many ways was prepared for the Charismatic
Movement by the decisions and spirit of the Vatican II Council. Protestants,
who previous to the council were "heretics," after the Council were only
"separated brethren" from which Roman Catholics could learn valuable
spiritual lessons. Some have gone so far as to say that Vatican II resulted
in the "Protestantization" of the Roman Catholic Church.[11] What Martin
Luther failed to do in the sixteenth century was accomplished at Vatican II
in the twentieth century. When one considers that the Charismatic Movement within the Roman Catholic Church happened as a result of Catholic
university students studying Pentecostal minister David Wilkerson's *The
Cross and the Switchblade* and Episcopalian John Sherrill's *They Speak with
Other Tongues,* the theory sounds plausible.

9. Rose, *Orthodoxy and the Religion,* 153–54.

10. See p. [***] above.

11. https://www.thecatholicthing.org/2011/11/19/the-protestantization-of
-the-church/.

The Orthodox Church, from the fifteenth and sixteenth centuries on, has felt a profound sense of encroachment by aggressive Roman Catholic and Protestant missionaries and naturally adopted a mode of defensiveness. While the Orthodox Church has been on the forefront of the Ecumenical Movement since the early twentieth century, its relationship to the Ecumenical Movement is very different from that of the Western churches. While most Protestant denominations would admit that they, as churches, do not theologically possess the "fullness of the faith," and that they in some way may err theologically, the Orthodox Church claims to be the "One, Holy, Catholic and Apostolic Church" and free of any and all theological error, and is involved in the Ecumenical Movement for the sole purpose of witnessing to Roman Catholics and Protestants of the fullness of the Orthodox faith, and calling them to return to the Orthodox fullness of the Christian Faith.[12] Because of this self-identity, the leaders of the Orthodox Church are very hesitant to ascribe authenticity to a spiritual movement that was born, and continues to thrive, outside of the Orthodox Church. To admit the legitimacy of the Charismatic Movement, outside the Orthodox Church would, for conservative Orthodox, be an admission that the Holy Spirit was, and continues, moving in a powerful and life-transforming way outside of the canonical boundaries of the Orthodox Church, which is ecclesiologically unacceptable. This would call into question the belief that the "fullness of the faith" resides within the sacramental and liturgical life of the Orthodox Church, or at least be an admission that the Holy Spirit does work and minister outside of the Orthodox Church.[13] To sum up the view of many of the leaders within the Orthodox Church:

> With its roots in the revivals of American Protestantism, the Charismatic movement embodies a spirituality that is foreign to Orthodoxy. Its origins, beliefs and practices are quite different than the sober spirituality of the Christian East.[14]

The author of the above statement goes even further and attributes the Charismatic Movement not just to Protestantism in general but specifically

---

12 https://www.academia.edu/6557817/_With_Seraphim_Danckaert_._Georges_Florovsky_in_Orthodox_Handbook_on_Ecumenism_Resources_for_Theological_Education_ed._Pantelis_Kalaitzidis_Thomas_FitzGerald_Cyril_Hovorun_Aikaterini_Pekridou_Nikolaos_Asproulis_Guy_Liagre_Dietrich_Werner_Volos_WCC_Regnum_Oxford_2014_pp._211–215.

13. Heers, *The Ecclesiological Renovation*, 167–81.

14. Morris, "The Charismatic Movement," 133.

to a "new form of the American civil religion of doctrinal relativism . . . ." He links what he perceives as the Charismatic Movements emphasis upon "instant spirituality" as a "concern of contemporary American society for immediate self-gratification."[15]

Second, the Movement was seen by many Orthodox clergy and laity as embracing the most radical elements of ecumenism. Some of the most virulent critiques have issued from the more conservative, anti-ecumenical ranks of the Orthodox Church. The most devastating analysis, as stated above, came from the pen of the Hieromonk Seraphim Rose.[16] An early convert to Orthodoxy from mainstream Protestantism, priest-monk of the conservative Russian Orthodox Church Outside Russia (ROCOR), abbot of St. Herman of Alaska Monastery in Platina, California and editor of the periodical *Orthodox Word,*[17] Rose, whose writings have wielded a very powerful influence over the thinking and opinions of Orthodox Christians in North America, not only identified the Charismatic Movement as a product of American Protestant revivalism but also seeks to label the Movement as "Christian Mediumism."[18] For Rose, the leaders of the Charismatic Movement evidenced characteristics similar to spiritualist mediums that channel "fallen spirits." This, in his opinion, was the source of the healings and "prophetic" gifts claimed by Charismatic ministers.[19] Rose, whose membership in ROCOR, also preconditioned him to harshly criticize the ecumenical character of the Movement. ROCOR reacted negatively to Orthodox participation in the official Ecumenical Movement, going so far as to label it a "pan-heresy."[20] This phrase, coined by Fr. Justin Popovic, a Serbian Orthodox priest, now a canonized a saint, conveyed that all the past heresies of the ages condemned by the Orthodox Church were summed up in the theology and spirituality propagated by the proponents of the Ecumenical Movement and their goal for "one world church," whose unity was based not in Orthodox Christian doctrine but some amorphous pan-Christian identity.[21] The ecumenical nature of the Charismatic Movement,

15. Ibid.

16. Christensen, *Not of This World.*

17. Damascene, *Father Seraphim Rose.*

18. Rose, *Orthodoxy and the Religion,* 160–76.

19. Ibid., 162.

20. Hieromonk [now Metropolitan] Amfilohije (Radovic), "Eulogy in Memory of Blessed Fr. Justin" http://www.orthodoxinfo.com/ecumenism/eulogy.aspx.

21. Christina Holland, "Against Ecumenism" http://www.orthodox.net/articles/

in which Charismatic Christians, regardless of denominational affiliation, whether Catholics, Protestant, or Orthodox, gathered together in conferences for joint prayer and worship, was interpreted by Rose as a clear violation of the canonical tradition of the Orthodox Church in which Orthodox Christians are forbidden to pray and worship with those who are "heretics" or "schismatics" and outside of the communion of the Orthodox Church.[22] For Rose, this was a strong reason why the Orthodox should reject the Movement as heretical. Roses' scathing denunciation of the Charismatic Movement was considered by many Orthodox laypeople to be the definitive Orthodox judgment on the origins and source of the Movement and is generally accepted by many of the rank and file members of the Orthodox Church in the English-speaking world. This being the case, and without any positive, or even nuanced analysis of the Charismatic Movement to the contrary, is it any wonder that the Movement was rejected in practice by the Orthodox Church in North America?

The third reason for the rejection of the Charismatic Movement was its linkage and almost exclusive association, at least in the minds of the hierarchy, especially those of the Greek Orthodox Archdiocese, with the Very Rev. Archimandrite Eusebius Stephanou. While Morris' critique gives a brief mention of Fr. Boris Zabrodsky, almost every other treatment of the Movement identifies Stephanou as the leader of the Charismatic Movement among Orthodox Christians and makes no mention of the other clergy or lay leaders within the Movement. This therefore led to the perception that everything Stephanou published or said was the definitive view, theologically and spiritually, of the Charismatic Movement among the Orthodox. Unfortunately, this was not a plus for the Movement, rather Stephanou's weaknesses and personal eccentricities became the face of the Movement to Orthodox leaders.

From the inception in 1968 of *The Logos*, Stephanou had a penchant for attacking and confronting the hierarchy of the Greek Orthodox Archdiocese. Even before his personal involvement with the Charismatic Movement, Stephanou ironically challenged Archbishop Iakavos' involvement in the Ecumenical Movement[23] as well as what Stephanou perceived as Iakavos'

against-ecumenism.html.

22. "The First Sorrowful Epistle of Metropolitan Philaret" http://www.orthodoxinfo. com/ecumenism/sorrow.aspx.

23. Stephanou. "The Need," 13–14.

hypocritical stand on civil rights.[24] Throughout the 1970s and 80s he continued to challenge the hierarchy in the pages of *The Logos*. Archbishop Iakavos, as well as Metropolitan Silas of New Jersey, Bishop Maximos of Pittsburgh, and Bishop Philip of Atlanta, felt the sting of his pen. However, the hierarchy were not the only ones to feel his ire. Priests who dared to challenge him, or priests involved in the Charismatic Renewal who refused to continue to partner with him, became the targets of his denunciations and judgment.[25]

Stephanou was also perceived to be spiritually boastful and arrogant. In several articles in *The Logos* he alluded to his "prophetic ministry" and suggested that he was the only Orthodox priest sounding the call for spiritual renewal in the Orthodox Church. Stephanou himself once wrote:

> The Rt. Reverend Methodius, bishop of Boston, remarked to me at one time: "What do you think you are? Some kind of prophet?" I replied: "I don't claim to be a prophet, although a large number of people testify that I exercise a prophetic ministry."[26]

Humility is one of the hallmark characteristics of Orthodox spirituality and those who make such boastful statements, rightly or wrongly, are immediately dismissed and their claims are seen as a sign of spiritual delusion or *prelest*. The *Church* (i.e. the people and the hierarchy) may discern that someone's ministry is prophetic or apostolic and declare it as such, but if *the person themselves* claims such a place they are spiritually suspect from the outset. Reflecting this opinion, Fr. Theodore Stylianopoulos, retired Professor of New Testament at Holy Cross Greek Orthodox School of Theology in Brookline, Massachusetts, who served

24. Stephanou. "The Revolt," 11.

25. Stethatos, *Voice of a Priest,* 115–22; 157–65. Both Emmert and Zabrodsky stated in interviews that working with Stephanou was extremely difficult. Emmert asserted that after he had written several articles for *The Logos,* after Stephanou embraced the Charismatic Movement, Stephanou informed him that he would have to donate $25 for each article he submitted to *The Logos* in order for it to be published. Emmert claims that he had some serious questions about what he perceived were classical Pentecostal leanings of Stephanou's theology and methodology. However, it was Stephanou's insistence on receiving money before printing any further articles by Emmert was the final reason for their parting ways, not because Emmert repudiated the Renewal, as asserted by Stephanou. (Athanasios Emmert, email message to author, August 14, 2010.) Zabrodsky likewise became uncomfortable with Stephanou's "Pentecostal methods" as well as what he perceived as Stephanou's obstinacies and refusal to cooperate with others. (Boris Zabrodsky, interview by author, Country Club Hills, IL, June 4, 2009.)

26. Stephanou, "Our 30th Anniversary," 1.

on an official Greek Orthodox Archdiocesan committee which investigated Stephanou's writings, wrote:

> Stephanou [was] by his own self-understanding . . . called by God
> to a special awakening and prophetic ministry . . . the personalities, attitudes, and actions, particularly of leaders in the charismatic movement among the Orthodox, definitely contributed to its
> alien character and alienation from the Church. They simply came
> across as pushy, emotional, overly self-assured, judgmental of the
> church and its people.[27]

Fourth, the Orthodox Church has always considered itself to be "charismatic" and therefore the leadership of the Church did not believe the Church was in need of a charismatic "renewal." If anything, the members of the Orthodox Church needed to rediscover and recover the authentic charismatic teachings and spirituality of the Church, remain faithful to the Church, and humbly practice the Orthodox faith daily. Few people articulated this as well as "a Monk of the Eastern Church," the pen name of Fr. Lev Gillet.[28]

Born in Insére, France in 1893, Gillet studied psychology and mathematics in Geneva, Switzerland. In 1919, after serving in World War I and spending three years as a POW of the Germans, Gillet joined the Benedictine Order as a monk. In 1928, he left the Catholic Church and was received as a priest in the Orthodox Church, of the Russian emigre community, in Paris. In 1938, he departed Paris for London and spent the remainder of his years in England until his death in 1980.[29] He was instrumental in forming the Fellowship of St. Alban and St. Sergius, an ecumenical study fellowship, active in France and England, which brought Orthodox and Anglican's together for annual conferences. Gillet writes in his classic work, *Orthodox Spirituality*, regarding the charismata:

> The gifts of the Spirit, which marked the beginnings of the Church
> are not things of the past. They have been given, they are given, to
> the Church for all times, . . . only their lack of faith inclines contemporary Christians to consider charismatic manifestations in
> our days exceptional. If they are exceptional it is because of a lack
> of faith similar to that which hindered Jesus at Nazareth (Matthew
> 13:58). But the power of the Holy Spirit is as alive today as it was

27. Fr. Theodore Stylianopoulos, e-mail message to author, March 11, 2009.

28. Behr-Sigel, *Lev Gillet*.

29. http://orthodoxwiki.org/Lev Gillet

in the days of the Book of Acts. The mighty works accomplished in the name of Jesus . . . can be accomplished now, if only we have faith (Mark 16:17, 18).[30]

Gillet also, articulating thoughts reminiscent of St. Symeon the New Theologian, suggests that there may be further experiences of the Holy Spirit separate and apart from the Mystery (sacrament) of Chrismation.

> The gift of the Holy Spirit cannot be exclusively identified with Chrism . . . in many modern cases we should not dare to deny the reality of a "baptism of the Spirit" conferred upon men who had not received it sacramentally . . . the grace of the Holy Spirit is already active in the baptism of water as well as the grace of the Father and the grace of the Son. But there is a special sending of the Spirit to man; and a baptism in water not completed by the baptism of the Holy Ghost would manifest a deficient Christian life. . . . [T]he question of Paul to the Ephesian disciples, "Did ye receive the Holy Spirit . . . ? [Acts 19:2] is asked of every one of us. It would not be enough to answer, "I have received the mystery or sacrament of the Spirit after my baptism, when I was anointed with Holy Chrism."[31]

Some Orthodox, as well as Pentecostal/Charismatic scholars, point to the later insertion of the *filioque* clause (". . . and the Son") by the Church in the West into the Nicene Creed, and the resultant theology developed over the centuries, to defend the insertion, as the cause for the Roman Catholic and Protestant Churches' deemphasizing the ministry of Holy Spirit in their theology and spirituality, and the need therefore for the contemporary Charismatic Movement to assist them in rediscovering the place of the Holy Spirit in the Church.[32]

The Orthodox Church's cautionary regard of the charismatic manifestations of the Holy Spirit can be summed up best in the words of Fr. Michael Harper, one-time leader of the Charismatic Movement and priest in the Church of England, who later joined the Antiochian Orthodox Church in Great Britain and was ordained an Orthodox priest and continued to participate, with the blessing of His Beatitude, Ignatius III (Hazim), the

---

30. Gilet, *Orthodox Spirituality*, 69, 72.

31. Ibid., 62–63.

32. Harper, *A Faith Fulfilled*, 175.

Patriarch of Antioch, in many European Charismatic gatherings, until his death in 2009.[33] Harper wrote:

> As a Church it has never questioned the presence of the gifts of the Spirit. It has also rightly seen the importance of proper discernment as to the source of power and the need to sanctify the human element in the presentation of these gifts to the Church and the world.[34]

Marginalized . . . Ignored . . . Dismissed

The Charismatic Movement in the Orthodox Church was but a "blip" on the radar screen of the twentieth century. Undoubtedly hundreds and thousands of Orthodox laypeople of the various jurisdictions were influenced by the Charismatic Movement, claiming personal spiritual renewal experiences that drew them closer to Christ and to the Orthodox Church, but overall the Movement's effect upon the hierarchy, leadership, and structure of the Church was negligible.[35] After unsuccessfully seeking to totally silence the most vocal and prolific leader of the Movement, Fr. Eusebius Stephanou, the Greek Orthodox Church's leadership effectively marginalized him, and by extension the entire Charismatic Movement among Orthodox Christians.

Over the years, Stephanou's influence and ministry among the Orthodox laity continued to wane. In many ways, Stephanou contributed to this marginalization. By refusing to accept parochial priestly ministry in the Greek Orthodox Archdiocese, and continuing to attack the Church's hierarchy both in print and in public addresses, he effectively cut himself

---

33. Michael Harper, email to author, May 05, 2009.

34. Harper, *A Faith Fulfilled*, 181.

35. Barrett and Johnson, "Global Statistics," 286, 288, 295. Barrett and Johnson, assert that there were 15,200 Orthodox Christian participants in the Renewal, tracing the beginning of the Charismatic Movement among the Orthodox to 1970. They further claim that by 1995 the number had risen to 2,941,900 Orthodox participants. It must be noted that these are global statistics and not confined to the United States and Canada. Likewise, these statistics also include Oriental Orthodox Charismatics who are members of the Armenian Apostolic, Coptic, Ethiopic, or Syrian churches who are not in communion with the Eastern Orthodox Churches who accept the Seven Ecumenical Councils. The author, even after a prolonged telephone conversation with Barrett, could not ascertain how he and Johnson arrived at these numbers and seriously questions their accuracy.

off from the day-to-day life and workings of the Church.[36] The building and maintenance of the Orthodox Renewal Center of St. Symeon the New Theologian took up Stephanou's time and energy from his previous itinerant preaching and teaching ministry, which had in the past kept him in contact with parish priests and Orthodox laypeople throughout the United States and Canada. While Stephanou's Brotherhood of St. Symeon the New Theologian continued to sponsor two Renewal conferences annually, corresponding to the two dates on the calendar dedicated to commemorating St. Symeon the New Theologian, over the years attendance at these conferences dwindled in number.[37] In the waning years of his life Stephanou felt that the Renewal Center in Florida was taking financial resources from the printing ministry of the Brotherhood. Finally, in 2011, against the advice and protestations of many people associated with the Brotherhood of St. Symeon, Stephanou sold the property.[38] Great irony lay in the fact that the Evangelical church ministry that bought the property was headed by a minister who had grown up in the Greek Orthodox Church and who left the Church because he felt it was lacking in spiritual fervor. After a brief illness, Archimandrite Eusebius died May 23, 2016 and was laid to rest in Destin, Florida.[39]

Since the death of Stephanou, Emmert, and Olekshy, no other Orthodox priests have taken up their "mantles," so to speak, and continued the work of promoting Charismatic Renewal in the Orthodox Church. While Zabrodsky continues to serve as an Orthodox parish priest he is not involved in what could be called charismatic activities, other than day-to-day

36. The author attended several "Renewal Conferences," between 2005 and 2009, sponsored by Stephanou and held at the Orthodox Renewal Center of St. Symeon the New Theologian in Destin, Florida during which the author heard Stephanou publicly on numerous occasions, during his talks to the conferees, verbally attack members of the hierarchy of the different Orthodox jurisdictions.

37. The author first attended and spoke at the fall 1992 Renewal Conference sponsored by the Brotherhood of St. Symeon the New Theologian in Destin, Florida. Approximately sixty people, from throughout the United States, attended that conference. The author returned to Destin and attended Renewal conferences in 2008 and 2009 at which less than fifteen to twenty people were in attendance. Likewise, the author served as a member of the Board of Trustees of the Brotherhood of St. Symeon the New Theologian from 2008 to 2010. As of September 2016, the author serves as Spiritual Advisor to the Brotherhood.

38. Personal interviews with Fr. Mark Hodges, Mr. John Kanniaris and Mr. Joseph Abatte, all members of the Board of Trustees of the Brotherhood of St. Symeon the New Theologian. n.d.

39. http://ocl.org/memory-archimandrite-eusebius-stephanou/.

pastoral ministry, in which in many cases he continues to exercise the charismata.[40] Likewise, there are no Orthodox parishes that could be characterized as Charismatic, nor are there any Orthodox Charismatic prayer groups that continue to function. *The Logos* and *Theosis* have ceased publication and only *The Orthodox Evangelist,* now published by the Brotherhood of St. Symeon the New Theologian, continues to call for the "Charismatic" Renewal of the Orthodox Church.[41]

While the Charismatic Movement in the Orthodox Church in North America may no longer exist, there is no doubt that there are still hundreds, and perhaps thousands, of Orthodox Christians, clergy, and laity alike, throughout the United States and Canada who in the past were influenced by the Movement directly or indirectly and that that influence left a permanent and continued mark upon their spiritual lives to this day.[42] Certainly, some are serving as priests and deacons, others as members of parish councils, Sunday School teachers, and catechism instructors. Others may teach in Orthodox colleges and seminaries and some may serve in higher positions in the institutional agencies of various Orthodox jurisdictions. Unfortunately, it is just as certain that others have left the Orthodox Church and may now minister in or attend other Evangelical or Pentecostal/Charismatic denominations or churches, or worse may have forsaken the Christian faith altogether. The heartbreaking fact is that wherever they are today their voices were marginalized, either by neglect or outright hostility, and because of it the Orthodox Church lost more than it gained.

---

40. Emmert, who regularly taught a Bible study group in his parish, related to the author that whenever the occasion arose, he openly shared with the Bible Study attendees his Charismatic experiences.

41. Stephanou, *A Manual,* 9. Written to commemorate the fortieth anniversary of Stephanou's involvement in "Renewal Ministry" he also states that it was written to "bring into a sharper focus what makes this Renewal Ministry different and distinct from any other renewal endeavors in the Orthodox Church, either contemporary or of the past." Also, "Firstly, it will remind those already part of our renewal ministry why it has a special calling from God for the whole Body of Christ, the Orthodox Church. Secondly, it will serve to help those who are newcomers to St. Symeon's ministry to grasp with greater precision its true scope, as well as the basic dimensions that make the calling it has received from the Lord truly distinctive. It must be made clear that this labor of faith is both evangelical and prophetic."

42. This statement is based upon the personal contacts of the author with hundreds of Orthodox Christians who have not repudiated their spiritual experiences in the Charismatic Movement and yet remain faithful, practicing and supporting members of the Orthodox Church.

Only time will tell exactly what influence the Charismatic Renewal had upon the life of the Orthodox Church in North America. Perhaps the large numbers of former Evangelical and Pentecostal/Charismatic converts who have joined the Orthodox Church in North America over the past twenty-five years have had an even greater impact upon the life of the Church than an organized movement.[43] Especially those converts, who have not "burned their bridges," spiritually speaking, whose spiritual lives were positively formed by their experience in the Charismatic Movement, have in time been the catalyst for general spiritual renewal in the Orthodox Church. While this study has attempted to give a brief glimpse into the lives of those who served as leaders of the Charismatic Movement, further investigation into the lives of the many lay men and women who were involved in the Movement would give a more full-orbed picture of the overall influence of the Movement.

Nonetheless, the Orthodox Church in North America has yet to definitively and theologically speak on the Charismatic Movement. Priests and some theologians have attempted to answer certain of the clearly excessive and heretical aspects of the Movement. However, the Orthodox Church in North America has yet to address the overall issue of the ongoing charismatic life in the Church. No thorough, serious, or authoritative study has been undertaken to give guidance to or provide spiritual formation for Orthodox laity who have been endowed with certain charisms that do not easily fit within the framework of the ordained Orthodox priesthood or the monastic life. With the growth of Athonite-style monasticism in America, as seen in the proliferation of both men and women's monasteries throughout the continent over the last decade, and the tensions they have produced between the monastics, clergy, laity, and

43. Gilquist, *Becoming Orthodox*, 4. While there is no definitive research on the number of Evangelicals in North America (United States and Canada), that have over the last couple of decades converted to the Orthodox Church, Gilquist's work states that there were 2,000 members of the Evangelical Orthodox Church (EOC) that were chrismated in 1987 as members of the Orthodox Church of the Antiochian Orthodox Christian Archdiocese of North America. Large numbers of former Evangelicals have also converted to the Orthodox Church through the Greek Archdiocese, Orthodox Church in America, Russian Orthodox Church Outside of Russia, and a number of other Orthodox jurisdictions in North America. Gilquist's book only deals with a specific group of Evangelicals (the EOC) and does not include individual Evangelicals or Pentecostal/Charismatics who have become members of the Orthodox Church. Over the past several years a half dozen or so communities of the Charismatic Episcopal Church have become members of the Antiochian Orthodox Christian Archdiocese.

hierarchy, it is clear that the pastoral leadership of the Orthodox Church is not addressing the great needs of everyday spiritual life among the rank and file laity.[44] These monastic communities draw great numbers of Orthodox lay pilgrims who are less than satisfied with the spiritual fare offered to them weekly on the parochial level. Unfortunately, this neo-monastic movement in North America, especially those communities established by Elder Ephraim of Mount Athos, is decidedly anti-Charismatic, as well as anti-Ecumenical, in its outlook. It is the age-old tensions of the institutional church versus the charismatic church. Perhaps the North American Charismatic Movement of the 1960s–90s is over and has run its course. However, the Holy Spirit, Who is ever active and moving, may yet find the soil of the Orthodox Church a fertile home for His renewing, reviving, and transformational ministry, as its theologians and leaders claim it already to be. Perhaps the following quote, attributed to the fourth-century Church Father, St. Athanasius the Great of Alexandria, is appropriate here: *"Become what you are."*[45]

44. www.orthodoxforum.com/topic.asp?TOPIC_ID=220 and www.rickross.com/groups/ephraim.html.

45. Also the title of a book by English philosopher and interpreter of Eastern thought for Westerners, Alan W. Watts, and the subtitle of German philosopher Friedrich Nietzsche's autobiography, *Ecce Homo.*

Afterword

THIS BOOK HAS PROVIDED a long-overdue history of the Charismatic Movement in the Eastern Orthodox Church in America. Nothing of its scope, depth, and insight has previously been written. It is a pioneering work of enduring significance, and as such, all future studies of the Charismatic Movement in the Orthodox Church will likely build on its achievements.

Dr. Timothy Cremeens has offered several reasons why the Charismatic Movement did not "take" in the Orthodox Church. Some of the most important reasons included lack of acceptance by the bishops due to fear, hostility, or indifference; resistance to the integration of set patterns of Orthodox spirituality with the exuberant behaviors of charismaticism; and the lack of effective leadership within the movement itself. Not observed in this study, however, were the renewal efforts of the religious education department of the Greek Orthodox Archdiocese in the 1980s and 1990s (as distinct from the jurisdictions of the Antiochian Archdiocese and Orthodox Church in America). Priests and laymen alike became the focus of the Church's singular efforts to bring about spiritual renewal through retreats and publications. Although individuals were positively impacted by such efforts, the Greek Orthodox Archdiocese fell short of its hope to enliven its communities. Similar conditions exist in other Orthodox jurisdictions in America.

Looking back, much has changed in American Orthodoxy since 1995 (the end of Cremeens's research). Orthodox leadership in the Charismatic Movement has shifted away from visible to less visible figures. There are currently no spiritual leaders that have taken up the mantel of such prominent figures as the late Father Eusebius Stephanou (+ May 23, 2016).[1] There are

1. At present, the *Brotherhood of St. Symeon the New Theologian* in Marimar Beach, Florida, continues Stephanou's ministry through two of his closest lay disciples, Joseph

also no local charismatic churches that can be found within the American Orthodox community. Yet, a noticeably evangelical spirit is clearly present in a small number of churches scattered throughout all Orthodox jurisdictions. Many of these churches have priests and/or parishioners who have joined the Orthodox Church from Charismatic or Evangelical backgrounds. Father Timothy Cremeens is himself evidence of that. Moreover, since 1987,[2] the entrance of former Protestant Evangelicals into the Antiochian Orthodox Church has enlivened a number of Orthodox Churches in nearly all jurisdictions. Evangelical converts have had a leavening affect on the spiritual quality of church life while also serving as a catalyst for indigenizing the faith on American soil. Nevertheless, the ethnic focus of various ecclesiastical jurisdictions is still alive and well, though not as prominent in some as it once was. The flames of spiritual renewal today are dowsed far more by centuries of religious formalism, liturgical fundamentalism, the appeal of a rigid monastic-type culture, and the sterile objectification of theology. In this context, Orthodoxy nevertheless appears to be on the cusp of an exciting intellectual renaissance in the twenty-first century which holds promise for spiritual renewal in the Orthodox world. But that time has not yet come. The spiritual condition of the contemporary Church still mirrors many of the spiritual inconsistencies faced by St. Symeon the New Theologian in the tenth to eleventh centuries: reliance on formal theology and clericalism more than the life-giving Spirit of Truth.

Father Timothy's book has demonstrated that the Orthodox Church has within it all that is necessary for authentic spiritual renewal. But such renewal can happen only if the Church is true to its own charismatic identity by avoiding the extremes of ecclesiastical minimalism and entrenched religious formalism. For genuine renewal to take place, the gospel of Jesus Christ must be made clear, central and compelling for each person in each generation. If the purpose of renewal is to enthrone Jesus Christ in His place of Lordship over individual lives, and in the practical life of the Church, then educational programs, theological lectures, publications, and retreats that rely more on human efforts than the Holy Spirit will prove as futile today as they have in the past. If renewal is to be genuine and lasting, it must start with a personal commitment to Jesus Christ as Lord and Savior. One must never assume that just because people attend Church they are genuine Christians. Conversion must be preached from time to time

---

Abbate and Symeon McKnight.

2. Nassif, "Evangelical Denomination," in *Christianity Today*, 40.

and integrated sporadically into the educational programs of the Church. Like St. Anthony of Egypt who became a more deeply committed disciple after hearing the gospel in Church, parishioners today must likewise deny themselves, take up the cross and follow Christ. Conscious decisions of repentance and faith must be made. Conversion may come about suddenly in a Damascus Road kind of experience (as emphasized by St. Symeon), or gradually as one increases in his or her obedience to the gospel (as taught by saints Mark the Ascetic and Makarios of Egypt). Either way—suddenly or gradually—without the renewing grace of baptism, and a "conscious awareness" of God's presence in the heart, spiritual life will not blossom. To that end, St. Symeon the New Theologian exhorts:

> *Do not say, "It is impossible to receive the Holy Spirit"; Do not say, "It is possible to be saved without Him." Do not say, then, that "one can possess Him without knowing it."* . . . *This is a thing never impossible, my friends, but on the contrary altogether possible for those who so wish it."* (Hymn 27)

Bradley Nassif, PhD

Professor of Biblical and Theological Studies,
North Park University (Chicago)

Bibliography

Abbott, Walter M., ed. *The Documents of Vatican II*. London: Chapman, 1966.

Afanasiev, Nicholas. *The Church of the Holy Spirit*. Notre Dame, IN: University of Notre Dame Press, 2007.

Alert, Craig D. *A High View of Scripture?* Grand Rapids: Baker, 2007.

Alexander, Donald L. *Christian Spirituality: Five Views of Sanctification*. Downers Grove: IL: Inter-Varsity, 1988.

Alfeyev, Hilarion. *Architecture, Icons and Music of the Orthodox Church*. Vol. III of *The Orthodox Church*. Yonkers, NY: St. Vladimir's Seminary Press, 2014.

———. *Doctrine and Teaching of the Orthodox Church*. Vol. II of *The Orthodox Church*. Yonkers, NY: St. Vladimir's Seminary Press, 2012.

———. *History and Canonical Structure of the Orthodox Church*. Vol. I of *The Orthodox Church*. Yonkers, NY: St. Vladimir's Seminary Press, 2011.

———. *St. Symeon the New Theologian and Orthodox Tradition*. Oxford: Oxford University Press, 2000.

———. *Worship and Liturgical Life of the Orthodox Church*. Vol. IV of *The Orthodox Church*. Yonkers, NY: St. Vladimir's Seminary Press, 2016.

Altschul, Paisius, ed. *An Unbroken Circle: Linking Ancient African Christianity to the African-American Experience*. St. Louis: Brotherhood of St. Moses the Black, 1997.

———. *Wade in the River: The Story of the African Christian Faith*. Kansas City, MO: Cross Bearers, 2001.

Anderson, Allan H. *African Reformation: African Initiated Christianity in the 20th Century*. Trenton, NJ: Africa World, 2001.

———. *An Introduction to Pentecostalism: Global Charismatic Christianity*. Cambridge: Cambridge University, 2004.

———. *Spreading Fires: The Missionary Nature of Early Pentecostalism*. Maryknoll, NY: Orbis, 2007.

Anderson, Allan H., and Edmond Tang, eds. *Asian and Pentecostal: The Charismatic Face of Christianity in Asia*. 2nd ed., Oxford: Regnum, 2011.

Anderson, Robert Mapes. *Vision of the Disinherited*. New York: Oxford University Press, 1979.

Applegate, Andrew. "The Orthodox Church Process of Canonization/Glorification, and the Life of Blessed Archbishop Arseny." *The Canadian Journal of Orthodox Christianity*, 10, no. 1, (2015) 1–34.

Archer, Kenneth J. *A Pentecostal Hermeneutic of the Twenty-First Century: Spirit, Scripture and Community.* London: T. & T. Clark, 2004.

Asamoah-Gyadu, J. Kwabena. *Contemporary Pentecostal Christianity.* Oxford: Regnum, 2013.

Ashanin, Charles. "THE LOGOS: A Sign and Symbol to Orthodox Christians. How the Prophetic and Charismatic Ministry Can Promise a New Vitality to the Church." *The Logos,* 5, no. 1 (1972) 3–4.

Azkoul, Michael. *Once Delivered to the Saints: An Orthodox Apology for the New Millennium.* Seattle: Saint Nectarios, 2000.

Badcock, Gary. *Light of Truth & Fire of Love: A Theology of the Holy Spirit.* Grand Rapids: Eerdmans, 1997.

Bagiackas, Joseph. *The Future Glory: The Charismatic Renewal and the Implementation of Vatican II.* South Bend, IN: Charismatic Renewal Services, 1983.

Bajis, Jordan. *Common Ground: An Introduction to Eastern Christianity for the American Christian.* Minneapolis: Light & Life, 1996.

Balmer, Randall, *Mine Eyes Have Seen the Glory: A Journey into the Evangelical Subculture of America.* Oxford: Oxford University Press, 1989.

Barnett, Donald Lee, and Jeffrey P. McGregor. *Speaking in Tongues: A Scholarly Defense.* Seattle: Community Chapel, 1986.

Barnett, Maurice. *The Living Flame: Being a Study of the Gift of the Spirit in the New Testament.* London: Epsworth, 1953.

Bartleman, Frank. *How Pentecost Came to Los Angeles.* Los Angeles: Bartleman, 1925.

Barton, Stephen C., ed. *Holiness: Past and Present.* London: T. & T. Clark, 2003.

Basham, Don. *Face Up with a Miracle.* Monroeville, PA: Whitaker House, 1971.

———. *A Handbook on Holy Spirit Baptism.* New Kensington, PA: Whitaker House, 1999.

———. *The Miracle of Tongues.* Old Tappan, NJ: Revell, 1973.

Basil of Caesarea. *On the Holy Spirit.* Translated by David Anderson. Crestwood, NY: St. Vladimir's Seminary Press, 1980.

Bassett. Paul M., and William M. Greathouse. *The Historical Development.* Vol. 1 of *Exploring Christian Holiness.* Kansas City, MO: Beacon Hill, 1985.

Bauman, Michael, and Martin I. Klauber, eds. *Historians of the Christian Tradition.* Nashville: Broadman & Holman, 1995.

Beacham, Doug. *G. B. Cashwell.* Franklin Springs, GA: LifeSprings Resources, 2006.

Bennett, Dennis and Rita. *The Holy Spirit and You.* Plainfield, NJ: Logos International, 1971.

———. *How to Pray for the Release of the Holy Spirit.* Plainfield, NJ: Logos International, 1985.

———. *Nine O'clock in the Morning.* Plainfield, NJ: Logos International, 1970.

Berger, Teresa, and Bryan D. Spinks, eds. *The Spirit in Worship-Worship in the Spirit.* Collegeville, MN: Liturgical, 2009.

Bernard, David K. *Practical Holiness: A Second Look.* Vol. IV of *Series in Pentecostal Theology.* Hazelwood, MO: World Aflame, 1985.

Bilaniuk, Petro B. T. *Theology and Economy of the Holy Spirit: An Eastern Approach.* Bangalore, India: Dharmaram, 1980.

Bishops' Liaison Committee with the Catholic Charismatic Renewal. *A Pastoral Statement on the Catholic Charismatic Renewal.* Washington, DC: Office of Publishing and Promotion Services, Unites States Catholic Conference, 1984.

Bittlinger, Arnold, ed. *The Church is Charismatic: The World Council of Churches and the Charismatic Renewal.* Geneva: WCC Renewal and Congregational Life, 1981.

Bixler, R. H., ed. *The Spirit is-a-Movin'.* Carol Stream, IL: Creation House, 1974.

Blane, Andrew, ed. *Georges Florovsky: Russian Intellectual, Orthodox Churchman.* Crestwood, NY: St. Vladimir's Seminary Press, 1993.

Blumhofer, Edith L., Russell P. Spittler, and Grant Wacker, eds. *Pentecostal Currents in American Protestantism.* Urbana, IL: University of Illinois Press, 1999.

Boone, Pat. *A New Song.* Carol Stream, IL: Creation House, 1970.

Borlase, Craig. *William Seymour: A Biography.* Lake Mary, FL: Charisma House, 2006.

Bradford, Brick. *Releasing the Power of the Holy Spirit.* Oklahoma City: Presbyterian Charismatic Communion, 1983.

Brand, Chad Owen. *Perspectives on Spirit Baptism.* Nashville: Broadman & Holman, 2004.

Braun, John. *Divine Energy: The Orthodox Path to Christian Victory.* Ben Lomond, CA: Conciliar, 1991.

Breck, John. *Scripture in Tradition: The Bible and Its Interpretation on the Orthodox Church.* Crestwood, NY: St. Vladimir's Seminary Press, 2001.

Bredesen, Harald. *Yes, Lord.* Plainfield, NJ: Logos International, 1972.

Brooks, Noel. *Scriptural Holiness.* Franklin Springs, GA: Advocate, 1967.

Brown, Dale. *Understanding Pietism.* Nappanee, IN: Evangel, 1996.

Brown, Michael. *Authentic Fire: A Response to John MacArthur's Strange Fire.* Lake Mary, FL: Excel, 2014.

Bruce, F. F. *Tradition: Old and New.* Grand Rapids: Zondervan, 1970.

Brunk II, George R., ed. *Encounter with the Holy Spirit.* Scottsdale, PA: Herald, 1972.

Bucke, Emory Stephens, ed., *The History of American Methodism.* 3 vols. New York: Abingdon, 1964

Budgen, Victor. *The Charismatics and the Word of God.* Welwyn, UK: Evangelical, 1985.

Bulgakov, Sergius. *The Comforter.* Grand Rapids: Eerdmans, 2004.

———. *The Orthodox Church.* Crestwood, NY: St. Vladimir's Seminary Press, 1988.

Burdon, Adrian. *Authority and Order: John Wesley and His Preachers.* Farnham, UK: Ashgate, 2005.

Burgess, Stanley, ed. *Encyclopedia of Pentecostal and Charismatic Christianity.* New York: Routledge, 2006.

———. *The Holy Spirit: Ancient Christian Traditions.* Peabody, MA: Hendrickson, 1984.

———. *The Holy Spirit: Eastern Christian Traditions.* Peabody, MA: Hendrickson, 1989.

———. *The Holy Spirit: Medieval Roman Catholic and Reformation Traditions.* Peabody, MA: Hendrickson, 1997.

———, ed. *The New International Dictionary of Pentecostal Charismatic Movements.* Grand Rapids: Zondervan, 2002.

Butler, C. S. *Test the Spirits: An Examination of the Charismatic Phenomenon.* Welwyn, UK: Evangelical, 1985.

Byrne, James E. *Living in the Spirit: A Handbook on Catholic Charismatic Christianity.* New York: Paulist, 1975.

Cabie, Robert. *The Eucharist.* Vol. 2 of *The Church at Prayer.* Edited by A. G Martimort; translated by Matthew J. O'Connell. Collegeville, MN: Liturgical, 1986.

Cage, Gary T. *The Holy Spirit: A Sourcebook with Commentary.* Reno, NV: Charlotee House Publishers, 1995.

Callen, Barry L. *The Holy River of God: Currents and Contributions of the Wesleyan Holiness Stream of Christianity.* Spring Valley, CA: Aldersgate, 2016.

Campbell, Bob. *Baptism in the Holy Spirit: Command or Option?* Monroeville, PA: Whitaker, 1973.

Campbell, Joseph E. *What to Believe and Why About Sanctification.* Franklin Springs, GA: The Publishing House, 1952.

Cantalamessa, Raniero. *Come, Creator Spirit: Meditations on Veni Creator.* Collegeville, MN: Liturgical, 2003.

———. *Sober Intoxication of the Spirit.* Cincinnati, OH: Servant, 2005.

———. *Sober Intoxication of the Spirit Part Two.* Cincinnati, OH: Servant, 2012.

Catanello, Ignatius A. "The Effects of the Charismatic Movement on Local Ecumenism: Descriptive Research." PhD diss., New York University, 1983.

Carteledge, Mark J. *Encountering the Spirit: The Charismatic Tradition.* Maryknoll, NY: Orbis, 2006.

Chakos, John. "The Charismatic Revival and its Implications for Orthodoxy." *Concern* X, no. 3 (1975) 6–9.

Chan, Simon. *Pentecostal Theology and the Christian Spiritual Tradition.* Sheffield, UK: Sheffield Academic Press, 2000.

Chervin, Ronda. *Why I Am a Charismatic: A Catholic Explains.* Liguori, MO: Liguori, 1978.

Cho, Paul Yongi, with Harold Hostetler. *Successful Home Cell Groups.* South Plainfield, NJ: Bridge, 1981.

Chondropoulos, Sotos. *Saint Nekarios—A Saint for Our Times.* Translated by Peter and Aliki Los. Brookline, MA: Holy Cross Orthodox Press, 1989.

Christensen, Damascene. *Father Seraphim Rose: His Life and Works.* Platina, CA: St. Herman of Alaska Brotherhood, 2003.

Christensen, Michael J., and Jeffrey A. Wittung, eds. *Partakers of the Divine Nature: The History and Development of Deification in the Christian Traditions.* Grand Rapids: Baker, 2007.

Christenson, Larry. *The Charismatic Renewal among Lutherans.* Minneapolis: Lutheran Charismatic Renewal Services, 1975.

———. *A Message to the Charismatic Renewal.* Weymouth, MA: Dimension, 1972.

———. *Welcome, Holy Spirit: A Study of Charismatic Renewal in the Church.* Minneapolis: Augsburg, 1987.

Cirlot, Felix L. *The Early Eucharist.* London: SPCK, 1939.

Clark, Randy. *Authority to Heal.* Shippensburg, PA: Destiny Image, 2016.

———. *The Essential Guide to the Power of the Holy Spirit.* Shippensburg, PA: Destiny Image, 2015.

———. *The Healing Breakthrough: Creating an Atmosphere of Faith for Healing.* Minneapolis, MN: Chosen, 2016.

———. *Power to Heal.* Shippensburg, PA: Destiny Image, 2015.

Clark, Steve. *Baptized in the Spirit and Spiritual Gifts.* Pecos, NM: Dove & Ann Arbor, MI: Servant, 1976.

Collins, Kenneth J. *The Scripture Way of Salvation: The Heart of John Wesley's Theology.* Nashville: Abingdon, 1997.

Committee for Pastoral Research and Practice, National Conference of Catholic Bishops. United States Catholic Conference, 1975.

Congar, Yves. *I Believe in the Holy Spirit.* Translated by David Smith. 3 vols. New York: Seabury, 1983.

———. *The Meaning of Tradition.* Translated by A. N. Woodrow. New York: Hawthorn, 1964.

———. *Report from Rome II: The Second Session of the Vatican Council.* London: Chapman, 1964.

———. *Tradition and Traditions; A Historical and Theological Essay.* Translated by Michael Naseby and Thomas Rainborough. New York: Macmillan, 1967.

Coniaris, Anthony. *Achieving Your Potential in Christ: Theosis.* Minneapolis: Light and Life, 1993.

———. *Introducing the Orthodox Church: Its Faith and Life.* Minneapolis: Light and Life, 1982.

Conn, Charles. W. *Like A Mighty Army.* Cleveland, TN: Church of God, 1955.

Cooke, Bernard. *Power and the Spirit of God: Toward an Experience-Based Pneumatology.* Oxford: Oxford University Press, 2004.

Cooper-Rompato, Christine F. *The Gift of Tongues: Women's Xenoglossia in the Later Middle Ages.* University Park, PA: Pennsylvania State University Press, 2010.

Cordes, Paul Josef. *Call to Holiness: Reflections on the Catholic Charismatic Renewal.* Collegeville, MN: Liturgical, 1997.

Corey, George S., Peter E. Gilquist, Anne Glynn Mackoul, Jean Sam, Paul Schneirla, eds. *The First One Hundred Years: A Centennial Anthology Celebrating Antiochian Orthodoxy in North America.* Englewood, NJ: Antakya, 1995.

Coulter, Dale, and Amos Yong, eds. *The Spirit, the Affections and the Christian Tradition.* Notre Dame, IN: University of Notre Dame Press, 2016.

Cox, Harvey. *Fire from Heaven: The Rise of Pentecostal Spirituality and the Reshaping of Religion in the 21st Century.* Cambridge, MA: De Capo, 2001.

Cremeens, Timothy. "The Pentecostal-Charismatic Movement: An Introduction for Orthodox Christians." M.Div. diss., St. Vladimir's Orthodox Theological Seminary, 1993.

———. *St. Symeon the New Theologian.* Destin, FL, Brotherhood of St. Symeon the New Theologian, VHS, 1992.

———. "St. Symeon the New Theologian: An Eastern Orthodox Model for Charismatic Spirituality." Paper presented at the annual meeting of the Society for Pentecostal Studies, Springfield, MO, 12 November 1992, Vol. 2, V. 1–29.

Crowe, Terrence Robert. *Pentecostal Unity: Recurring Frustration and Enduring Hopes.* Chicago: Loyola University Press, 1993.

Dabney, Lyle. "Saul's Armor: The Problem and the Promise of Pentecostal Theology Today." *Pneuma* 23, no. 1 (2001) 115–46.

Davies, J. G. *The Spirit, the Church and the Sacraments.* London: The Faith, 1954.

Dayton, Donald W. *Theological Roots of Pentecostalism.* Peabody, MA: Hendrickson, 1987.

Dayton, Donald W., and Robert K. Johnston. *The Variety of American Evangelicalism.* Knoxville: University of Tennessee Press, 1991.

Dempster, Murray W., Byron D. Klaus, and Douglas Petersen, eds. *The Globalization of Pentecostalism: A Religion Made to Travel.* Oxford: Regnum, 1999.

Derstine, Gerald. *Following the Fire.* Plainfield, NJ: Logos International, 1980.

———. *Visitation of God to the Mennonites.* Bradenton, FL: Gospel Crusade, 1961.

Dieter, Melvin. *The Holiness Revival of the Nineteenth Century.* Lanham, MD: Scarecrow, 1996.

Dillenschneider, Clement. *The Holy Spirit and the Priest: Toward and Interiorization of Our Priesthood.* St. Louis: Herder, 1965.

Dories, David. "Edward Irving and the 'Standing Sign' of Spirit Baptism." In *Initial Evidence: Historical and Biblical Perspectives on the Pentecostal Doctrine of Spirit Baptism*, edited by Gary McGee, 41–56. Peabody, MA: Hendrickson, 1991.

Dorr, Donal. *Remove the Heart of Stone: Charismatic Renewal and the Experience of Grace.* New York: Paulist, 1978.

Du Plessis, David. *A Man Called Mr. Pentecost: David Du Plessis as told to Bob Slosser.* Plainfield, NJ: Logos International, 1977

———. *The Spirit Bade Me Go.* Plainfield, NJ: Logos International, 1977.

Durasoff, David. *Bright Wind of the Spirit.* New York: Prentice Hall, 1972.

Durham, William. *Articles Written by Pastor Durham Taken from the Pentecostal Testimony.* Los Angeles: np., nd..

Edwards, Jonathan. *Religious Affections.* Goodyear, AZ: Diggory, 2007.

Elbert, Paul, ed. *Essays on Apostolic Themes.* Peabody, MA: Hendricksen, 1985.

El-Meskeen, Matta. *Orthodox Prayer Life: The Interior Way.* Crestwood, NY: St. Vladimir's Seminary Press, 2003.

Emmert, Athanasius. "Come, Holy Spirit!" *The Logos* 5, no. 3 (1972) 8–9.

———. "The Glory Is His Alone." *The Logos* 5, no. 6 (1972) 8–9.

———. *Israel in Prophecy.* Homewood, IL: St. Nicholas Orthodox Church, 2 Audiocassettes, n.d.

———. "Making the Power of the Holy Spirit Our Own: The Wonderful Promise of God." *The Logos,* 5, no. 2 (1972) 8–9.

———. "The Pentecostal Power Inherent in the Orthodox Church." *The Logos,* 5, no. 4 (1972) 8–10.

———. "The Power of the Holy Spirit: A Need for Our Day." *The Logos* 5, no. 1 (1972) 14–16.

———. "The Unfamiliar is Threatening to Some Orthodox: Why the Charismatic Movement Is Not Foreign to Orthodoxy." *The Logos,* 5, no. 5 (1972) 11–13.

Engelsviken, Tormod. "The Gift of the Spirit: An Analysis and Evaluation of the Charismatic Movement from a Lutheran Theological Perspective." PhD diss., Aquinas Institute of Theology, Dubuque, 1981.

Ensley, Eddie. *Sounds of Wonder: A Popular History of Speaking in Tongues in the Catholic Tradition.* New York: Paulist, 1977.

Erb, Peter C., ed. *Pietists—Selected Writings.* New York: Paulist, 1983.

Ervin, Howard M. *These Are Not Drunken as Ye Suppose.* Plainfield, NJ: Logos, 1967.

Espinosa, Gastón. *William Seymour and the Origins of Global Pentecostalism.* Durham, NC: Duke University Press, 2014.

Estabrooks, Spencer. "A Continuing Pentecost: The Experience of the Holy Spirit in Orthodox Christianity (with a View to Dialogue between Orthodox Christians and Pentecostals)." *Canadian Journal of Orthodox Christianity,* 1, no. 1 (2006) 1–20.

Farkas, Thomas George. "William H. Durham and the Sanctification Controversy in Early American Pentecostalism." PhD diss., Southwestern Baptist Theological Seminary, 1993.

Faupel, D. William. *The Everlasting Gospel.* Sheffield, UK: Sheffield Academic Press, 1996.

Fee, Gordon D. *Listening to the Spirit in the Text.* Grand Rapids, Eerdmans, 2000.

Ferguson, Charles W., *Methodists and the Making of America: Organizing to Beat the Devil.* Austin, TX: Eakin, 1983.

Fields, Anne. *From Darkness to Light: How One Became a Christian in the Early Church.* Ben Lomond, CA: Conciliar, 1997.

Flannery, Austin, ed. *Vatican Council II: The Conciliar and Post Conciliar Documents.* Grand Rapids: Eerdmans, 1992.

———, ed. *Vatican Council II: More Post Conciliar Documents.* Collegeville, MN: Liturgical, 1982.

Florovsky, Georges. *Aspects of Church History.* Belmont, MA: Nordland, 1975.

———. *Bible, Church, Tradition: An Eastern Orthodox View.* Vaduz, Liechtenstein: Buchervertriebsanstalt, 1987.

———. *The Byzantine Ascetic and Spiritual Fathers.* Vaduz, Liechtenstein: Buchervertriebsanstalt, 1987.

———. *The Byzantine Fathers of the Fifth Century.* Vaduz, Liechtenstein: Buchervertriebsanstalt, 1987.

———. *The Byzantine Fathers of the Sixth to the Eighth Century.* Vaduz, Liechtenstein: Buchervertriebsanstalt, 1987.

———. *Christianity and Culture.* Belmont, MA: Nordland, 1974.

———. *Creation and Redemption.* Belmont, MA: Nordland, 1976.

———. *The Eastern Fathers of the Fourth Century.* Vaduz, Liechtenstein: Buchervertriebsanstalt, 1987.

———. *Ecumenism I: A Doctrinal Approach.* Vaduz, Liechtenstein: Buchervertriebsanstalt, 1987.

———. *Ecumenism II: A Historical Approach.* Vaduz, Liechtenstein: Buchervertriebsanstalt, 1987.

———. *The Ways of Orthodox Theology: Part One.* Belmont: MA: Nordland, 1979.

———. *The Ways of Orthodox Theology: Part Two.* Vaduz, Liechtenstein: Buchervertriebsanstalt, 1987.

Flower, J. Roswell "The Birth of the Pentecostal Movement." *The Pentecostal Evangel,* no. 1907 (November 26, 1950), 3, 12–14.

Ford, J. Massingberd. *The Spirit and the Human Person: A Meditation.* Dayton, OH: Pflaum, 1969.

Foster, K. Neill. *Help! I Believe in Tongues: A Third View of the Charismatic Phenomenon.* Minneapolis: Bethany Fellowship, 1975.

Frame, Randall. "UnOrthodox Behavior?" *Christianity Today* 37, no. 18 (1993) 57.

Freeman, Jean "Encountering the Holy Spirit Through Healing" *Theosis,* vol. 1, no. 7 (1978) 7.

Frodsham, Stanley. *With Signs Following: The Story of the Pentecostal Revival in the Twentieth Century.* Springfield, MO: Gospel, 1946.

Frost, Evelyn. *Christian Healing.* London: Mowbray, 1940.

Frost, Robert. *Aglow with the Spirit.* Plainfield, NJ: Logos International, 1971.

———. *Overflowing Life.* Plainfield, NJ: Logos International, 1972.

———. *Set My Spirit Free.* Plainfield, NJ: Logos International, 1973.

Fudge, Thomas A. *Christianity without the Cross: A History of Salvation in Oneness Pentecostalism.* Parkland, FL: Universal, 2003.

Gabriel, Anthony. *The Ancient Church on New Shores: Antioch in North America.* n.p. 2015.

———. "Lest We Forget Archpriest Paul Schneirla on the 100th Anniversary of His Birth." *The Word,* vol. 60, no. 4. (April 2016) 10–12.

Galvano, Stephen, ed. *Fiftieth Anniversary of the Christian Church of North America, 1927–1977.* Sharon, PA: General Council of the Christian Church of North America, 1977.

Gaustad, Edwin S., and Mark Noll, eds. *A Documentary History of Religion in America*. 2 vols. 3rd ed. Grand Rapids: Eerdmans, 2003.

Gavrilia, Nun. *Mother Gavrilia: The Ascetic of Love*. Pierias, Greece: Tertios, 1999.

Gelpi, Donald. *Charism and Sacrament: A Theology of Christian Conversion*. New York: Paulist, 1976.

————. *Pentecostalism: A Theological Viewpoint*. New York: Paulist, 1971.

Gilbertson, Richard. *The Baptism of the Holy Spirit: The Views of A. B. Simpson and His Contemporaries*. Camp Hill, PA: Christian, 1993.

Gilet, Lev. *Orthodox Spirituality: An Outline of the Orthodox Ascetical and Mystical Tradition*. Crestwood, NY: St. Vladimir's Seminary Press, 1987.

————. *The Year of Grace of the Lord*. Crestwood, NY: St. Vladimir's Seminary Press, 1980.

Gillespie, Thomas W. *The First Theologians: A Study in Early Christian Prophecy*. Grand Rapids: Eerdmans, 1994.

Goergen, Donald J. *Fire of Love: Encountering the Holy Spirit*. New York: Paulist, 2006.

Goff, James R. and Grant Wacker, eds. *Portrait of a Generation: Early Pentecostal Leaders*. Fayetteville, AR: University of Arkansas Press, 2002.

————. *White unto Harvest: Charles F. Parham and the Missionary Origins of Pentecostalism*. Fayetteville: University of Arkansas Press, 1988.

Goodman, Felicitas D. *Speaking in Tongues: A Cross-Cultural Study of Glossolalia*. Chicago: University of Chicago Press, 1972.

Goss, Ethel E. *The Winds of God*. Hazelwood, MO: World Aflame, 1958.

Gresham, Jr., John L. *Charles G. Finney's Doctrine of the Baptism of the Holy Spirit*. Peabody, MA: Hendrickson, 1987.

Grudem, Wayne. *The Gift of Prophecy in the New Testament and Today*. Wheaton, IL: Crossway, 1988.

Gundry, Stanley, and James Stamoolis, eds. *Three Views on Eastern Orthodoxy and Evangelicalism*. Grand Rapids: Zondervan, 2004.

Hamilton, Michael P., ed. *The Charismatic Movement*. Grand Rapids, Eerdmans, 1975

Hanson, R. P. C. *The Search for the Christian Doctrine of God*. Grand Rapids: Baker Academic, 2010.

————. *Tradition in the Early Church*. London: SCM, 1962.

Harakas, Stanley Samuel. *Of Life and Salvation: Reflections on Living the Christian Life*. Minneapolis: Light and Life, 1996.

Harper, Michael. *As at the Beginning: The Twentieth-Century Pentecostal Revival*. London: Hodder and Stoughton, 1965.

————. *A Faith Fulfilled: Why are Christians across Great Britain Embracing Orthodoxy?* Ben Lomond, CA: Conciliar, 1999.

————. *Power for the Body of Christ*. London: Fountain Trust, 1965.

Harrell Jr., David Edwin. *All Things are Possible: The Healing and Charismatic Revivals in Modern America*. Bloomington, IN: Indiana University Press, 1975.

Harris, Ralph W. *Spoken by the Spirit; Documented Accounts of "Other Tongues" from Arabic to Zulu*. Springfield, MO: Gospel, 1973.

Hatch, Alden. *A Man Called John: The Life of Pope John XXIII*. New York: Hawthorn, 1963.

Haughey, John C. *The Conspiracy of God the Holy Spirit in Men*. Garden City, NY: Doubleday, 1973.

————, ed. *Theological Reflections on the Charismatic Renewal*. Ann Arbor, MI: Servant, 1978.

Hausherr, Irénée. *The Name of Jesus*. Kalamazoo, MI: Cistercian, 1978.

———. *Spiritual Direction in the Early Christian East*. Kalamazoo, MI: Cistercian, 1990.

Hayford, Jack W. *The Beauty of Spiritual Language*. Dallas: Word, 1992.

Hayford, Jack W., and David S. Moore. *The Charismatic Century: The Enduring Impact of the Azusa Street Revival*. New York: Time Warner, 2006.

Hazim, Patriarch Ignatius IV. *The Resurrection and Modern Man*. Crestwood, NY: St. Vladimir's Seminary Press, 1985.

Healey, John B. *Charismatic Renewal: Reflections of a Pastor*. New York: Paulist, 1976.

Heers, Peter. *The Ecclesiological Renovation of Vatican II: An Orthodox Examination of Rome's Ecumenical Theology Regarding Baptism and the Church*. Simpsonville, SC: Uncut Mountain, 2015.

Heyer, Robert, ed., *Pentecostal Catholics*. New York: Paulist, 1974.

Heyrman, Christine Leigh. *Southern Cross: The Beginnings of the Bible Belt*. New York: Knopf, 1997.

Hitchcock, James, and Gloriana Bednarski. *Catholic Perspectives: Charismatic*. Chicago: Moore, 1980.

Hocken, Peter. *Azusa, Rome, and Zion: Pentecostal Faith, Catholic Reform, and Jewish Roots*. Eugene, OR: Pickwick, 2016.

———. *The Challenges of the Pentecostal, Charismatic and Messianic Jewish Movements: The Tension of the Spirit*. New York: Routledge, 2016.

———. *Pentecost and Parousia: Charismatic Renewal, Christian Unity, and the Coming Glory*. Eugene, OR: Wipf and Stock, 2013.

Hoekema, Anthony A. *Tongues and Spirit-Baptism: A Biblical and Theological Evaluation*. Grand Rapids: Baker Book House, 1981.

Hogan, Bob. *Celebrating a Charismatic Jubilee: A Fresh Look at Charismatic Renewal and the Charismatic Dimension of the Church*. Locust Grove, VA: Catholic Charismatic Renewal Service Committee, 2016.

Hogue, Richard. *Tongues: The Theological History of Christian Glossolalia*. Mustang, OK: Tate, 2010.

Holland, Christina. "Against Ecumenism." http://www.orthodox.net/articles/against-ecumenism.html (accessed August 28, 2010).

Hopko, Thomas. *Bible and Church History, Vol. II of The Orthodox Church: An Elementary Handbook on the Orthodox Church*. New York: The Department of Religious Education, The Orthodox Church in America, 1976.

———. *Doctrine, Vol. I of The Orthodox Church: An Elementary Handbook on the Orthodox Church*. New York: The Department of Religious Education, The Orthodox Church in America, 1976.

———. *The Fullness of God: Essays on Orthodoxy, Ecumenism and Modern Society*. Crestwood, NY: St. Vladimir's Seminary Press, 1982.

———. *The Spirit of God*. Wilton, CT: Morehouse-Barlow, 1976.

———. *Spirituality. Vol. IV of The Orthodox Church: An Elementary Handbook on the Orthodox Church*. New York: The Department of Religious Education, The Orthodox Church in America, 1976.

———, ed. *Women and the Priesthood*. Crestwood, NY: St. Vladimir's Seminary Press, 1992.

———. *Worship. Vol. II of The Orthodox Church: An Elementary Handbook on the Orthodox Church*. New York: The Department of Religious Education, The Orthodox Church in America, 1976.

Hollenweger, Walter. *Pentecostalism: Origins and Developments Worldwide.* Peabody, MA: Hendrickson, 1997.

————. *The Pentecostals: The Charismatic Movement in the Churches.* Minneapolis: Fortress, 1972.

Hovenden, Gerald. *Speaking in Tongues: The New Testament Evidence in Context.* London: Sheffield Academic Press, 2002.

Hummel, Charles. *Fire in the Fireplace,* Downers Grove, IL: Inter-Varsity, 1994.

Humphrey, Edith M. *Ecstasy and Intimacy: When the Holy Spirit Meets the Human Spirit.* Grand Rapids: Eerdmans, 2006.

Hunt, Stephen, Malcolm Hamilton, and Tony Walter, eds. *Charismatic Christianity: Sociological Perspectives.* New York: St. Martin's, 1997.

Hunter, Harold. "Tongues-Speech: A Patristic Analysis." *Journal of the Evangelical Theological Society,* 23, no. 2 (1980) 125–37.

Iakovos, Archbishop. "Exorcism and Exorcists in Orthodox Tradition," *Upbeat,* 7, no. 8 (May/June 1974) 15–19.

Irenaeus of Lyons. *Against Heresies.* Translated by ANF 1, 1885. Reprint. Grand Rapids: Eerdmans, 1987.

Jacobson, Douglas. *Thinking in the Spirit: Theologies of the Early Pentecostal Movement.* Bloomington, IN: Indiana University Press, 2003.

Johns, Cheryl Bridges. *Pentecostal Formation: A Pedagogy among the Oppressed.* Sheffield, UK: Sheffield Academic, 1993.

Johnson, Ann. "Home Pages: Prosphora," *Orthodox Outlook* 97 (May-June 2002) 24–26.

Johnson, Luke Timothy. *Religious Experience in Earliest Christianity.* Minneapolis: Fortress, 1998.

Jones, Charles Edwin. *The Charismatic Movement: A Guide to the Study of Neo-Pentecostalism with Emphasis on Anglo-American Sources.* 2 vols. Metuchen, NJ: American Theological Library Association and Scarecrow, 1995.

————. *A Guide to the Study of the Pentecostal Movement.* 2 vols. Metuchen, NJ: American Theological Library Association and Scarecrow, 1983.

————. *The Holiness-Pentecostal Movement: A Comprehensive Guide.* Lanham, MD: American Theological Library Association and Scarecrow, 2008.

Jungman, Josef A. *The Early Liturgy: To the Time of Gregory the Great.* Translated by Francis Brunner Notre Dame, IN: University of Notre Dame Press, 1959.

Kagarise, Robby J. *Paul's Charismatic Imperatives.* Blandford Forum, UK: Deo, 2014.

Kärkkäinen, Veli-Matti. *One with God: Salvation as Deification and Justification.* Collegeville, MN: Liturgical, 2004.

Karmiris, John. *The Status and Ministry of the Laity in the Orthodox Church.* Brookline, MA: Holy Cross Orthodox, 1994.

Kay, William K., and Anne E. Dyer. *Pentecostal and Charismatic Studies.* London: SCM, 2004.

Kelsey, Morton. *Tongues Speaking: The History and Meaning of Charismatic Experience.* New York: Crossroads, 1981.

Kelso, Scott. *Ice on Fire: A New Day for the 21st Century Church.* Nashville: Nelson, 2006.

Kerr, John Stevens. *The Fire Flares Anew: A Look at the New Pentecostalism.* Philadelphia: Fortress, 1974.

King, Joseph Hilary. *From Passover to Pentecost.* Franklin Springs, GA: Advocate, 1976.

Kizhakkeparampil, Isaac. *The Invocation of the Holy Spirit as Constitutive of the Sacraments According to Cardinal Yves Congar.* Rome: Gregorian University Press, 1995.

Kostlevy, William, ed. *Historical Dictionary of the Holiness Movement*. Lanham, MD: The Scarecrow, 2009.

Krestiankin, John. *May God Grant You Wisdom! The Letters of Fr. John Krestiankin*. Wildwood, CA: St. Xenia Skete, 2007.

Krivocheine, Basil. *In the Light of Christ*. Crestwood, NY: St. Vladimir's Seminary Press, 1986.

Küng, Hans. *The Church*. Garden City, NY: Image, 1976.

————. *Infallible?* London: Collins, 1977.

LaBerge, Agnes N. O. *What God Hath Wrought*. n.d. Reprint. New York: Garland, 1985.

Land, Stephan J. *Pentecostal Spirituality*. Sheffield, UK: Sheffield Academic Press, 2001.

Langdon, Joseph. *How the Holy Spirit Brings Us to Christ*. OR #44, Fort Wayne, IN, Service Committee for Orthodox Spiritual Renewal. Audiocassette, n.d.

Laurentin, René. *Catholic Pentecostalism: An In-depth Report on the Charismatic Renewal by a Renowned International Theologian*. Garden City, NY: Doubleday, 1977.

Lawler, Mary. *Marcus Garvey: Black Nationalist Leader*. New York: Chelsea House, 1988.

Lederle, H. I. *Treasures Old and New*. Peabody, MA: Hendrickson, 1988.

————. *Theology with Spirit: The Future of the Pentecostal & Charismatic Movements in the 21ˢᵗ Century*. Tulsa, OK: Word & Spirit, 2010.

Lesser, R. H. *The Holy Spirit and Charismatic Renewal*. Bangalore: Asian Trading Corporation, 1996.

Lie, Geir. "E. W. Kenyon: Cult Founder or Evangelical Minster: An Historical Analysis of Kenyon's Theology with Particular Emphasis on the Roots and Influences." Master's diss., Norwegian Lutheran School of Theology, 1994.

Limouris, Gennadios, ed. *Come, Holy Spirit Renew the Whole Creation*. Brookline, MA: Holy Cross Orthodox, 1991.

Lossky, Vladimir. *Dogmatic Theology: Creation, God's Image in Man, & the Redeeming Work of the Trinity*. Yonkers, NY: St. Vladimir's Seminary Press, 2017.

MacArthur, John. *The Charismatics: A Doctrinal Perspective*. Grand Rapids: Zondervan, 1978.

————. *Charismatic Chaos*. Grand Rapids: Zondervan, 1992.

————. *Strange Fire: The Danger of Offending the Spirit with Counterfeit Worship*. Nashville: Thomas Nelson, 2013.

Macchia, Frank D. *Baptized in the Holy Spirit*. Grand Rapids: Zondervan, 2006.

————. "Justification through New Creation: The Holy Spirit and the Doctrine by which the Church Stands or Falls." *Theology Today* 58, no. 2 (2001) 202–17.

————. "The Tongues of Pentecost: A Pentecostal Perspective on the Promise and Change of Pentecostal/Roman Catholic Dialogue." *Journal of Ecumenical Studies*, 35, no. 1 (1998) 1–18.

Mackey, J. P. *The Modern Meaning of Tradition*. New York: Herder & Herder, 1963.

MacNutt, Francis. *Healing*. Notre Dame, IN: Ave Maria, 1974.

————. *The Nearly Perfect Crime: How the Church Almost Killed the Ministry of Healing*. Grand Rapids: Chosen, 2005.

————. *Overcome by the Spirit*. Tarrytown, NY: Revell, 1990.

————. *The Practice of Healing Prayer: A How-To Guide for Catholics*. Frederick, MD: The Word Among Us, 2010.

Mahan, Asa. *Baptism of the Holy Spirit*. Clinton, NY: Williams, n.d.

Macarius of Egypt. *Intoxicated with God: The Fifty Spiritual Homilies of Macarius*. Translated by George A. Maloney. Denville, NJ: Dimension, 1978.

Maloney, George. *The Breath of the Mystic*. Denville, NJ: Dimension, 1974.

———. *Invaded by God: Mysticism and the Indwelling Trinity*. Denville, NJ: Dimension, 1979.

———. *The Jesus Prayer*. Pecos, NM: Dove, 1974.

———. *Jesus, Set Me Free!* Denville, NJ: Dimension, 1977.

———. *Listen, Prophets!* Denville, NJ: Dimension, n.d.

———. *Mystic of Fire and Light*. Denville, NJ: Dimension, 1975.

———. *Prayer of the Heart*. Notre Dame: Ave Maria, 1981.

———. *Uncreated Energy: A Journey into the Authentic Sources of Christian Faith*. Amity, NY: Amity House, 1987.

Malony, H. Newton, and A. Adams Lovekin. *Glossolalia: Behavioral Science Perspectives on Speaking in Tongues*. Oxford: Oxford University Press, 1985.

Mansfield, M. Robert. *Spirit & Gospel in Mark*. Peabody, MA: Hendricksen, 1987.

Mansfield, Patti Gallagher. *As by a New Pentecost: The Dramatic Beginning of the Charismatic Catholic Renewal*. Phoenix, AZ: Almor Deus, 2016.

Marcoux, Marcene. *Cursillo, Anatomy of a Movement: The Experience of Spiritual Renewal*. New York: Lambeth, 1982.

Marshall, Catherine. *The Helper*. Waco, TX: Chosen, 1978.

Martin, David, and Peter Mullen, ed. *Strange Gifts: A Guide to Charismatic Renewal*. Oxford: Blackwell, 1984.

Martin, George, ed. *Scripture and the Charismatic Renewal*. Ann Arbor, MI: Servant, 1979.

Martin, Ralph. *Fire on the Earth: What God is Doing in the World Today*. Ann Arbor, MI: Servant, 1975.

———. *The Life-Changer: How You Can Experience Freedom, Power and Refreshment in the Holy Spirit*. Ann Arbor, MI: Servant, 1990.

———, ed. *New Wine, New Skins*. New York: Paulist, 1976.

———. *Unless the Lord Build the House: The Church and the New Pentecost*. Notre Dame, IN: Ave Maria, 1971.

Martinez, Archbishop Luis M. *The Sanctifier*. Boston: Pauline & Media, 2003.

Marty, Martin E. *Modern American Religion, Volume 1: The Irony of It All: 1893–1919*. Chicago: University of Chicago Press, 1987.

Matthews, David, L. *The Perfecting of the Saints: How Pentecostal Terminology Is Bewitching the Charismatic Movement*. Malta, OH: Sozo Ministries, 1977.

Mazza, Enrico. *Mystagogy: A Theology of Liturgy in the Patristic Age*. Translated by Matthew J. O'Connell. New York: Pueblo, 1989.

McCarthy, Timothy G. *The Catholic Tradition: Before and After Vatican II, 1878–1993*. Chicago: Loyola University Press, 1994.

McClymond, Michael, ed. *Encyclopedia of Religious Revivals in America*. 2 vols. Westport, CT: Greenwood, 2007.

McDonnell, Kilian. *Catholic Pentecostalism: Problems in Evaluation*. Pecos, NM: Dove, 1970.

———. *The Charismatic Movement in the Churches*. New York: Seabury, 1976.

———, ed. *The Holy Spirit and Power: The Catholic Charismatic Renewal*. New York: Doubleday, 1975.

———. *The Other Hand of God: The Holy Spirit as the Universal Touch and Goal*. Collegeville, MN: Liturgical, 2003.

———, ed. *Presence, Power, Praise: Documents on the Charismatic Renewal*. 3 vols., Collegeville, MN: Liturgical, 1980.

———. *Toward a New Pentecost for a New Evangelization*. Collegeville, MN: Liturgical, 1993.

McDonnell, Kilian, and Arnold Bittlinger, *The Baptism of the Holy Spirit as an Ecumenical Problem*. Ann Arbor, MI: Word of Life, 1972.

McDonnell, Kilian, and George T. Montague. *Christian Initiation and Baptism in the Holy Spirit*. Collegeville, MN: Liturgical, 1991.

McGee, Gary B., ed. *Initial Evidence: Historical and Biblical Perspectives on the Pentecostal Doctrine of Spirit Baptism*. Peabody, MA: Hendrickson, 1991.

———. *Miracles, Missions, and American Pentecostalism*. Maryknoll, NY: Orbis, 2010.

———. *People of the Spirit: The Assemblies of God*. Springfield, MO: Gospel, 2004.

McIntire, C. T., ed. *God, History and Historians*. New York: Oxford University Press, 1977.

McManners, John, ed. *The Oxford Illustrated History of Christianity*. Oxford: Oxford University Press, 1990.

Meyendorff, John. *Byzantine Theology*. New York: Fordham University Press, 1979.

———. *Imperial Unity and Christian Divisions: The Church 450–680 A.D.* Crestwood, NY: St. Vladimir's Seminary Press, 1989.

———. *The Primacy of Peter*. Crestwood, NY: St. Vladimir's Seminary Press, 1992.

———. *St. Gregory Palamas and Orthodox Spirituality*. Crestwood, NY: St. Vladimir's Seminary Press, 1974.

Middleton, Herman A. *Precious Vessels of the Holy Spirit: The Lives & Counsels of Contemporary Elders of Greece*. Thessalonica: Protecting Veil, 2003.

Miller, Donald E., and Ymamori, Tetsunao. *Global Pentecostalism: The New Face of Christian Social Engagement*. Berkeley: University of California Press, 2007.

Minns, Denis. *Irenaeus*. London: Chapman, 1994.

Monios, Constantine M. "BEHOLD: I Make All Things New!" *The Logos,* 5, no. 3 (March 1972) 14–16.

———. "A Breath of Spiritual Fragrance." *The Logos,* 5, no. 2 (February 1972) 10–11.

———. "A Happy Priest." *The Logos,* 5, no. 5 (May 1972) 9–10.

Montague, George. *The Holy Spirit: Growth of a Biblical Tradition*. New York: Paulist, 1976.

———. *The Spirit and His Gifts*. New York: Paulist, 1974.

Moon, Tony. *From Plowboy to Pentecostal Bishop: The Life of J. H. King*. Lexington, KY: Emeth, 2017.

Moore, David. *The Shepherding Movement*. London: T. & T. Clark, 2003.

Moore, Lazarus. Translated by *St. John Climacus: The Ladder of Divine Ascent*. Etna, CA: Eastern Orthodox Books, 1973.

Moran, Gabriel. *Scripture and Tradition: A Survey of the Controversy*. New York: Herder & Herder, 1963.

Morfessis, Anthony. *God Made Me for His Plans*. Johnstown, PA: Shepherd, 1980.

Morgan-Wynne, John Eifion. *Holy Spirit and Religious Experience in Christian Literature ca. AD 90–200*. Milton Keynes, UK: Paternoster, 2006.

Moriarty, Michael G. *The New Charismatic: A Concerned Voice Responds to Dangerous New Trends*. Grand Rapids: Zondervan, 1992.

Morris, John Warren. *The Charismatic Movement: An Orthodox Evaluation*. Brookline, MA: Holy Cross Orthodox, 1984.

Moser, Maureen Beyer. *Teacher of Holiness: The Holy Spirit in Origen's Commentary on the Epistle to the Romans*. Piscataway, NJ: Gorgias, 2005.

Mühlen, Heribert. *Charismatic Theology: Initiation in the Spirit*. New York: Paulist, 1978.

Munk, Gerald W. "The Charismatic Experience in Orthodox Tradition." *Theosis*, 1, no. 7 (1978) 1–3.

n.a. "A Discussion with Father Khodre." *Upbeat*, 2, no. 4 & 5 (April-May 1969) 28–33.

n.a. "Ann Arbor Site of Orthodox Conclave." *Logos Journal*, 4, no. 3 (May-June 1974) 64–65.

n.a. "Fort Wayne Site of Orthodox Conference." *Logos Journal*, 5, no. 3 (May-June, 1975) 74.

Needham, N. R. *2000 Years of Christ's Power Part One: The Age of the Early Church Fathers*. London: Grace Publications Trust, 1997.

Nassif, Bradley. "Evangelical Denomination Gains Official Acceptance into the Orthodox Church." *Christianity Today* 31, no. 3, (February 1987) 40.

———. "Greek Orthodox Church Tries to Muzzle a Popular Charismatic Priest." *Christianity Today* 27, no. 18, (November 25, 1983) 53.

Neitz, Mary Jo. *Charisma and Community: A Study of Religious Commitment with the Charismatic Renewal*. New Brunswick, NJ: Transaction, 1987.

Neumann, Peter D. *Pentecostal Experience: An Ecumenical Encounter*. Eugene, OR: Pickwick, 2012.

Nicodemos of the Holy Mountain. *Concerning Frequent Communion of the Immaculate Mysteries of Christ*. Translated by George Dokos, Des, OR: Uncut Mountain, 2006.

———. *The Philokalia*. Translated by G. E. H. Palmer, Philip Sherard, Kalistos Ware, 4 vols. London: Faber and Faber, 1977–95.

Nicozisin, George. *Born Again Christians, Charismatics, Gifts of the Holy Spirit: An Orthodox Perspective*. New York: Greek Orthodox Department of Religious Education, n.d.

———. *The Hope of the Hopeless, the Savior of the Tempest-Tossed: Sermons by Father George Nicozisin*. n.p., 1985.

———. *Speaking in Tongues an Orthodox Perspective*. New York: Greek Orthodox Department of Religious Education, n.d.

Nissiotis, Nikos A. "The Unity of Scripture and Tradition: An Eastern Orthodox Contribution to the Prolegomena of Hermeneutics." *The Greek Orthodox Theological Review*, XI (1965–66) 183–208.

Noll, Mark. *The Rise of Evangelicalism: The Age of Edwards, Whitefield and the Wesleys*. Downers Grove, IL: IVP, 2003.

Norwood, Frederick A. *The Story of American Methodism*. Nashville: Abingdon, 1974.

O'Connor, Edward D. *Pope Paul and the Spirit: Charisms and Church Renewal in the Teaching of Paul IV*. Notre Dame, IN: Ave Maria, 1978.

Oden, Thomas, ed. *Phoebe Palmer: Selected Writings*. New York: Paulist, 1988.

Oh, Gwang Seok. *John Wesley's Ecclesiology: A Study in Its Sources and Development*. Lanham, MD: Scarecrow, 2008.

Okholm, Dennis. *Monk Habits for Everyday People*. Grand Rapids: Brazos, 2007.

Oleksa, Michael, ed. *Alaskan Missionary Spirituality*. Mahwah, NJ: Paulist, 1987.

Oliver, Jeff. *Early Prophetic and Spiritual Gifts Movements. Book One Pentecost to the Present: The Holy Spirit's Enduring Work in the Church*. Newbury, FL: Bridge-Logos, 2017.

———. *Reformations and Awakenings. Book Two of Pentecost to the Present: The Holy Spirit's Enduring Work in the Church*. Newbury, FL: Bridge-Logos, 2017.

———. *Worldwide Revivals and Renewal. Book Three of Pentecost to the Present: The Holy Spirit's Enduring Work in the Church*. Newbury, FL: Bridge-Logos, 2017.

Orsini, Joseph. *The Cost in Pentecost.* Plainfield, NJ: Logos International, 1977.

————. *Hear My Confession.* Plainfield, NJ: Logos International, 1971.

Osborn, Eric. *Irenaeus of Lyons.* Cambridge: Cambridge University Press, 2001.

Papacostas, Seraphim. *Repentance.* Athens: The Zoe Brotherhood of Theologians, 1958.

Papadopoulos, Stylianos. *The Garden of the Holy Spirit: Elder Iakovos of Evia.* Clearwater, FL: Orthodox Witness, 2007.

Patterson, Eric, and Edmund Rybarczyk. *The Future of Pentecostalism in the United States.* Lanham, MD: Rowan & Littlefield, 2007.

Pederson, Duane, with Bob Owens. *Jesus People.* Glendale, CA: Regal, 1971.

Pelikan, Jaroslav. *The Emergence of the Catholic Tradition 100–600.* vol. 1 of *The Christian Tradition: A History of the Development of Doctrine.* Chicago: University of Chicago Press, 1971.

————. *The Spirit of Eastern Christendom 600–1700.* vol. 2 of *The Christian Tradition: A History of the Development of Doctrine.* Chicago: University of Chicago Press, 1974.

Peters, John Leland. *Christian Perfection and American Methodism.* Grand Rapids: Francis Asbury, 1985.

Plowman, Edward E. "Mission to Orthodoxy: The 'Full Gospel.'" *Christianity Today* 18, no. 14 (April 18, 1974) 44–45.

Poloma, Margaret M. *The Charismatic Movement: Is There a New Pentecost?* Boston: Twayne, 1982.

Prange, Erwin E. *The Gift is Already Yours.* Plainfield, NJ: Logos International, 1973.

Purves, Jim. *The Triune God and the Charismatic Movement.* PTMS. Carlisle, UK: Paternoster, 2004.

Quebedeaux, Richard. *The New Charismatics: The Origins, Development and Significance of Neo-Pentecostalism.* Garden City, NY: Doubleday, 1976.

————. *The New Charismatics II: How a Christian Renewal Movement Became Part of the American Religious Mainstream.* New York: Harper & Row, 1983.

Raboteau, Albert. *Slave Religion: The "Invisible Institution" in the Antebellum South.* New York: Oxford University Press, 2004.

————. *A Sorrowful Joy: The Spiritual Journey of an African-American Man in Late Twentieth Century America.* New York: Paulist, 2002.

Rahner, Karl. *Most Recent Writing. Vol. IV of Theological Investigations.* Translated by Kevin Smyth. New York: Seabury, 1974.

Ramírez, Daniel. *Migrating Faith: Pentecostalism in the United States and Mexico in the Twentieth Century.* Chapel Hill, NC: University of North Carolina Press, 2015.

Ranaghan, Kevin, and Dorothy Ranaghan. *Catholic Pentecostals.* New York: Paulist, 1969.

————. *The Spirit in the Church.* New York: Seabury, 1979.

Ratzinger, Joseph. *Called to Communion: Understanding the Church Today.* San Francisco: Ignatius, 1996.

Rea, John. *The Layman's Commentary on the Holy Spirit.* Plainfield, NJ: Logos International, 1972.

Robeck, Jr., Cecil M. *The Azusa Street Mission and Revival.* Nashville: Thomas Nelson, 2006.

————. *Charismatic Experiences in History.* Peabody, MA: Hendrickson, 1985.

Robeck, Jr., Cecil M., and Amos Yong, eds. *The Cambridge Companion to Pentecostalism.* New York: Cambridge University Press, 2014.

Roberson, Dave. *The Walk of the Spirit-The Walk of Power: The Vital Role of Praying in Tongues.* Tulsa, OK: Dave Roberson Ministries, 1999.

Roberts, Oral. *The Baptism of the Holy Spirit and the Value of Speaking in Tongues Today.* Tulsa, OK: Oral Roberts Evangelistic Association, 1964.

Robins, R. G. *Pentecostalism in America.* Santa Barbara, CA: Praeger, 2010.

Rogers Jr., Eugene F. *After the Spirit: A Constructive Pneumatology from Resources Outside the Modern West.* Grand Rapids: Eerdmans, 2005.

Rose, Seraphim. *Orthodoxy and the Religion of the Future.* Platina, CA: St. Herman of Alaska Brotherhood, 1975.

Runyan, Theodore, ed. *What the Spirit is Saying to the Churches.* New York: Hawthorn, 1975.

Ruthven, John. *On the Cessation of the Charismata: The Protestant Polemic on Postbiblical Miracles.* Sheffield, UK: Sheffield Academic Press, 1993.

Ryan, John J. *The Jesus People.* Chicago: Life in Christ, 1970.

Rybarczyk, Edmund. *Beyond Salvation: Eastern Orthodoxy and Classical Pentecostalism on Becoming Like Christ.* PTMS. Carlisle, UK: Paternoster, 2004.

Sandage, Jerry, ed. *Roman Catholic/Pentecostal Dialogue (1977–1982): A Study in Developing Ecumenism.* Frankfurt am Main: Lang, 1987.

Satyavrata, Ivan. *The Holy Spirit: Lord and Life-Giver.* Downers Grove, IL: IVP Academic, 2009.

Scanlan, Michael. *Let the Fire Fall.* Steubenville, OH: Franciscan University, 2016.

———. *A Portion of My Spirit.* St. Paul, MN: Carillon, 1979.

Schmemann, Alexander. *The Eucharist: The Sacrament of the Kingdom.* Translated by Paul Kachur. Crestwood, NY: St. Vladimir's Seminary Press, 1988.

———. *For the Life of the World.* Crestwood, NY: St. Vladimir's Seminary Press, 1973.

———. *Introduction to Liturgical Theology.* Crestwood, NY: St. Vladimir's Seminary Press, 1986.

Schreck, Alan. *A Mighty Current of Grace: The Story of the Catholic Charismatic Renewal.* Frederick, MD: The Word Among Us, 2017.

Schultz, Hans-Joachim. *The Byzantine Liturgy: Symbolic Structure and Faith Expression.* Translated by Matthew J. O'Connell. New York: Pueblo, 1986.

Sherrill, John. *They Speak with Other Tongues.* Tappan, NJ: Revell, 1973.

Shelton, James B. *Mighty in Word and Deed: The Role of the Holy Spirit in Luke-Acts.* Peabody, MA: Hendricksen, 1991.

Simmons, Dale H. *E. W. Kenyon and the Postbellum Pursuit of Peace, Power, and Plenty.* Lanham, MD: Scarecrow, 1997.

Smail, Tom, Andrew Walker, Nigel Wright. *Charismatic Renewal: The Search for a Theology.* London: SPCK, 1993.

Small, Franklin. *Living Waters: A Sure Guide for Your Faith.* Winnipeg: The Columbia Press Limited, n.d.

Smith, Raynard D., ed. *With Signs Following: The Life and Ministry of Charles Harrison Mason.* St. Louis, MO: Christian Board of Publication, 2015.

Snyder, Howard. *The Divided Flame: Wesleyans and the Charismatic Renewal.* Grand Rapid: Francis Asbury, 1986.

Spittler, Russell P., ed. *Perspectives on the New Pentecostalism.* Grand Rapids: Baker Book House, 1976.

Stagg, Frank., E. Glenn Hinson, Wayne E. Oates. *Glossolalia: Tongue Speaking in Biblical, Historical, and Psychological Perspective.* Nashville: Abingdon, 1967.

Stoekoe, Mark, and Leonid Kishkovsky. *Orthodox Christians in North America 1794–1994.* Wayne, NJ: Orthodox Christian Publications Center, 1995.

Staniloae, Dumitru. *Tradition and Modernity in Theology.* Iasi, Romania: Center for Romanian Studies, 2002.

Stephanou, Eusebius. *The Baptism in the Holy Spirit: An Orthodox Understanding.* M11, Fort Wayne, IN, Logos Ministry for Orthodox Renewal, Audiocassette, n.d.

———. *Belief and Practice in the Orthodox Church.* n.p., n.d.

———. *Charisma and Gnosis in Orthodox Thought.* Fort Wayne, IN: Logos Ministry, 1975.

———. *The Charismata in the Early Church Fathers.* Destin, FL: St. Symeon the New Theologian Orthodox Brotherhood, n.d.

———. "The Charismatic Witness as the Church Congress." *The Logos,* 5, no. 7 (August-September 1972) 22–23.

———. *Chrismation, the Hidden Sacrament.* Destin, FL: n.p., 1988.

———. *The Holy Spirit Glorifies Jesus.* M10, Fort Wayne, IN: Logos Ministry for Orthodox Renewal, Audiocassette, 1973.

———. "How the Quickening Spirit is Stirring the Orthodox Church." *The Logos,* 5, no. 4 (April 1972) 3–5.

———. *A Manual on the Basic Principles of Orthodox Renewal.* Destin, FL: St. Symeon the New Theologian, 2008.

———. "The Mighty Outpouring of the Holy Spirit in Our Day." *The Logos,* 5, no. 1 (January 1972) 12–14.

———. "The Need for Vision and Sense of Mission" *The Logos,* 1, no. 4 (April 1968) 13–14.

———. "Our 30th Anniversary" *The Orthodox Evangelist,* 30, no. 1 (January-February 1997) 1–2.

———. "Preparing for the Charismatic Conference of July 1973." *The Logos,* 6, no. 1 (January-February 1973) 16–18.

———. "Priestly Authority in the Charismatic Renewal." *The Logos,* 6, no. 2 (March–April 1973) 12–13.

———. "The Proposed Orthodox Charismatic Conference." *The Logos,* 5, no. 9 (November 1972) 5.

———. "Rekindling the Gift of God for a More Effectual Witness." *The Logos,* 5, no. 6 (June-July 1972) 17–20.

———. *Renewal Pains in the Orthodox Church.* Fort Wayne, IN: Logos Ministry, 1982.

———. "The Revolt of the American Negro: An Orthodox Christian Evaluation" *The Logos,* 1, no. 2 (February 1968) 11–12.

———. *Sacramentalized But Not Evangelized.* Destin, FL: St. Symeon the New Theologian, 2005.

———. *Selected Passages from the Writings of St. Symeon the New Theologian.* Destin, FL: Brotherhood of St. Symeon the New Theologian, 1979.

———. "Sharing in the Spirit" *The Logos,* 17, no. 4, (July-August 1984) 3–4.

———. *Sounding the Trumpet in the Orthodox Church.* Destin, FL: St. Symeon the New Theologian, 2005.

———. "The Undying Flame of Pentecost." *The Logos,* 5, no. 8 (October 1972) 14–17.

Stephens, Rand J. *The Fire Spreads: Holiness and Pentecostalism in the American South.* Cambridge, MA: Harvard University Press, 2008.

Stethatos, Maria. *The Voice of a Priest Crying in the Wilderness.* El Cajon, CA: CSN, 2008.

Stethatos, Niketas. *The Life of Saint Symeon the New Theologian* Translated by Richard P. H. Greenfield. Cambridge: Harvard University Press, 2013.

Stibbe, Mark. *Times of Refreshing: A Practical Theology of Revival for Today*. London: Marshall Pickering, 1995.

Stiles, J. E. *The Gift of the Holy Spirit*. Old Tappan, NJ: Revell, 1971.

Stoeffler, F. Earnest, ed. *Continental Pietism and Early American Christianity*. Grand Rapids: Eerdmans, 1976.

Stott, John R. W. *Baptism and Fullness: The Work of the Holy Spirit Today*. Downers Grove, IL: InterVarsity, 1976.

Stronstad, Roger. *The Charismatic Theology of St. Luke*. Peabody, MA: Hendrickson, 1984.

Stroud, Marilyn. "The Hebden Mission—Our Canadian Azusa?" *Testimony*, 90, no. 5 (May 2009) 27.

St. Tikhon's Monastery. *The Book of Needs*. Vol. 1, *Holy Mysteries*. South Canaan, PA: St. Tikhon's Seminary Press, 2000.

Stylianopoulos, Theodore. *Christ Is in Our Midst: Spiritual Renewal in the Orthodox Church*. Brookline, MA: Greek Orthodox Archdiocese Department of Religious Education, 1981.

———. *The Good News of Christ*. Brookline, MA: Holy Cross Orthodox, 1991.

———. *The Way of Christ: Gospel, Spiritual Life and Renewal in Orthodoxy*. Brookline, MA: Holy Cross Orthodox, 2002.

Suenens, Leon J. Cardinal, and Dom Helder Camara. *Charismatic Renewal and Social Action: A Dialogue*. Ann Arbor, MI: Servant, 1979.

———. *Ecumenism and Charismatic Renewal: Theological and Pastoral Orientations*. Ann Arbor, MI: Servant, 1978.

———. *The Holy Spirit, Life-Breath of the Church*. 3 vols. Oppem-Meise, Belgium: FIAT Association, 2001.

———. *A New Pentecost?* Translated by Francis Martin. New York: Seabury, 1975.

Sullivan, Francis. A. *Charisms and Charismatic Renewal: A Biblical and Theological Study*. Ann Arbor: MI: Servant, 1982.

Suurmond, Jean-Jacques. *Word and Spirit at Play: Towards a Charismatic Theology*. Grand Rapids: Eerdmans, 1994.

Swete, Henry Barclay. *The Holy Spirit in the Ancient Church*. Grand Rapids: Baker, 1966.

———. *The Holy Spirit in the New Testament*. Grand Rapids: Baker, 1964.

Symeon the New Theologian. *The Discourses*. Translated by C. J. deCatanzaro. New York: Paulist, 1980.

———. *The First Created Man*. Translated by Seraphim Rose. Platina, CA: St. Herman of Alaska Brotherhood, 1994.

———. *Hymns of Divine Love*. Translated by George Maloney. Denville, NJ: Dimension, 1976.

———. *Letter on Confession* Translated by George Gabriel. Dewdney, BC: Synaxis, 1997.

———. *On the Mystical Life: The Ethical Discourses*. Translated by Alexander Golitzin. 3 vols. Crestwood, NY: St. Vladimir's Seminary Press, 1995–97.

———. *The Practical and Theological Chapters and the Three Theological Discourses*. Translated by Paul McGuckin. Kalamazoo, MI: Cistercian, 1982.

Synan, Vinson, ed. *Aspects of Pentecostal-Charismatic Origins*. Plainfield, NJ: Logos International, 1975.

———. *The Century of the Holy Spirit*. Nashville: Thomas Nelson, 2001.

———. *Charismatic Bridges*. Ann Arbor, MI: Word of Life, 1974.

———. *The Holiness-Pentecostal Movement in the United States*. Grand Rapids: Eerdmans, 1971.

———. *The Holiness-Pentecostal Tradition.* Grand Rapids: Eerdmans, 1997.

———. *In the Later Days: The Outpouring of the Holy Spirit in the Twentieth Century.* Ann Arbor, MI; Servant, 1984.

———. *The Old-Time Power: A History of the Pentecostal Holiness Church.* Franklin Springs, GA: Advocate, 1973.

———. *The Twentieth-Century Pentecostal Explosion.* Altamonte, FL: Creation House, 1987.

———. *Under His Banner: History of Full Gospel Business Men's Fellowship International.* Costa Mesa, CA: Gift, 1992.

Synan, Vinson, and Daniel Woods. *Fire Baptized: The Many Lives and Works of Benjamin Hardin Irwin.* Lexington, KY: Emeth, 2017.

Synan, Vinson, and Amos Yong, eds. *Global Renewal Christianity. Europe and North America.* Vol. 4. Lake Mary, FL: Charisma House, 2017.

———, eds. *Global Renewal Christianity. Asia and Oceania.* Vol. 1. Lake Mary, FL: Charisma House, 2016.

Synan, Vinson, Amos Yong, and J. Kwabena Asamoah-Gyadu, eds. *Global Renewal Christianity. Africa.* Vol. 3. Lake Mary, FL: Charisma House, 2016.

Synan, Vinson, Amos Yong, and Miguel Álvarez, eds. *Global Renewal Christianity. Latin America.* Vol. 2. Lake Mary, FL: Charisma House, 2016.

Synan, Vinson, and Charles R. Fox, Jr. *William J. Seymour: Pioneer of the Azusa Street Revival.* Alachua, FL: Bridge-Logos, 2012.

Synan, Vinson, and Ralph Rath. *Launching the Decade of Evangelism.* South Bend, IN: North American Renewal Service Committee, 1990.

Tarasar, Constance J., and John H. Erickson, eds. *Orthodox America 1794–1976: Development of the Orthodox Church in America.* Syosset, NY: The Orthodox Church in America Department of History and Archives, 1975.

Terry-Thompson, A. C. *The History of the African Orthodox Church.* New York: Beacon, 1956.

Theological-Historical Commission for the Great Jubilee of the Year 2000. *The Holy Spirit, Lord and Giver of Life.* New York: Crossroad, 1997.

Thomas, Stephen. *Deification in the Eastern Orthodox Tradition: A Biblical Perspective.* Piscataway, NJ: Gorgias, 2007.

Tomlinson, A. J. *Sanctification, a Peculiar Treasure.* Cleveland, TN: Committee on Doctrine, Cleveland, TN: The Church of God of Prophecy, n.d.

Torrance, Thomas F. *Theology in Reconciliation: Essays Towards Evangelical and Catholic Unity in East and West.* Grand Rapids: Eerdmans, 1975.

Trader, Alexis. *In Peace Let Us Pray to the Lord: An Orthodox Interpretation of the Gifts of the Spirit.* Salisbury, MA: Regina Orthodox, 2002.

Trevett, Christine. *Montanism: Gender, Authority and the New Prophecy.* Cambridge: Cambridge University Press, 1996.

Trifa, Valerian D. *Holy Sacraments for Orthodox Christians.* Jackson, MI: The Romanian Episcopate of America, n.d.

Tsirpanlis, Constantine. *Introduction to Eastern Patristic Thought and Orthodox Theology.* Collegeville, MN: Liturgical, 1991.

Tuttle, Jr., Robert G. *Mysticism in the Wesleyan Tradition.* Grand Rapids: Francis Asbury, 1989.

Tugwell, Simon, George Every, Peter Hocken, and John Orme Mills. *New Heaven? New Earth? An Encounter with Pentecostalism.* Springfield, IL: Templegate, 1977.

Turner, Max. *The Holy Spirit and Spiritual Gifts.* Carlisle, UK: Paternoster, 1996.

Urshan, Andrew. *The Life of Andrew Bar David Urshan.* Stockton, CA: Apostolic, 1967.

Vagaggini, Cyprian. *Theological Dimensions of the Liturgy: A General Treatise on the Theology of the Liturgy.* Translated by Leonard J. Doyle and W. A. Jurgens. Collegeville, MN: Liturgical, 1976.

Vicher, Lukas, ed. *Spirit of God, Spirit of Christ: Ecumenical Reflections on the Filioque Controversy.* London: SPCK, 1981.

Volf, Miroslav. *After Our Likeness: The Church as the Image of the Trinity.* Grand Rapids: Eerdmans, 1998.

Von Campenhausen, Hans. *Ecclesiastical Authority and Spiritual Power in the Church of the First Three Centuries.* Peabody, MA: Hendrickson, 1997.

Wagner, C. Peter. *The Third Wave of the Holy Spirit: Encountering the Power of Signs and Wonders.* Ann Arbor, MI: Vine, 1988.

Wakefield, Gavin. *Alexander Boddy, Pentecostal Anglican Pioneer.* London: Paternoster, 2007.

Walker, Andrew, and Costa Carras, eds. *Living Orthodoxy in the Modern World.* London: SPCK, 1996.

———. *Notes from a Wayward Son: A Miscellany.* Eugene, OR: Cascade, 2015.

———. "The Orthodox Church and the Charismatic Movement." In *Strange Gifts? A Guide to the Charismatic Movement,* edited by David Martin and Peter Mullen, 192–207. Oxford: Blackwell, 1984.

———. "Thoroughly Modern: Sociological Reflections on the Charismatic Movement from the End of the Twentieth Century." In *Charismatic Christianity: Sociological Perspectives,* edited by Stephen Hunt, Malcolm Hamilton and Tony Walter, 17–42. New York: St. Martin's, 1997.

Walsh, Vincent M. *A Key to the Charismatic Renewal in the Catholic Church.* Wynnewood, PA: Key of David, 1974.

Walston, Rick. *The Speaking in Tongues Controversy.* Eugene, OR: Wipf & Stock, 2003.

Waldvogel, Edith Lydia. "The 'Overcoming Life': A Study in the Reformed Evangelical Origins of Pentecostalism." PhD diss., Harvard University Press, 1977.

Ware, Kallistos. "Orthodoxy and the Charismatic Movement" *Eastern Churches Review* 5, no. 2 (1973) 182–86.

———. *The Power of the Name: The Jesus Prayer in Orthodox Spirituality.* Oxford: SLG, 1974.

Ware, Timothy. *The Orthodox Church.* New York: Penguin, 1980.

Warner, Laceye. "Spreading Scriptural Holiness: Theology and Practices of Early Methodism for the Contemporary Church." *The Asbury Journal* 63: No. 1 (2008) 115–38.

Wegman, Herman. *Christian Worship in East and West: A Study Guide in Liturgical History.* Translated by Gordon W. Lathrop. New York: Pueblo, 1985.

Welker, Michael, ed. *The Work of the Spirit: Pneumatology and Pentecostalism.* Grand Rapids: Eerdmans, 2006.

Wesley, John. *A Plain Account of Christian Perfection.* Cincinnati: Methodist Book Concern, 925.

———. *The Letters of Rev. John Wesley.* Edited by John Telford. 8 vols. London: Epsworth, 1931.

Westerlund, David. *Global Pentecostalism: Encounter with Other Religious Traditions.* London: I. B. Tauris, 2009.

Wheelock, Donald Ray. "Spirit Baptism in American Pentecostal Thought." PhD diss., Emory University Graduate School, 1983.

Winslow, Jack C. *Christa Seva Sangha*. Westminster, UK: Society for the Propagation of the Gospel in Foreign Parts, 1930.

Wild, Robert. *Enthusiasm in the Spirit*. Notre Dame, IN: Ave Maria, 1975

Wilgen, Ralph M. *The Rhine Flows into the Tiber: A History of Vatican II*. Rockford, IL: TAN, 1985.

Wilkerson, David, with Elizabeth Sherrill, John Sherrill. *The Cross and the Switchblade*. New York: Random House, 1963.

Wilkerson, Gary. *David Wilkerson: The Cross, the Switchblade and the Man Who Believed*. Grand Rapids: Zondervan, 2014.

Wilkinson, Michael, ed. *Canadian Pentecostalism: Transition and Transformation*. Montreal: McGill-Queen's University Press, 2009.

Williams, J. Rodman. *The Era of the Spirit*. Plainfield, NJ: Logos International, 1971.

———. *The Gift of the Holy Spirit Today*. Plainfield, NJ: Logos International, 1980.

———. *Renewal Theology: Systematic Theology from a Charismatic Perspective*. Grand Rapids: Zondervan, 1996.

Williams, J. Rodman. *The Pentecostal Reality*. Plainfield, NJ: Logos International, 1972.

Wilson, Mark W., ed. *Spirit and Renewal: Essays in Honor of J. Rodman Williams*. Sheffield, UK: Sheffield Academic Press, 1994.

Wood, Laurence. *The Meaning of Pentecost in Early Methodism: Rediscovering John Fletcher as John Wesley's Vindicator and Designated Successor*. Lanham, MD: Scarecrow, 2002.

Word of God. *The Life in the Spirit Seminars Team Manual (Catholic Edition)*. Ann Arbor, MI: Servant, 1979.

Yeide, Harry. *Studies in Classical Pietism: The Flowering of the Ecclesiola*. New York: Lang, 1997.

Yong, Amos. "As the Spirit Gives Utterance: Pentecost, Intra-Christian Ecumenism and the Wider Oikoumene." *International Review of Mission* 92, no. 366 (2003) 299–314.

———. *The Spirit Poured Out on All Flesh: Pentecostalism and the Possibility of Global Theology*. Grand Rapids: Baker Academic, 2005.

Young, Alexey. *The 12-Step Program and Orthodox Spirituality*. Beaumont: TX, Antiochian Christian Orthodox Radio Network (ACORN), 2 Audiocassettes, n.d.

Zabrodsky, Fr. Boris. *The Sacraments in the Charismatic Experience*. H10, Fort Wayne, IN, Logos Ministry for Orthodox Renewal, Audiocassette, n.d.

Zacharias, Archimandrite. *The Hidden Man of the Heart (1 Peter 3:4) The Cultivation of the Heart in Orthodox Christian Anthropology*. Waymart, PA: Mount Thabor, 2008.

Zizioulos, John. *Being as Communion*. Crestwood, NY: St. Vladimir's Seminary Press, 1985.

Zodhiates, Spiros. *Tongues*. Ridgefield, NJ: AMG, 1974.